MIDDLE PUGET SOUND

AFOOT & AFLOAT

SECOND EDITION

Marge & Ted Mueller

THE
MOUNTAINEERS

Published by
The Mountaineers
1001 SW Klickitat Way, Suite 201
Seattle, Washington 98134

First edition 1990. Second edition: first printing 1997, second printing 2000

Published simultaneously in Great Britain by Cordee, 3a DeMontfort Street, Leicester, England, LE1 7HD

Manufactured in the United States of America

Edited by Dana Lee Fos
Maps by Marge and Ted Mueller
All photographs © Marge and Ted Mueller
Cover design by Watson Graphics
Book design and layout by Gray Mouse Graphics

Cover photograph: *Cyclists pause at Seacrest Park to admire the Seattle skyline;* insets: *Entering the small locks; clamdigging on Hood Canal; kayaks at Poulsbo.*
Frontispiece: *Winslow Wharf Marina in Eagle Harbor, Bainbridge Island*

Library of Congress *Cataloging-in-Publication* Data
Mueller, Marge.
     Middle Puget Sound, afoot & afloat / Marge & Ted Mueller. — 2nd ed.
        p.   cm.
     Revised ed. of: Middle Puget Sound and Hood Canal afoot and afloat. © 1990.
     Includes bibliographical references and index.
     ISBN 0-89886-498-4
     1. Outdoor recreation—Washington (State)—Puget Sound.   2. Outdoor
recreation—Washington (State)—Puget Sound—Directories.   3. Puget Sound
(Wash.)—Guidebooks.   4. Marinas—Washington (State)—Puget Sound—
Guidebooks.   I. Mueller, Ted.   II. Mountaineers (Society)   III. Title.
GV191.42.W2M84   1997
796.5'025'16432—dc20   96–46945
                                                                    CIP

CONTENTS

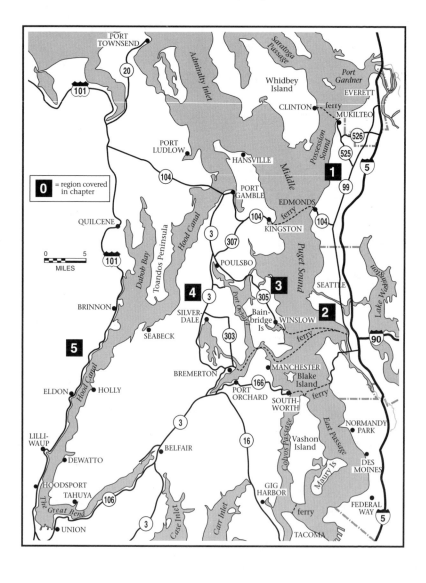

CHAPTER FIVE: HOOD CANAL   187

APPENDICES   239

INDEX   250

LEGEND

building	anchorage	street or paved road ——
park office	float, dock, or pier	highway
lighthouse	artificial or natural reef	parking area
campsite	trail	freeway
marsh	railroad	ferry route --------------------
mooring buoy	gravel road	park boundary

A family heads back from the beach at Dosewallips State Park.

PREFACE

The *Afoot and Afloat* series operates on the premise that one of the great attractions of the water and shores of Puget Sound is its diversity. This series describes not only the broad natural and historical range of the sound, but also the many activities that are associated with it. It is our hope the books will lure beachgoers to some heretofore undiscovered cranny and expand their understanding of this fascinating environment.

While this series focuses more on the surroundings than on the facilities to be found, it is understood that facilities often enable visitors to enjoy the marine environment, so brief descriptions of marinas and campgrounds are included.

WHERE IS "MIDDLE PUGET SOUND"?

This volume of the *Afoot and Afloat* series includes the waters lying between the southern tip of Whidbey Island and the northern end of Vashon Island. Although Hood Canal is not part of the sound, it is included as an added bonus because it adjoins the area called Middle Sound.

The broad seaway on which the major population centers of western Washington front, and on which thousands of boats travel daily, ought to have a nice all-inclusive name. Unfortunately, it doesn't. In precise geographic language "Puget Sound" applies only to the channels south of a line drawn from Port Townsend on the Olympic Peninsula to Admiralty Head on Whidbey Island. That leaves a whole chunk of Washington's inland waters without a name. True, some of these, such as the Strait of Juan de Fuca, Saratoga Passage, and Rosario and Haro Straits, have specific names, but the area still lacks an official, overall name that weather reports, government agencies, the populace in general, and beleaguered writers, especially, can use.

From time to time various labels have been proposed to the State Board of Geographic Names. The most recent suggestion was *Whulje* (loosely translated as "big saltwater"), the original Native American name for this inland sea. While the word has a lot going for it historically, it doesn't trip lightly over the tongue, and it was rejected.

Officialdom aside, however, many local people (as well as most state agencies) commonly consider Puget Sound to be all of Washington's inland waters that run north from Olympia to the Canadian border and west to the Pacific Ocean. Because that designation was used for our companion volume, *North Puget Sound, Afoot and Afloat,* it follows that the areas described in this book must be considered "Middle Puget Sound."

*   *   *

The locations in this book were surveyed over a period of several years and rechecked just prior to publication of this second edition; however, changes to facilities do occur. The authors and The Mountaineers would appreciate knowing of any such changes so future editions can be updated. Please address comments to the authors in care of The Mountaineers Books, 1001 SW Klickitat Way, Suite 201, Seattle, WA 98134.

Marge and Ted Mueller
July 1996

INTRODUCTION

Middle Puget Sound boasts more population and more boats than any other section of Washington's inland waterways. The waterway teems with activities of giant freighters plowing up and down the channel, ferries churning back and forth, bevies of white-crowned sailboats driven in the wind, cruisers of every size bustling about, and fishing boats bobbing on the tides. From cities and towns along its shores stream thousands of recreation seekers, some headed for distant vacation lands, but many looking for nearby diversions.

And the diversions *are* here—beaches and parks draw people for a wide array of activities, ranging from fishing to sand castle building, from birdwatching to sunbathing. Parks and public shorelands are sandwiched between real estate developments and tucked in obscure crannies of quiet bays. They range from multipurpose facilities of several hundred acres to narrow beach accesses offering only a chance to drag a boat to the water and toss it in.

GETTING AROUND

Time was when the only way to travel around the Puget Sound area was by boat. Forests blanketed most of the shoreline so thickly that even walking was difficult; the communities that sprang up as the land was settled were linked by sailing ships and rowboats. Because waterways provided easy channels of travel, time was better spent clearing land for farming or cutting timber for mills than undertaking the Herculean task of road building.

Even as cities grew, the water remained the transportation mainstay; steamboats joined the wind- and muscle-powered vessels, and a network of sturdy little packets moved passengers and goods throughout the channels, sloughs, and navigable rivers. These workhorses, known as the Mosquito Fleet, were active on the sound for nearly 70 years, until the road system finally reached all communities, and the state took over the operation of the ferry system.

Thanks to today's extensive highway network, it is not necessary to use a boat (ferries included) to reach most of the fine saltwater recreation

The wildlife area at Spencer Island, near Everett, lies just a short distance from major highways.

sites on Middle Puget Sound and Hood Canal. The exceptions are the public beaches managed by the Department of Natural Resources (the DNR beaches)—many of these can be approached only by boat, because the uplands above the mean high tide level are private, and crossing this land would be trespassing.

Land Access

On the east side of Puget Sound, the major north–south freeway is Interstate 5; for most recreation sites outside of urban areas this book uses I-5 as a reference point. In some cases the predecessor of I-5, old Highway 99, is referred to when it is closer to the beaches than I-5 and offers a more convenient approach. In urban areas directions generally are given starting from major arterials in the vicinity. Although the authors are Seattle-based, we try to avoid the provincialism of assuming all readers of this book use Seattle as a reference point.

The Kitsap Peninsula can be reached from the south end by leaving I-5 in Tacoma and heading north on State Highway 16, reaching the peninsula via the Tacoma Narrows Bridge. Still another route is via U.S. 101 from Olympia to Shelton, then to the Kitsap Peninsula on either State Highway 3 or 106.

The east side of Hood Canal, which is lightly populated, is only minimally accessible by road. A county road extension of State Highway 300 west of Belfair skirts the north edge of the canal's "bend" as far as Tahuya. It then turns inland and wanders, sometimes paved, sometimes not, through dense forest to touch the east side of the canal at only a couple of small bays with no public access. Not until the vicinity of Seabeck, near the north end of the canal, are public recreational sites again accessible by land. North of Seabeck the huge Bangor Naval Base locks up the shore access until Lofall, the old Hood Canal ferry terminal.

The west side of Hood Canal can be reached from the south through Olympia and Shelton via U.S. 101, a very scenic highway running along the complete length of the west shoreline of the canal. From the north end of Kitsap Peninsula, the Hood Canal Bridge (on State Highway 104) provides a route to the west side of the canal.

Ferry Access

Although it is not essential, by far the most convenient means of reaching the Kitsap Peninsula, Bainbridge Island, and Hood Canal from the east side of Puget Sound is the Washington State Ferry System. Two ferry routes leave from the Colman Terminal, Pier 52, on the Seattle waterfront. One crosses the sound, then winds through narrow Rich Passage to arrive at Bremerton on the Kitsap Peninsula; the other runs straight across the sound to Winslow, on the east side of Bainbridge Island.

A ferry leaving the east side of Puget Sound at Fauntleroy, south of Seattle's Lincoln Park, reaches the Kitsap Peninsula at Southworth, with an intermediate stop at Vashon Island. North of Seattle, a ferry route runs from Edmonds, on the east side of the sound, to Kingston, on the north end of the Kitsap Peninsula.

The ferries are easy to use; simply drive to the terminal area, inform the cashier of your destination if leaving from the Colman Terminal or Fauntleroy (all other terminals have only one destination option), purchase a ticket, and follow the attendant's instructions. Fares are collected for car, driver, and passengers on the westbound runs, but only for car and driver on eastbound ones. At terminals lacking a separate passenger loading ramp, passengers will be boarded and discharged from the car deck before any auto traffic moves. Bicyclists also enter and leave the car deck of the ferry ahead of vehicle traffic.

On holidays and busy summer weekends, don't expect a guaranteed spot for your car or camper on the next departing ferry. Vehicular loads are often too heavy for even the largest of superferries, and delays of one or more sailings do occur. Bring a book, some games, a picnic snack, and a sense of humor, and relax while cooling your heels with the crowd in the large asphalt holding lot.

A passenger-only ferry operates on a limited schedule between Bremerton and Seattle, and periodically more of this type of commuter ferry is advocated for other routes, especially as locations on the east side of the sound become popular bedroom communities for workers in downtown Seattle. As of the publication of this book, a private company has also applied to the state for permission to run passenger-only ferries on the sound. Maybe in the future Puget Sound transportation will come full circle with the re-creation of a full-blown Mosquito Fleet of small boats handling smaller loads of passengers and maybe even cargo!

Boat Access

Boating is a pleasant way of getting around Middle Puget Sound, and for those who choose to travel this way ample boating facilities are available. Many of the state, city, and county parks have mooring buoys, floats, and launch ramps. When these facilities are not provided, boaters usually can anchor out and approach the shore in dinghies, kayaks, or other boats small enough to be beached. No fee is charged for day-use of dock, floats, or buoys; however, boaters using state parks are required to pay for overnight tie-up.

A number of bays are totally surrounded by private property. Dropping a hook for a lunch stop or overnight stay in these bays is permitted, but private shores should be respected.

Boats cruising on Puget Sound are subject, of course, to such details as depth of keel, levels of tide, and submerged reefs and rocks. Kayaks and other small paddle-propelled boats can travel with impunity, strong winds and tidal currents excepted. Boats moored in the sheltered freshwater of Lake Washington and Lake Union, or those headed from the sound into freshwater destinations, must work their way through the locks at Shilshole Bay. The trauma of doing this is directly related to the number of inexperienced or indifferent skippers waiting to go through in the locking. (Locking procedures are described in detail in chapter 2.)

Using This Book

Information summaries at the beginning of many of the site descriptions describe the facilities and recreation to be found at that site. If a location is very small, and the recreation is limited to a single activity such as boat launching or picnicking, the summaries are omitted.

A quick reference matrix at the back of the book provides an easy way to locate the best spot for a particular activity, such as camping, boat launching, or scuba diving.

The map sketches are drawn in perspective to give a general feel for the area. They might be adequate for general travel, although navigational charts are essential for water travel. A list of charts and more detailed maps is included in appendix B.

PUBLIC RECREATION SITES ON MIDDLE PUGET SOUND AND HOOD CANAL

Public Parks

Public shorelands on Middle Puget Sound and Hood Canal fall under the jurisdiction of a number of different governmental agencies. Most parks are owned and maintained by either city, county, or state park departments, although a few owe their existence to one of several local port authorities.

Facilities vary widely from park to park. Camping is available at Seal Rock Forest Camp and at many state parks. County parks on Middle Sound are day-use only; a few are minimally developed or poorly maintained. Roughly half of these county parks have launch ramps. Facilities at public shoreline accesses provided by various port authorities tend toward launch ramps and fishing piers, with some limited picnicking facilities. A quick reference chart listing the facilities of each of the parks is in appendix C.

Because of their nearness to large population centers, city parks can have a downside. They tend to be quite crowded on weekends, holidays, and sunny summer days. Several suffer a summer inundation of younger people and, unless tightly policed, attendant problems of crowds of cars, raucous music, alcohol, and drugs. Seattle's downtown waterfront parks, unfortunately, have their share of vagrants who have drifted there to sleep off their last hangover and harass passersby into contributing to their next.

DNR Beaches and Other Public Lands

Aside from parks, substantial stretches of public beach are owned by the Washington State Department of Natural Resources (DNR). Most of these shorelands are public only up to mean high water line; property above that is privately owned. As a result, most DNR beaches are not accessible via land unless they are a continuation of a beach in front of some other public property.

At one time the DNR attempted to mark the boundaries of public beaches with distinctive black-and-white posts at high water line, but they abandoned the effort because of problems they had maintaining these markers. Similar black-and-white posts are now used to identify offshore geoduck leases—do not confuse these with DNR markers.

A number of publications available from the DNR give general locations and boundaries of their public beaches. Use care to avoid trespassing on private property; adjacent beaches are usually liberally posted if they are private, but do not assume unposted property is public. This book attempts to give you guidelines for locating boundaries, where possible.

Theler Wetlands Nature Trail, near Belfair, is a splendid example of an ecologically sensitive area that also provides public recreation.

In addition to beaches owned by the DNR, several other public beaches are administered by the Washington State Parks and Recreation Department as State Park Recreational Tidelands.

Launching Facilities

Public launching facilities are available at some city, county, and state parks; a few more are provided by the Washington State Department of Fish and Wildlife and some of the various port authorities. These are all paved ramps; however, the depth of water at the end of the various ramps and the condition of the beaches beyond them vary widely. Some lead out to shallow beaches that become extensive mudflats at low tide, making them usable only at high water. At other launch sites there are sharp drop-offs not far beyond the end of the ramp. Exercise care using any launch facility until you are familiar with it.

The condition of the ramps themselves also varies widely, with some receiving only cursory maintenance. The best of ramps are multilane, with adjoining boarding floats provided for the convenience of loading supplies and passengers. One such facility is found at Marine Park in Everett. Several of these larger ramps are divided into two sets of lanes; one set is reserved for launching boats; the other set is for retrieving them. At most ramps users are charged a launching fee, either collected by on-site support personnel or voluntarily deposited at a nearby collection station.

Marinas and beach resorts also have launching facilities; most have slings adequate for handling power boats up to 30 feet or more. Launching facilities at some resorts may not be available during off-season months. Commercial facilities are subject to economic vagaries—resorts and marinas might go out of business or be expanded to accommodate sudden popularity.

Marina Facilities

Middle Puget Sound has the largest and most elaborate marinas in the state, with every amenity for boat, captain, and crew: fuel, groceries, ice, fishing equipment and bait, restaurants, shops, marine repair and supplies, water, power, restrooms, showers, laundry, and, frequently, attractions for stir-crazy kids. But not all marinas fit this description; there are also a number of sleepy boathouses, moldering in disrepair, that rent a few kicker boats each day to neighborhood anglers. The description of each area in this book begins with an information list of facilities available at each marina at the time of publication.

Commercial or port authority-run marinas normally set aside one or more docks for guest moorage, available for a daily fee. Many marinas will also sublease to guest boaters, on a daily basis, the slips of resident boats away for a period of time. Moorage fees generally cover use of all marina facilities with the exception of dockside power, which is available for an additional fee. Some marinas accept advance registration, either by mail, telephone, or boat radio. If arriving without prior arrangements, check in at the fuel dock or marina office immediately upon arrival to be assigned and pay for a vacant slip.

A few of the larger marinas have a tidal grid—a "poor man's drydock"—consisting of a stable platform below water level and some adjoining pilings to which boaters tie their craft. As the tide goes out, the keel of the boat settles on the platform and the pilings support it for the duration of the low tide; the boat is thus exposed for maintenance and repair. Numbers painted on the side of the pier or pilings (the "grid") indicate the depth of the water at the platform. Use of a tidal grid or other special-purpose facilities requires prior arrangement with the marina office.

RECREATION ON MIDDLE PUGET SOUND AND HOOD CANAL

A wide variety of recreational opportunities are available on Middle Puget Sound and Hood Canal, ranging from boating, paddling, beachcombing, shellfish harvesting, fishing, scuba diving, birdwatching, swimming, and sunbathing to bicycling, hiking, and camping. Several museums and a bounty of historical markers recall the exploration, settlement, and key events in the growth of the region. Recreation is here for all ages and all levels of energy, with appeal to tourists and residents alike.

Boating

Puget Sound residents do like their boating. You have only to take a quick look at the forest of masts in the Everett, Shilshole Bay, or Elliott Bay marinas, or glance at the parking lots full of boat trailers at any of the larger launch sites, to quickly establish that fact. Billowing sails and throbbing motors don't tell the whole story, however; peek into any small, secluded bay and you will probably find a group of kayakers quietly paddling in search of shoreline sights that the crews of larger boats may never take time to find. Boating is diverse, but regardless of the size or shape of your aquatic transportation certain fundamentals and cautions apply to all who use these waterways.

Chartering and Renting. Boating in the area is readily available to those who do not own a boat; over two dozen firms offer charter services for boats ranging from small weekenders to large luxury yachts. Charter operators will insist on proof of adequate boat handling and navigation skills before renting their vessels to an unknown sailor and, if not impressed with the candidate's abilities, may require a quick boating course or the company of a paid skipper to protect their investment. All required safety gear is included with the rental.

On a lesser scale, a deposit fee will rent a small outboard-powered craft from any of several boathouses and resorts in the area for a day's fishing at a local hot spot.

Paddling. Each passing year sees greater interest in the sport of kayaking, and it is rare to spend a day on the water without spotting several of these sleek, muscle-powered craft poking into shallow backwaters where only they have the draft to venture. More experienced kayakers may even make a cross-sound trip, providing weather and tidal current conditions are favorable.

Kayak and canoe rentals, as well as training in their use, are available at several locations around the sound; outdoor groups in the area also offer training courses as well as provide the safety and camaraderie of group-sponsored outings.

One disadvantage to kayaking is that paddlers are limited in the distance that they can cover in a day, and a multiday trip requires campsites along the shoreline at convenient intervals. The Washington Water Trails Association (WWTA) is an organization of paddlers formed in 1990, with an ambitious dream—the creation of a marine trail system with a chain of campsites that are a reasonable day's paddle apart. The Cascadia Marine Trail, as envisioned, would link 150 miles of inland waterways all the way from the southern reaches of Puget Sound to the Canadian border (and dreaming farther, to Alaska!). Currently the WWTA has successfully forged relationships with Washington State Parks, the DNR, and other city and county parks departments who have designated primitive shoreside campsites on their properties.

These campsites, which may be used only by persons in muscle-powered boats, are accessible from the water at points where craft can easily be beached and carried ashore. Sanitation facilities are available at or near the campsites, but other amenities are limited—often the site is just a spot level enough for a tent. Open fires either are not permitted or are strongly discouraged, and potable water is available only at those sites that are associated with other fully developed camping facilities.

An annual permit is required for use of Cascadia Marine Trail campsites, and a nominal overnight camping fee is also charged for the use of campsites in state parks. As of 1996, there are five Cascadia Marine Trail sites in the region covered by this book, and additional sites are being negotiated. For more information contact the WWTA at the address listed in appendix A.

Boating Safety. Because of the sheer number of boaters enjoying the waters of Puget Sound and Hood Canal, it is inevitable that some of them will disregard the requirements of safe boating. One need only to approach the locks at Shilshole Bay on a busy summer weekend to realize some boaters lack the skills, courtesy, and sobriety necessary to make an outing pleasurable for their fellow boaters. Anyone starting into boating should take one of the boating safety courses provided by the local U.S. Power Squadron. Information on time and location of these courses can be obtained from the U.S. Coast Guard.

Although on Middle Puget Sound or Hood Canal a boat is never more than a couple of miles from the nearest shoreline, navigational hazards and potential bad weather still mandate that every boater be thoroughly familiar with the skills of coastal navigation and possess the tools and navigational charts required to put this knowledge to use.

Sailing on Admiralty Inlet near Port Ludlow

The illustrative maps in this book are intended for general information only. They are not intended to replace a *good navigation chart*. A list of current NOAA charts for this area is in appendix B.

Vessel Traffic. Middle Puget Sound is heavily used by commercial vessels, naval vessels, ferries, fishing boats, and recreational boats, making it seem downright crowded at times. As any boating course graduate knows, there are rules-of-the-road specifying who stays clear from whom under what conditions; however, don't risk life, limb, and the hull of your boat assuming another captain knows those rules and will follow them. A sailboat skipper shouting "Starboard tack!" at a large power vessel closing at high speed might end up getting his satisfaction in maritime court—after he has been fished from the icy sound.

To bring more order to large vessel traffic, the Coast Guard has installed a Vessel Traffic Service (VTS) on Puget Sound. Northbound and southbound traffic lanes have been designated down the center of the sound, and those are marked on all navigation charts of the area. The ½-nautical-mile-wide traffic lanes lie on either side of a ¼-nautical-mile-wide separation zone, which has midchannel buoys marking every point at which the lanes alter direction. Radar stations are located at key points on the sound to track vessel traffic; all radar signals feed into the Coast Guard VTS Center on Pier 36 on the Seattle waterfront.

Vessels over 300 gross tons, vessels carrying passengers for hire, vessels engaged in commercial towing, and dredges or floating plants are required to participate in the vessel traffic control system. Communication with the VTS Center takes place over VHF channel 14; boaters concerned with the location of large-vessel traffic can monitor this frequency for information. Smaller commercial and recreational vessels generally don't participate in the VTS; however, they will probably appear on the center radar, depending on their size and radar reflectance. These boats may contact the center in emergencies, and the center will provide assistance, if possible.

Another potential traffic problem, especially at night during commercial salmon fishing season, is the dozens of fishing boats with nets deployed; at times they seem to blanket an area. Proper lights on fishing boats and nets should identify areas to avoid, but a sharp lookout is required to spot these lights and avoid running into nets.

Weather. Summer favors Puget Sound and Hood Canal with mild temperatures, moderate weather, and light winds—the major weather concern is avoiding a painful sunburn. However, sudden summer storms do come up occasionally; in other seasons the waters in this area can at times be downright nasty and dangerous. Prevailing storm winds come from the southwest; the shift of wind to that direction, plus a falling barometer, bodes of worsening weather.

This section of Puget Sound has a particular weather anomaly known as a "convergence zone." Low-level winds from the west off the ocean split as they encounter the Olympic Mountains: a portion loops south around the mountain range then back down the sound; another portion loops north through the Strait of Juan de Fuca and then up the sound. When these two fronts of winds meet head-on (generally in the area between Seattle and Everett), a violent local weather front is sometimes created, with localized high winds, rain, and at times thunder and lightning.

The long, open, unobstructed north–south channels of Puget Sound and Hood Canal provide plenty of fetch for strong storm winds to build up substantial seas. When wind-built waves are met by tidal currents from the opposite direction, sharp choppy seas can result, making for uncomfortable, if not unsafe, boating. The best defense against being caught by adverse weather conditions is a regular monitoring of the NOAA weather channel, VHF channel WX1 (FM 162.550 MHz).

Fog. The temperature differential between the always-cold sound and summer-warmed beaches creates ideal conditions for formation of fog, especially in late night and early morning hours. Although this fog generally lifts by midday, a planned early departure might have to be delayed, or navigation skills will be severely tested in the blank white wall of surrounding mist.

Rocks and Shoals. Most serious navigational hazards in this area are marked with lights, buoys, or other navigational markers. However, with a potential tidal variation of 16 to 20 feet at extreme tides, normally submerged and safe rocks and reefs can come dangerously close to the surface at extreme minus tides, and underwater shoals and bars can become a four-hour or more resting place for the sailor who doesn't keep a wary eye on the chart, tide table, and depth sounder. When anchoring for the night, check tide levels at the time and for the duration of your stay to make sure you have enough water under you during that period and that the proper length of anchor rode has been payed out.

Tidal Current. Tide level and tidal currents are related, but definitely not synonymous. The *tide* refers to the change in depth of the water due to gravitational influences of the sun and moon and other esoteric things such as barometric pressure. In Puget Sound there are two highs and two lows in any tidal cycle of approximately 25 hours. As the vertical water level rises and falls, the volume of water at any point must move in and out of the area, resulting in horizontal *tidal currents*. The direction and velocity of the current are determined not only by the tidal cycle, but also by the channel involved and by any shoreline or underwater obstructions.

Tidal currents in Middle Puget Sound range from virtually zero along the east shoreline to 2 knots or more in Admiralty Inlet near Foulweather Bluff. In the narrower channels, such as Agate Passage, Rich Passage, and Port Washington Narrows, tidal currents of up to 4 knots can be expected. The impact of such currents on small, low-powered boats or hand-powered kayaks is obvious—you can be going full-steam ahead into a strong current and still be moving backwards.

Tidal current tables are printed annually and are keyed to stations identified on the NOAA small-craft chart portfolio. A combination of the charts and current tables will give a good approximation of the current strength and direction that you can expect to encounter in a given area.

Walking and Hiking

"Hiking" is probably a misnomer for the foot-bound recreation described in this book, because trails in the parks included here rarely exceed a mile or so one way, and elevation gained and lost is seldom more than 100 to 200 feet. Such short walks have their interest and charm, however, as more time can be spent observing the surrounding sights, smells, colors, flowers, and wildlife when there is less pressure to cover a long distance. There certainly is a wide variety of things to see on these walks. Even urban Discovery Park, for example, is visited by over 200 species of birds and includes a dozen varieties of trees, an equal or greater selection of shrubs, 40 or more types of herbs, ferns, and mosses, more than 50 species of beach life, and a showcase-lesson in Puget Sound geology in its beach bluffs.

Beach walks of up to a couple miles in length can be found in some locations where DNR beaches are accessible from public uplands. Many beach walks are very dependent on tide levels; a wide, gently tapering beach can disappear within four or five hours beneath an incoming tide. Because many beaches lie below steep bluffs or impenetrable brush, note the time of the next tide change and plan your walk to avoid getting trapped in some uncomfortable or unsafe place by the incoming tide. Tide tables are available at bookstores and marine supply stores, and daily predictions are published in most area newspapers.

Bicycling

Nearly all the areas covered in this book are well suited for bicycling, and many are quite popular for both one-day and extended bicycle trips. Because traffic tends to keep to the inland highways and freeways, many of the shoreline roads are lightly traveled.

On weekends the ferries to Bainbridge Island disgorge dozens of bicyclists intent on some variation of a loop trip around the island (or in early spring the competitive challenge of the "Hilly Chilly"). Most of the roads on Bainbridge Island have wide shoulders usable for bike lanes, and the roads around the perimeter of the island are reasonably level, although some crossing the island can be a real challenge, climbing and dropping over successive ridges and valleys.

U.S. 101 along Hood Canal is also popular for longer trips and, with a few exceptions, has shoulders wide enough for safe and comfortable bicycling. Highway 106 along the south side of the bend of Hood Canal is another well-used bicycle route; however, the road is narrow and twisted and traffic is generally heavy, so more caution is advised on this trip.

A number of bicycle tours in this area are described in detail in the two books *Bicycling the Backroads Around Puget Sound* and *Bicycling the Backroads of Northwest Washington*. Both are by Bill and Erin Woods and are published by The Mountaineers.

In Washington, bicyclists are required to use the right side of the road, the same as vehicular traffic, and to travel single file or, on wide roads, no more than two abreast. Bicyclists are not permitted to stack up a line of traffic behind them; if one starts to build, cyclists should pull over at the nearest safe spot and permit traffic to pass. Courtesy is the byword, and consideration by bicyclists for the requirements of auto traffic will increase the chances that such consideration will be reciprocated.

Camping

Forest Service campgrounds and those state parks offering camping provide both tent and RV camping at individual sites. Some also provide a group campsite, available by reservation only. A host of private resorts in the area also offer camping; most resorts stack campsites side-by-side with little individual privacy.

As of 1996, state parks in the Middle Sound area at Belfair, Dosewallips, Manchester, and Scenic Beach will accept campsite reservations via a telephone reservation system run jointly with the state of Oregon. Refer to appendix A for phone numbers. Camping at other sites is presently on a first-come, first-served basis. Fees are collected nightly for all campsites, and campgrounds are closed after 10:00 P.M. Picnic areas cannot be used for overflow camping.

Beach Exploration

Although most of the beaches in this area are heavily used, low tides uncover a wide variety of saltwater plants and animals for examining and photographing. Park regulations prohibit removal of any beach life except for food use; consideration for other future beach explorers as well as for the environment dictates that nothing be destroyed or taken from any of the beaches. All plants and animals play a vital role in the environment and food chains; their removal can only lead to deterioration of the beach ecology. Even empty shells and pockmarked driftwood may serve as future homes for small marine creatures and are better left on the beach than stuffed in a sack and forgotten on someone's back porch.

Harvesting Seafood—Fishing, Scuba Diving, and Beach Foraging

Licenses and Limits. Within the areas covered in this book, the Washington State Department of Fish and Wildlife requires a Food Fish License and a Puget Sound Enhancement License for taking cod, pollock, hake, flatfish, herring, anchovies, candlefish, sardines, lingcod, greenlings, mackerels, rockfish, sculpin, sea bass, shad, sharks, skates, surf and pile perch, halibut, salmon, and sturgeon. In addition, a Salmon-Catch Record Card is required for any migratory salmon fishing. A Shellfish/Seaweed License is required to gather crabs, goose barnacles, mussels, octopuses, oysters, razor clams, scallops, sea cucumbers, sea urchins, shrimp, soft- and hardshell clams, squid, and seaweed.

It is the responsibility of the individual to be aware of all regulations regarding size, limits, methods of harvesting, seasons, restricted sites, and license requirements. A free, annually published pamphlet, *Fishing in Washington,* put out by the Department of Fish and Wildlife outlines license requirements and other regulations. The guide is available from that department and is also found in most sporting goods stores.

Scuba Diving. To take food fish, scuba divers must have a Food Fish License and, to take shellfish, a Shellfish/Seaweed License. It is unlawful to fish for or take salmon, octopuses, or crabs using underwater spearfishing gear. With the exception of regulations regarding lingcod, all bag limits, size, season, and area restrictions for fishing apply to scuba divers as well.

Digging Holes on the Beach. State regulations require that holes dug on a beach for purposes of gathering clams *must always* be refilled. The incoming tide might take three or four cycles to fill holes; in the meantime small marine animals trapped on top of the pile are exposed to the sun and may die of dehydration.

Oyster Gathering. It is unlawful

When gathering oysters at the beach, bring a bucket and a knife with you, and shuck the oysters there.

to remove oyster shells from the beach; the shells are hosts for oyster larvae that will die if the shells are removed. Take a bucket and an oyster knife to the beach with you and shuck oysters where you find them.

Paralytic Shellfish Poisoning (Red Tide)

When the Washington State Department of Health periodically issues a "red tide warning" and closes particular beaches on Puget Sound, the public usually reacts with confusion or skepticism. A clearer understanding of the phenomenon of red tide will lead to a greater respect for its dangers.

The name "red tide" itself contributes to some of the public's confusion, for it is not always visibly red, it has nothing at all to do with the tide, and not all red algae are harmful. Paralytic shellfish poisoning (PSP) is a serious illness caused by *Gonyaulax catenella,* a toxic, single-celled, amber-colored algae present in small numbers at all times in the water. During the spring, summer, and fall, certain environmental conditions may combine to permit a rapid multiplication or accumulation of these microscopic organisms. Most shellfish toxicity occurs when the concentrations of *G. catenella* are too sparse to discolor the water; however, the free-floating plants sometimes become so numerous that the water appears to have a reddish cast—thus the name "red tide."

Bivalve shellfish such as clams, oysters, mussels, and scallops, which feed by filtering seawater, may ingest millions of the organisms and concentrate the toxin in their bodies. The poison is retained by most of these shellfish for several weeks after the occurrence of the red tide; butter clams can be poisonous for much longer.

When the concentration of the toxin in mollusks reaches a certain level, it becomes hazardous to humans who eat them. The toxins cannot be destroyed by cooking, and cannot be reliably detected by any means other than laboratory analysis. Symptoms of PSP, beginning with the tingling of the lips and tongue, may occur within a half hour of ingestion. The illness attacks the nervous system, causing loss of control of arms and legs, difficulty in breathing, paralysis, and, in extreme cases, death.

Shellfish in all counties on Puget Sound are under regular surveillance by the State Department of Health. PSP (or red tide) warnings are issued and some beaches are posted when high levels of toxin are detected in tested mollusks. Warnings are usually publicized in the media; the state toll-free hotline, listed in appendix A, has current information as to which beaches are closed to shellfish harvesting. Crabs, abalone, shrimp, and fin fish are not included in closures because there have been no recorded cases of PSP in the Northwest caused by eating those animals.

Pollution. Pollution, both chemical and biological, has so thoroughly contaminated beaches in King County that harvesting of bottomfish, crab, or shellfish is not recommended along any of its shores. Similar problems afflict several beaches and bays in metropolitan areas of Kitsap and Snohomish Counties and some limited areas on Hood Canal in Mason and Jefferson Counties. Fish and shellfish from these areas have been found to have high levels of pollutants in their body tissues. A continuous diet of such animals can pose a health hazard. Hazardous beaches are generally posted. If in doubt, inquire.

SAFETY CONSIDERATIONS

Boating and beach travel entail unavoidable risks that every traveler assumes and must be aware of and respect. The fact that an area is described in this book is not a representation it will be safe for you. The areas described herein vary greatly in the amount and kind of preparation needed to enjoy them safely. Some areas might have changed since this book was written, or conditions may have deteriorated. Weather conditions can change daily or even hourly, and tide levels and tidal currents will also vary considerably. An area that is safe in good weather at low or slack tide might be completely unsafe during inclement weather or at times of high tide or maximum tidal current. You can meet these and other risks safely by exercising your own independent judgment and common sense. Be aware of your own limitations and those of your vessel and of conditions when or where you are traveling. If conditions are dangerous or if you are not prepared to deal with them safely, change your plans. Each year many people enjoy safe trips in the waters and on the beaches of Middle Puget Sound and Hood Canal. With proper preparation and good judgment, you can too.

EMERGENCY ASSISTANCE

The overall legal authority in all unincorporated areas of Washington State rests with the county sheriff or county police. Within city limits, the local city police force has legal authority. Port authority police have jurisdiction on port property only, although in most cases they are cross-deputized in other local police forces. Emergencies or complaints should be referred to the authority having jurisdiction; telephone numbers are listed in appendix A.

Within state and county parks, the park manager or ranger assumes emergency assistance responsibilities. Not all parks have resident managers; appendix A provides the locations of managers responsible for unmanned parks.

The U.S. Coast Guard has the primary responsibility for safety and law enforcement on Puget Sound and Hood Canal waters. Marine VHF channel 16 is constantly monitored by the Coast Guard and should be the most reliable means of contact in cases of emergencies on the water. The Coast Guard monitors Citizens Band channel 9 at some locations and times but has no commitment to a full-time radio watch on this channel. Several volunteer groups do an excellent job of monitoring the CB emergency frequency and will assist with relaying emergency requests to the proper authorities.

With growing use of cellular telephones, the cellular providers in the Puget Sound area provide a quick-dial number, *CG, that immediately connects the caller to the Coast Guard Vessel Traffic Service Center in Seattle. This center coordinates all marine safety and rescue activities for the region.

A NOTE ABOUT SAFETY

Safety is an important concern in all outdoor activities. No guidebook can alert you to every hazard or anticipate the limitations of every reader. Therefore, the descriptions of roads, trails, routes, and natural features in this book are not representations that a particular place or excursion will be safe for your party. When you follow any of the routes described in this book, you assume responsibility for your own safety. Under normal conditions, such excursions require the usual attention to traffic, road and trail conditions, weather, terrain, the capabilities of your party, and other factors. Because many of the lands in this book are subject to development and/or change of ownership, conditions may have changed since this book was written that make your use of some of these routes unwise. Always check for current conditions, obey posted private property signs, and avoid confrontations with property owners or managers. Keeping informed on current conditions and exercising common sense are the keys to a safe, enjoyable outing.

The Mountaineers

Sailing on Port Gardner, with Mount Baker in the distance

CHAPTER ONE

POSSESSION SOUND AND EDMONDS

Boating spots are usually thought of in two categories—places you go to and places you leave from. In Washington, the wonderful change-of-pace destinations like the San Juans, Port Townsend, or Poulsbo fall in the first group. In the latter category are spots boaters do not usually think of stopping at unless the motor suddenly develops palsy, or (worse yet) it is discovered that all the food for the weekend is still sitting at home on the kitchen table.

To Puget Sound boaters, marinas and bays along Possession Sound usually fall in this second group—they are too close to home to offer a convenient first night's stop, or too much like home to provide a real change of pace. A stop along Possession Sound can, however, be a real bonus. Boaters can add one more pleasurable day to the weekend by leaving the home slip in Seattle or points south on Friday afternoon and pausing somewhere along Possession Sound for the night before continuing north. Or they can use this as a last stop on a vacation trip before making the final leap for the locks.

For those not in transit to vacation getaways, Possession Sound offers beaches aplenty for a day's enjoyment wading in the waves, sculpting sand castles, lolling against sun-splashed driftwood, or casting a fishing line. For small craft, Possession Sound beaches and marinas offer ideal launch points for local exploration or fishing. Scuba divers also relish the opportunity to probe the underwater world within a short jaunt from home.

Captain George Vancouver, who was the first European explorer to venture into these waters, anchored off Gedney Island in June of 1792, after exploring the southern reaches of Puget Sound. In taking possession of all the inland waters in the name of King George III of England, he gave this arm of Admiralty Inlet its name.

"Possession Sound" is a somewhat pretentious name for this body of water, which is, in truth, just one more wandering arm of Puget Sound

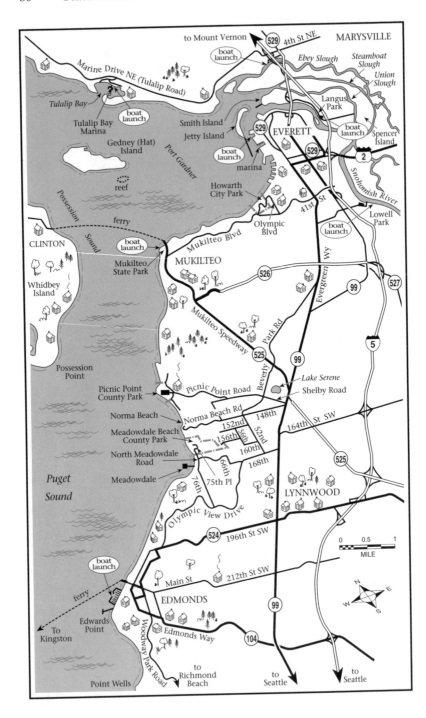

itself. It bulges into Port Gardner, a broad basin south of the confluence of Saratoga Passage and Port Susan. A large part of the east side of this basin is a dredged mudflat at the mouth of the Snohomish River, baring at low tide. A dredged channel leads into Everett, the major city on this body of water.

Gedney (Hat) Island

A long subterranean shelf reaches south from Camano Head to Gedney Island, in the middle of Possession Sound. This is a popular year-round salmon fishing area. To provide more habitat for fish, and thus improve fishing and scuba diving in the area, an artificial reef of massive chunks of broken concrete has been placed just off Gedney Island. The reef, marked by buoys, lies ½ mile south of the island.

All of the island is private; residents reach it by private boat or via the private ferry. The small marina lying behind a breakwater on the northeast side is for the use of island residents only. Avoid cruising too close to the south or east side of the island, as shoal water extends some distance from shore. In calm weather, the north side of the island offers some anchorages.

TULALIP BAY

The Tulalip Indian Reservation spreads along the shore between Kayak Point and Everett. The center of the reservation shoreline is marked by the small, shallow indentation of Tulalip Bay. The slender finger of Skayu Point frames the south side of the entrance to the bay. The north side of the bay is dotted with submerging rocks; the hull of the *Hicira*, a gas scow that burned and sank in 1919, lies in these rocks. When entering the bay, favor the north side once past the entrance rocks to avoid drying shoals found near the center of the bay. The bay ranges just 1 to 2 fathoms deep at mean lower low water, making it suitable only for shallow-draft vessels.

Tulalip Bay Marina

Facilities: Boat launch (ramp), guest moorage, groceries, cafe, bait, fuel, restrooms (no showers)

A small marina lies behind a short rock jetty at the center of the eastern shore of Tulalip Bay. The marina's 100 slips primarily provide full-time moorage for tribal fishing boats; however, a few slips are open for day-by-day rental for visiting boaters. Check with the marina office or grocery store for available moorage. A steep, concrete, single-lane launch

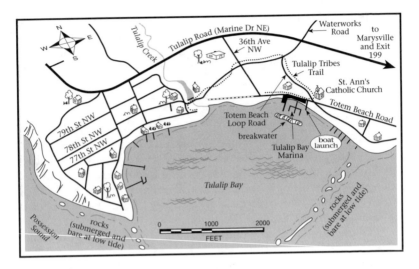

ramp with an adjoining boarding float is located at the south end of the marina area; there is ample parking in the vicinity.

To reach the marina by land, take Exit 199 (Marysville, Tulalip) from I-5. At the intersection with 4th Street NE, turn west and follow the main highway, Marine Drive NE (also marked Tulalip Road), for 6 miles to Waterworks Road, where signs lead west to the marina. Historic St. Ann's Catholic Church, built in 1904, sits prominently on the hillside above the marina.

Tulalip Bay Marina

Tulalip Tribes Trail

A ¾-mile-long walking loop along roads above the Tulalip Bay Marina offers insights into the history and way of life of the Tulalip Tribe. Each of eight stations has a large informational display with historical photos and narrative. Short posts nearby identify plants and shrubs and describe the uses made of the plants by the Tulalips. The stations on the trail are found just above the marina along Totem Beach Road, and on the hillside above on Totem Beach Loop Road and Waterworks Road. The path between the stations is marked with rather obscure, rust-colored painted pipes.

THE SNOHOMISH RIVER ESTUARY

Between Marysville and Everett the Snohomish River meanders soundward, dividing into a braided network of sloughs, backwaters, and channels. The main channel of the Snohomish River is navigable by large boats for about ¾ mile east of the I-5 overpass. A railroad swing bridge and several highway bridges—some fixed, some opening—cross the channel. The least vertical clearance of the fixed bridges is 56 feet. Several marinas are located near the mouth of the river, at Ebey Slough, at Union Slough, and on the main channel. All have haulouts and marine repair, but none provide guest facilities.

Small boats put in along the channel can explore the maze of quiet sloughs or cruise out to the bustling activity of Port Gardner. The tidal influence on the lower Snohomish estuary is significant, so paddle-powered trips should be planned with the tidal current in mind.

Either from boats or from trails that edge the shores watch for the wide variety of gulls, ducks, shorebirds, and herons that frequent the estuary. You may also spot deer, river otter, raccoon, and coyote that live in the grassy marshes.

Ebey Slough Launch Ramp

A public launch ramp on the most northerly of the Snohomish River sloughs provides access to the many channels of the estuary. To reach it, leave I-5 at Exit 199 (Marysville, Tulalip). In Marysville turn south on Beach Avenue, the first intersection to the east after leaving the freeway. Follow Beach Avenue south to a T-intersection with First Street and then head west. Just after the street ducks under I-5, a single-lane launch ramp is on the left, facing on Ebey Slough. A dirt parking area beside the road under the freeway has space for three or four cars with trailers. Park well off the road, as logging machinery and trucks make heavy use of the road during working days. Don't park inside the concrete barriers—they mark logging company property, and you will be towed.

Langus Riverfront Park and Trail (City of Everett)

Park Area: 54 acres; 5,700 feet of shoreline
Facilities: Boat launch (ramp), float, fishing pier, restrooms, picnic tables, racing shell launch, picnic shelter, riverside trail
Attractions: Boating, paddling, fishing, hiking, bicycling, birdwatching, picnicking, views

This Everett city park on the main channel of the Snohomish River offers landscaped picnic sites and an excellent two-lane concrete launch ramp with adjoining boarding floats. The south end of the park also has a concrete float used for launching racing shells and other hand-carried boats or for fishing. Several picnic tables lining this short stretch of open shoreline overlook the river and provide a place to munch a sandwich and watch birds or boats, whichever is your fancy. At the north end of the park a short fishing pier offers another opportunity to drop a line into the river. Northeast, above the downstream channel, the icy cone of Mount Baker rises, and to the west loom the sharp summits of Whitehorse, Three Fingers, and Mount Pilchuck.

To reach the park, leave I-5 North at Exit 195 (Port of Everett, Marine View Drive) in Everett or I-5 South at Exit 198 (Highway 529, Marine View Drive); either exit leads to Highway 529. Leave Highway 529 from either direction at the first available exit between the Snohomish River and Union Slough, then head southwest parallel to the highway to reach an intersection, on the east side of the highway near the north bank of the

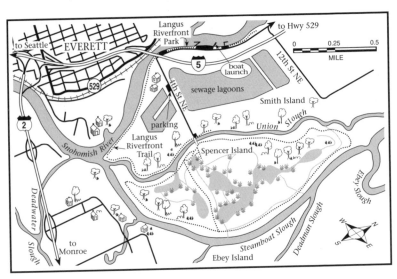

Canada geese snooze at Langus Riverfront Park, below the snowy sentinel of Mount Pilchuck.

Snohomish River. The road passes the large area for dry storage of boats at Dagmar's Landing. At a Y-intersection at 12th Street NE, a little over ¼ mile south of Dagmar's, bear south, and in another ½ mile reach the park, which is tucked between the river and the freeway.

Along the top of the dike a narrow, rough dirt path leads north, downriver along the water's edge for nearly a mile. A few small pocket beaches along the dike provide more spots to relax and watch the river creatures and activities. A parking lot at the south end of the park marks the start point of the Langus Riverfront Trail, a flat, 1½-mile-long paved path atop the dike along the east bank of the Snohomish River and the west bank of Union Slough. Benches dpotted along the bank provide spots to lounge in the sun and listen to and look for myriad birds and waterfowl that use the riverside as their home or hotel.

The trail starts out with less than auspicious scenery: the city sewage plant on one side, and grubby industrial Everett on the other side across the river. Blackberries, brush, and a deciduous forest soon mask the uglies. As the path bends north along Union Slough, the noise of civilization is damped by the surrounding greenery, and it becomes a quiet haven. In spring clumps of skunk cabbage flash golden blossoms through marsh mud, and trailside shrubs wear a delicate mantle of pink and red blossoms. The rotting hull of a long forgotten boat protrudes from the bottom of the slough.

At 1½ miles the bridge to Spencer Island is reached, and in another 100 yards the trail atop the dike peters out. Return to your car the way you came, or take a ¾-mile shortcut via 4th Street NE.

Spencer Island (Snohomish County)

Park Area: 1,117 acres; 13,000 feet of shoreline
Facilities: Trails, viewing platforms, interpretive signs, sani-cans
Attractions: Hiking, birdwatching, nature study, views

Don't plan for a quick hike through Spencer Island. Although the paths are easy and the distance is not far, you'll soon discover that a leisurely pace is needed to see, hear, and absorb all the wonders that are here. Birdwatchers report spotting more than 30 different species in a single outing.

The island, sandwiched between Union and Steamboat Sloughs, was once an industrial dumping ground for wood waste products from nearby lumber mill operations. Dikes were built here to protect local farms from flooding. The marshy island now stands as a premier example of habitat restoration. Beginning in 1990, the Snohomish County Parks Department, the state Department of Fish and Wildlife, and a group of volunteers joined forces to excavate debris from the north end of the island, creating a freshwater wetland pond and a cross-island levee. The north end of the island is preserved as a freshwater marsh environment for small mammals, migrating waterfowl, and other bird species that thrive in this habitat.

South of the levee the former dikes were breached to restore the flow of tidal saltwater to the remainder of the island. The hope is that the tidal flushing will create a transition zone for juvenile salmon headed from spawning grounds to sea. The saltwater will also kill non-native canary grass, allowing native plants to reestablish, and cause some of the deciduous forest on this end of the island to die, producing snags for nesting and resting sites for birds and bats.

Skunk cabbage on Spencer Island

Although the primary objective in restoring the island was habitat preservation, compatible recreational opportunities such as hiking, wildlife viewing, and seasonal hunting of migratory waterfowl are permitted.

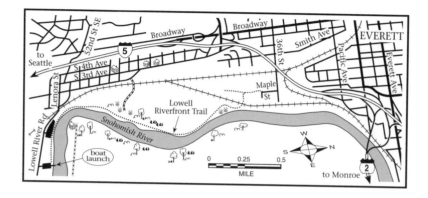

To reach the island, drive east from the south end of Langus Riverfront Park on 4th Street NE, which deadends at the bridge to Spencer Island. Parking is prohibited at the road end; the nearest parking area is a concrete slab just outside the fenced sewage lagoons about ½ mile from the road end.

A broad, bark-covered path circles the island. A cross-island trail atop the dike bisects the route, forming two trail loops. The south loop around the tidally influenced environment is 1¼ miles in length; the north loop around the freshwater marshes is just over 2 miles. Planked spur paths lead to observation platforms along the marsh area, and interpretive signs describe the environment and the restoration efforts. Cattails, marsh grass, and a bevy of birds close at hand are dramatically silhouetted by ice-clad peaks of the Cascades in the distance.

Lowell Riverfront Trail (City of Everett)

Park Area: 14 acres; 7,000 feet of shoreline
Facilities: Boat launch (ramp), trail, park benches, picnic tables, sani-can
Attractions: Birdwatching, paddling, fishing, bicycling, views

This beautiful riverfront trail runs along the west bank of the Snohomish River, following the route of an old railroad track. In the future, local government agencies plan to continue the riverside trail all the way to the town of Snohomish.

The south end of the park is anchored by a parking lot that accommodates about 55 cars and trailers. A two-lane, concrete boat launch ramp with boarding pier drops into the Snohomish River. Boaters launching here should remember the river level at this point is still very much affected by tidal levels.

North from the ramp area a level, paved path follows the river for 2½ miles. Walk slowly, watch, and listen for river and marshland inhabitants.

An artist paints distant mountains at Lowell Riverfront Trail.

Frogs croak from ponds, dozens of tiny birds flit and chatter among the bushes, cormorants sit on mid-river logs drying their wings, and leggy blue herons flap away as you approach. Picnic tables and benches along the trail invite you to stop and enjoy it all leisurely. At about 1 mile the path bends away from the river, separated from it by a cattail marsh, and continues north to the intersection of Maple Street and 38th Street, where there is another parking lot and sani-can.

To reach the south end of the trail leave I-5 at any exit signed to either Broadway or Everett City Center. Take Broadway south from downtown to the intersection with 52nd Street SE; here turn east onto Lowell Road. The road ducks under the freeway, takes a ½-block jog south at South 3rd Avenue, then continues downhill to the east, crosses the railroad tracks, and arrives at the main parking lot. The boat launch area is another ½ mile farther along Lowell River Road.

The north end of the trail can be reached by turning south from Pacific Avenue on Smith Avenue. In ½ mile turn east on 36th Street, which ducks under the freeway and crosses the railroad tracks, then traces the north end of a reclaimed landfill area. In two blocks turn south toward the recycling station to reach the parking lot at road end.

PORT GARDNER AND EVERETT

Many communities along Puget Sound were founded on the basis of a rumor and pure speculation. When railroad magnate Jim Hill visited Everett in February of 1892, he commented on the boom, joking he had seen only four tree stumps that hadn't been given a town name. Unlike the many waterfront communities that died on the vine without the stimulus of industry and investors' money, Everett grabbed the brass ring on the speculation merry-go-round when in 1893 it became the West Coast terminus of the Great Northern Railroad.

Although Everett had been one of the last towns to be established on Puget Sound, in the years immediately preceding the arrival of the railroad it grew from a handful of settlers to over 3,000 persons rushing to make their fortunes in the anticipated economic boom. These first entrepreneurs cleared patches of land and lived in tents and hastily erected shacks—a local coffin maker found his wares were more in demand for bunks than for burials. The frenzied growth was fueled in 1889 by the discovery of gold and silver at Monte Cristo in the mountains 40 miles to the east. By 1892 construction was underway in Everett on a huge smelter that would handle the rich ores soon to arrive from the high Cascades.

Once its future was assured by the railroad, Everett settled down to a period of population growth and industrial expansion, although the output

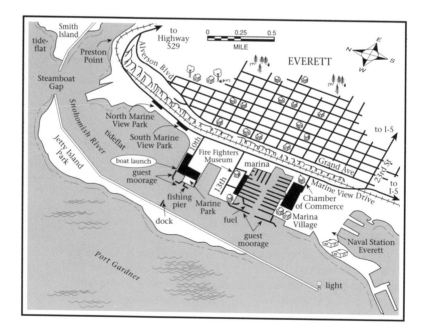

of the Monte Cristo mines was much more modest than had been anticipated. The economic depressions of 1893 and the 1930s affected the town, as they did all of the country, but the small metropolis on Port Gardner was able to ride out its difficulties and continue as an industrial center.

One of the most striking features of the town is its harbor. Back in 1895 town founder Henry Hewitt got the bright idea to divert the Snohomish River south along the waterfront to give the city a freshwater harbor. He planned to build a dike and a series of locks that would force the Snohomish River into a new channel. (Obviously this was before the days of environmental impact statements.) The rock dike was built; however, the mighty Snohomish was not to be domesticated, and it retaliated by dumping silt in its new channel, making it unusable for navigation. These engineering problems, coupled with financial difficulties, caused the project to be abandoned. A cut, called Steamboat Gap, was made through the dike at its north end, permitting the silt to collect in two settling basins. With locks now out of the question, the city was left with a rock breakwater serving nicely to shelter its (still saltwater) harbor.

Another major change to the Everett waterfront, Naval Station Everett, has recently been completed. In 1990 the Navy began construction of the base, and the first vessel arrived four years later. The 200-acre site along Port Gardner Bay is home base for the carrier *Nimitz*, as well as the cruisers, destroyers, and frigates of the seven-ship battle group.

Port of Everett Marina

Facilities: Guest moorage with power and water, restrooms, showers, laundry, marine pumpout station, fuel dock, haulouts (Travelifts, marine ways, hoist), groceries, restaurants, shopping, marine supply and repairs, boat charters and rental, farmers' market (Sundays in summer)

Over the years the Everett waterfront has seen a dramatic shift from a purely commercial status to a recreational one. Today the 2,000-plus slips in the Port of Everett boat harbor qualify it as the second largest marina on the West Coast, surpassed only by Marina Del Rey in California. The marina, lying behind the rock jetty, north of the commercial wharves, is easily spotted from either water or land—just watch for a forest of aluminum spars.

Two lighted markers are at the entrance to the dredged channel, at the south opening of the breakwater. Boats should enter well to the south to avoid a huge, buoy-marked shoal lying off the end of the Snohomish River and extending from Tulalip Bay to the southern end of the jetty. The main channel of the Snohomish River flows behind the dike, and the current can be quite strong, especially when it is combined with an outgoing tidal flow.

The marina basin lies between two 2,000-foot-long earth-filled piers. A network of floats extends from each of the piers, and a marine repair area with haulout slings is at the head of the basin. The Everett Yacht Club building on the north side is managed by the Port as a meeting and banquet facility. On the south pier is Marina Village, a collection of nice shops and restaurants done up in modern "olde-timey" decor; the marina administration office is on the east side of this complex.

Primary guest moorages are at the entrance to the basin on the two concrete floats that serve as a breakwater. When the river current is strong, docking at these outer floats can be difficult. The finger piers on the inside of the floats are fairly stable, but boats tied to the outside of the floats will be buffeted by the currents and boat wakes. Some permanent moorage slips are also sublet by the day when their boats are out of port. For boaters moored on the north section, it is more than a mile-long walk around the basin to facilities on the south, although it is just a short row— if you brought your dinghy. Visitors on the north side can pay for moorage at the west side of the Yacht Club building or the fuel dock to save a trip to the marina offices on the south side. A 100-foot-long disabled-accessible guest float can also be found at the east end of the marina.

By land the Port of Everett Marina is reached by leaving I-5 North at Exit 193 (Pacific Avenue, City Center) or I-5 South at Exit 194 (City Center, U.S. 2 E, Snohomish, Wenatchee) and driving west about 1½

Cyclists pause along the pier at the Port of Everett Marina.

miles to Marine View Drive. Turn north and in about 1¼ miles more the marina complex is reached.

Regular bus service connects Marina Village with downtown Everett, where there are services and shopping to meet every need. Merchants can provide information on schedules.

The Swiss chalet–style mansion at the entrance to the marina is worth a stop, whether visiting by land or water. The building was originally constructed in 1927 on the Everett waterfront as an office for the Weyerhaeuser sawmill. In 1938 the company moved it around Preston Point to a site up the Snohomish River just east of where the freeway crosses the channel. When the company closed its operations in Everett, they donated it to the city, and it was barged back downriver to its present site. It should certainly qualify as the most-traveled building around, as well as one of the most beautiful. It now serves as an office for the Chamber of Commerce (which has information about other interesting sites in Everett).

On the north side of the marina, on 13th Street, is a firefighters museum housed in an old fire station adjacent to a more modern one. The building is filled with memorabilia such as vintage hoses, nozzles, switchboards, fire helmets, and a few old fire engines. The museum is not staffed, so its historic treasures are viewed from outside through large windows.

North and South Marine View Parks (City of Everett)

Park Area: 4.5 acres; 1,200 feet of shoreline
Facilities: Park benches
Attractions: Viewpoint, walking

The city of Everett has turned a ½-mile stretch of shorefront along Port Gardner Bay into a pretty little viewing and strolling area. Although they are considered two separate parks, North and South Marine View Parks are really two car parking areas joined by a blacktop path, with several benches along the route. Up-close views are of rafts of thousands of logs waiting for the mill (or an extensive log-strewn mudflat at low tide) and lots of ducks, gulls, and cormorants. The more distant scene is of Possession Sound and blue-collar boats going about their daily work or pleasure cruisers headed for a day's leisure. An informational display at South Marine View Park tells some of the history of the area and describes local wildlife.

North Marine View Park is on West Marine View Drive, just as the street drops down from the bluff at the north end of the city; ¼ mile farther is the parking area for South Marine View Park. From here walks can continue south to the boat launch area of Marine Park or on to the Port of Everett Marina.

Marine Park (City of Everett)

Park Area: 21 acres; 710 feet of shoreline
Access: Land, boat
Facilities: Boat launch (ramp), floats, guest moorage, marine pumpout station, fishing pier and float, sailboard launch ramp, picnic tables, restrooms, passenger ferry to Jetty Island Park (summers only)
Attractions: Boating, picnicking, fishing, sailboarding (no kite flying)

This is, hands down, the best boat launch facility on Puget Sound. In a region that hypes itself as a boating capital, there ought to be many more like it. Located at the end of 10th Street, the concrete-surfaced launching area is 13 lanes wide, with a short boarding float between each pair of ramps. The adjacent parking lot has space for 300 vehicles and trailers. The ramps are well maintained, have a good slope, and have protection from weather. To facilitate use of the ramps, separate sections are designated for launching or retrieving boats. Concrete floats on the west side of the launch area serve both as a breakwater and guest moorage.

A pretty little grassy park on the bank south of the launch ramps offers picnic tables, benches, and nice views of both Jetty Island Park and the boating activities in the channel. A fishing pier and float in the river channel off the end of the park provide an opportunity for the boatless to share in the fun of angling. On the south edge of the park a single-lane concrete ramp drops to water level for launching sailboards. A large modern metal sculpture adds to the "first class" ambiance.

The first weekend in June, the park is the site of "Salty Sea Days," a nautical festival featuring pirates, parades, log-rolling contests, a barbecue, kayak races, fireworks, and numerous other fun events.

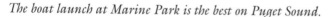

The boat launch at Marine Park is the best on Puget Sound.

Jetty Island Park (City of Everett)

Park Area: 160 acres; 13,200 feet of shoreline
Facilities: Picnic tables, latrines, dock, interpretive hut, free passenger ferry
   (summer only)

For years people took for granted the rock jetty that created the Everett harbor—it served nicely to shelter the moorages, it was a handy final resting place for old barges (which also served to stabilize the sand and silt), and it was an ideal seagull parking lot. Eventually the secret got out about what a great spot the jetty is, and now it is the darling of the Everett waterfront—and if you don't have your own boat to get there, the city will transport you!

The Jetty Island Park dock is across from the boat launch area at Marine Park, making it convenient for small boats to cross the ¼-mile-wide channel; if traveling in paddle-powered craft, be aware that the current can be strong at times. Kayakers will enjoy a circumnavigation of 2-mile-long Jetty Island, exploring hulks of beached barges and passageways around old pilings and logs. From July 1 through Labor Day, a city park's passenger ferry leaves from the Marine Park dock at regular intervals, taking visitors on the 10-minute jaunt to the jetty. The trip is a bargain—it's free!

Summer tides flowing over the long sandy shoals on the west side of Jetty Island are warmed to near-bathtub temperatures on sunny days; the sand is the best around for castle construction. A hands-on interpretive hut above the dock gives visitors the feel of the habitat, and free ranger-led activities are provided. Picnic tables are scattered in the beach grass at the top of the dike.

A large colony of sea lions frequents the island in winter and spring before heading to breeding grounds in southern California. They can often be seen hauled out on the beached barges at the southern end of the dike. Observe them from a distance, as they have little fear of humans and can be dangerous.

Howarth City Park (City of Everett)

Park Area: 28 acres; 3,960 feet of shoreline
Access: Land, boat
Facilities: Picnic tables, restrooms, hiking trails, tennis courts, horseshoe
   pits, children's play equipment
Attractions: Beachcombing, hiking, fishing

In the late 1800s, when railroads first arrived at Puget Sound and made their way to welcoming pioneer settlements, the logical route for tracks was the path of least resistance. Inland were ravines, hills, and dense forests, so the tracks were laid along the shoreline—between Seattle and

Everett some 30 miles of beachfront is consumed by railroad beds. As it traveled along the shore, the railroad cut across numerous small spits, leaving them exiled from the rest of the land. Several of these spits eventually became community parks, with elaborate pedestrian viaducts crossing the tracks. In fact, it almost seems the bridge architects were vying with one another to create the most unique design.

One of these parks, Howarth City Park, on the south side of Everett, spans not only the shoreline, but also an adjoining gully and bluff top. To find the park, leave I-5 at Exit 192 (Broadway, Naval Station, Port of Everett) and drive west on 41st Street SE, which eventually becomes Mukilteo Boulevard. At a small shopping center, turn north on Olympic Boulevard and follow this road as it circles through a residential area to a viewpoint marking the north end of the park; here are stunning views out over Possession Sound. The road then hairpins down to the lower entrance of the park. You may choose not to turn at the eastern intersection of Olympic Boulevard and continue west on Mukilteo Boulevard for another mile, to where the west end of the loop of Olympic Boulevard can be caught at Upper Howarth Park.

At the lower entrance to the park a road goes north, down the gully of Pigeon Creek No. 2, to a parking lot. From this entrance a trail also follows the west bank of the creek through thick brush and past some tiny waterfalls to reach the parking lot. From the west side of the lot, a trail crosses the creek and climbs a tier of stairs, reaching a railroad overpass. Across the tracks a spiral staircase winds around a remarkable castle-like, three-level tower to the beach. The grass-and-sand flat of the park is on a landfill behind a riprap bulkhead. Small boats can be landed on the beach in calm weather. There are no restroom facilities at the beach.

Southwest of the railroad overpass, stairs and a trail climb up the gulch to a viewpoint 100 feet above, on a curve of Olympic Boulevard, and to the upper portion of the park. A sign at the viewpoint tells of the area's past and includes historical photos of the park and the

The tower at Howarth City Park

construction of the first road between Everett and Mukilteo. Upper Howarth Park is the more "civilized" section, with grassy expanses, picnic tables, restrooms, tennis courts, horseshoe pits, and play equipment for kids.

MUKILTEO

Facilities: Ferry terminal, fishing pier, groceries, restaurants, stores, bait, boat rentals, gas, marine supplies and repairs
Attractions: Boating, fishing, beach walking

The early Native Americans called this point of land *Muckl-Te-Oh,* meaning "good camping." That this was a favored spot of the local Native Americans undoubtedly prompted Governor Isaac Stevens to choose it as one of three meeting sites on Puget Sound used for signing the treaty in which the Native Americans gave up their lands and agreed to live on reservations. Over 2,000 Native Americans from 22 different tribes met here in January of 1855 to be read the Point Elliot Treaty and have their chiefs place their marks on the document. Considering that they relinquished all of the territory from Tacoma north to the Canadian border and east to the crest of the Cascades in exchange for meager reservation lands and a monetary pittance, the Native Americans may now more appropriately call the site "Bamboozle."

A year after the signing of the Point Elliot Treaty, Morris H. Frost, a customs collector from Port Townsend, and J. D. Fowler, who had been running a saloon on Whidbey Island, established a trading post at Mukilteo to exchange flour, blankets, gunpowder, and other white man's goods for Native American furs. When the reservation lands were finally allotted and the Native Americans moved onto them, settlers began to establish claims at Mukilteo. By 1875, 10 streets had been laid out, and the new town had a modern steam-operated sawmill, salmon saltery, brewery, telegraph station, school, and several taverns and hotels.

By 1910 the town was booming, capitalizing on growth in nearby

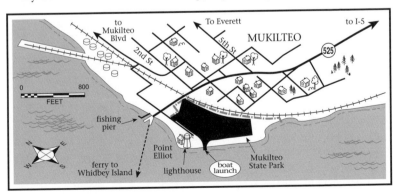

The Mukilteo lighthouse is near the ferry landing.

Everett. A powder mill established here was the largest on Puget Sound, surpassing in size the Dupont Powder Company south of Tacoma. At its peak it turned out 400,000 tons of explosives monthly for shipment throughout the West for use in land clearing, logging, railroad building, and mining. In September of 1930 the town boomed in quite another way, when the powder works was destroyed by a series of shattering explosions and fireworks, forcing the temporary evacuation of the town.

Earlier that same year the lumber mill had closed its doors, and when the vacant mill buildings burned to the ground eight years later in a spectacular fire, the industrial life of Mukilteo came to a resounding end. Today the town leads a quiet life as a suburb of Everett and a terminal for the ferry to Whidbey Island.

Mukilteo is reached by turning off I-5 at Exit 189 (Mukilteo, Whidbey Island Ferry, Highway 526 W) and driving west on Highway 526 and then north on 525. The ferry landing is at the bottom of the hill. Here, turn right to the town's shopping area or left to the state park.

The Mukilteo lighthouse, first staffed in 1906, is west of the ferry terminal, next to the state park. The lighthouse, with its handmade lens dating from 1858, is open to public tours Saturdays and Sundays, 1:00 P.M. to 4:00 P.M., April through September. Special tours can be arranged by calling City Hall at (425) 355-4141.

Mukilteo Fishing Pier

An L-shaped public fishing pier, operated by the Port of Everett, is on the east side of the Mukilteo ferry landing. In addition to fishing, it is a good place to watch the comings and goings of the nautical buses. The pier can be reached via a walkway angling off from the side of the ferry pier. A nearby boathouse has bait and tackle for sale.

Mukilteo State Park

Park Area: 17.6 acres; 1,495 feet of shoreline
Access: Land, boat
Facilities: Boat launch (ramp), boarding float, picnic tables, fireplaces, restrooms, concession stand
Attractions: Boating, fishing, walking, scuba diving, kite flying

This day-use park consists primarily of a three-lane boat launch ramp with adjoining boarding float and a large parking lot. When entering the park, turn left—traffic goes clockwise, rather than the expected counter-clockwise. Be aware that a fee is charged for parking in the first 60 or so spots just inside the park entrance. These slots, which are used primarily by commuters, are marked by painted stripes and numbers.

Although the boat ramp is heavily used, unfortunately it is considered one of the worst on Puget Sound. Launching is difficult because the point is exposed to westerly and southwesterly winds. When winds are strong, boaters are wise to drive north to Everett to launch. The ramp is also difficult to use at low tide because of the very gradual slope at its upper level. About 15 feet beyond the last piling of the boarding float, the ramp drops off sharply.

The nicest part of the state park is the picnic area stretching along the shore south from the launch ramp. Here are tables, fire stands, and a wide gravel beach for sunbathing. The chilly water is only for the brave or for those rare hot days when even Puget Sound water is inviting. Because the point picks up winds sweeping down Possession Sound, it is a grand spot for flying kites.

Picnic Point County Park (Snohomish County)

Park Area: 15 acres; 1,200 feet of shoreline
Access: Land, boat
Facilities: Picnic tables, fireplaces, sani-cans
Attractions: Picnicking, scuba diving

Picnicking is not required, but if you forget the lunch you'll regret it, because you'll want to stay all day. Picnic tables are on a grassy, maple-shaded flat, complete with a trickling stream. The sand and gravel beach below fans ever-outward, offering endless possibilities for sunbathing, castle building, or Frisbee throwing. Scuba divers who explore the seabed, which slopes gently down to 70 feet, find crabs, flounders, skates, sea pens, moon snails, and other sand-loving critters. Pollution, however, has made the beach unsafe for swimming, fishing, or taking of shellfish.

The park is midway between Mukilteo and Edmonds. One block south of the intersection of Highways 99 and 525, turn west from 99 onto Shelby Road. In about 1¼ miles Shelby crosses Beverly Park Road and becomes Picnic Point Road. At a Y-intersection in another ¾ mile, bear right as Picnic Point Road drops down a wooded gully to its end at a parking lot next to

The trail to the beach at Picnic Point County Park

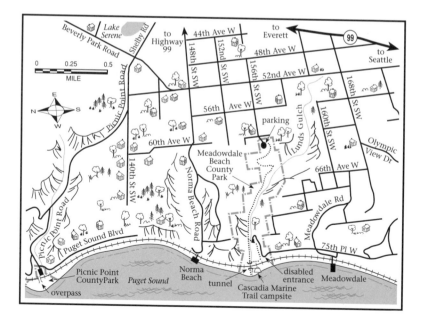

the railroad tracks. An elaborate concrete and steel pedestrian bridge (disabled accessible) crosses the tracks.

Norma Beach and Meadowdale

The small communities of Norma Beach and Meadowdale lie on the shore midway between Everett and Edmonds. For anglers, these places are significant because of their closeness to Possession Bar, a huge underwater shelf extending from the south end of Whidbey Island. The bar offers year-round fishing for a wide variety of fish, although salmon is the most sought-after prize.

In the past, two boathouses at Norma Beach and Meadowdale offered boat rentals, launching, gas, and supplies for anglers. Both have suffered financial difficulties and the facilities are somewhat the worse for the wear. Public boat rentals may or may not be available; if you are hoping to rent a boat from here, call first to check out the current viability of the businesses.

There are no public beaches at either location.

Meadowdale Beach County Park (Snohomish County)

Park Area: 95 acres; 1,000 feet of shoreline
Access: Land
Facilities: Picnic sites, picnic shelter, sani-cans, hiking trail, Cascadia Marine Trail campsite

This jewel-like park, lying between Norma Beach and Meadowdale, is a relatively recent addition to the Snohomish County Parks system. A 1¼-mile hike down the long wooded stretch of Lunds Gulch is required to reach the beach and its adjacent picnic area, although a lower access road and parking area are available for the disabled.

To drive to the main (upper) park entrance, turn west from Highway 99 at either 148th Street SW or 168th Street SW. Use either street to reach 52nd Avenue W, then follow 52nd to either 152nd Street SW or 160th Street SW. Go west four blocks on either street to 56th Avenue W and follow it to 156th Street SW. Turn west on 156th Street SW, which arrives at the park's upper parking lot in two blocks.

To reach the access for disabled persons, leave Highway 99 at 168th Street SW, and follow it west to 66th Avenue W. Turn north on 66th, then west on Meadowdale Road to 75th Place W. Follow 75th north to the park and the parking lot. This access is always gated. Disabled persons wishing to use it may obtain a keycard by telephoning the Snohomish County Parks and Recreation Division at the number listed in appendix A.

Check the map of the park and its trail at the kiosk at the upper parking lot before you head out. Just below the parking lot is the upper picnic area—

A bridge crosses Lunds Gulch near the lower picnic area at Meadowdale Beach County Park.

a grassy bowl with a few trees and a pair of picnic tables along its edge. The trail descends through second-growth alder, then switchbacks steeply down to the floor of the gully where moisture provided by Lunds Gulch Creek and side streamlets nurtures cedar, ferns, and salal.

On the floor of the gulch watch for several old cedar stumps, some up to 8 feet in diameter, that have springboard notches. These deep grooves were cut for springboards on which loggers stood when cutting the trees. Most of these huge stumps now boast new, smaller trees growing from their tops.

The trail continues through a cathedral arch of red alder, then breaks into the open a few hundred yards above the beach, where the ranger's residence and lower picnic area are reached. Wooden planks bridge the stream as it flows under the railroad tracks, through an underpass to the beach.

At the shore, look out to the south end of Whidbey Island and across the sound to the Olympic Mountains. The sand and gravel beach tapering gently out into the sound is ideal for wading; swimmers should be cautious, as there are sudden drop-offs in the water. The Cascadia Marine Trail campsite located here requires advanced reservation to assure access from the beach through the tunnel that leads to the upland portion of the park.

Sailboarding on Puget Sound off Edmonds

EDMONDS

From its elaborate underwater scuba diving park to its flower beds of blazing color, Edmonds has put a lot of effort into making its waterfront inviting as well as functional. The waterfront complex begins and ends with parks—and even has parks in-between. In the center of everything is the ferry terminal, with its giant boats sailing hourly to Kingston on the Kitsap Peninsula. Numerous postcards and travel brochures have carried photographs of this ferry gliding picturesquely into the scarlet sunset against the black silhouette of the Olympic Mountains.

By water, the Edmonds harbor is 9 nautical miles north of Seattle's Shilshole Bay, or 13 nautical miles south of Everett. To drive to Edmonds, leave I-5 at Exit 177 (Edmonds, Lake Forest Park, Highway 104), which is signed to Edmonds and the Kingston ferry. Highway 104 (Edmonds Way) goes directly into town. Stay left to avoid ending up in the waiting lanes of the ferry terminal.

A marshland west of the highway, just as the road enters town, is a 23-acre wildlife sanctuary. The wetland was partially filled to build a shopping mall, but fortunately this section was saved in its natural state. The forest of cattails attracts large numbers of red-winged blackbirds as well as other marsh-loving birds.

The Edmonds business district, with its wide range of stores and services, is within walking distance of the waterfront. The small complex on the waterfront has several stores, including one selling fresh seafood.

Harbor Square, a large shopping center west of Edmonds Way (Highway 104) at the foot of Dayton Street, includes a hotel and shops that sell everything from marine supplies to lingerie. Old Mill Town, which has shopping with turn-of-the-century atmosphere, is at Dayton Street and 5th Avenue S. Because of the area's popularity with scuba divers, air fills and other needed supplies are available in the town.

Walk two blocks north of Mill Town, past a prettily spurting fountain, to find the Chamber of Commerce and Edmonds Museum (open Tuesdays, Thursdays, Saturdays, and Sundays, 1:00 P.M. to 4:00 P.M.), just north of the corner of 5th Avenue N and Main Street. The Chamber of Commerce is in an interesting historic log cabin.

In 1870 a severe storm chanced to force the canoe of logger George Brackett onto the beach here. Brackett was so impressed with the spot that he purchased land north of Edwards Point, where he built a wharf and general store. The town's main claim to historic fame came in 1890 when, falling 2 short of the 72 signatures necessary for filing the petition to incorporate the town, Brackett added the names of two of his oxen, Bolivar and Isaac, to the document. When, thanks to his oxen, the town was incorporated, he became its first mayor.

A more recent source of fame for the town are the many Olympic athletes the town has produced. Twelve Olympic competitors have hailed from Edmonds (perhaps a record for a city of this size); one of the waterfront parks has been dedicated in their honor.

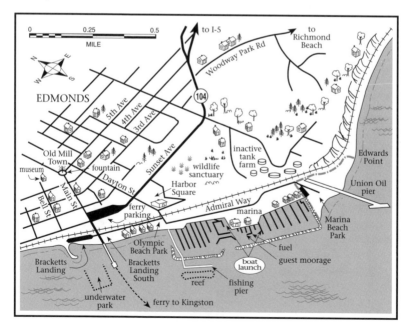

Port of Edmonds Marina

Facilities: Guest moorage with power and water, diesel, gas, boat launch (sling), restrooms, showers, ice, bait, tackle, groceries (limited), boat charters and rentals, marine supplies and repair, picnic tables, restaurants

Although the guest boating facilities at the Port of Edmonds Marina are small, they are exceptionally nice. Most of the 900-slip yacht basin is covered and private. The entrance to the marina is in the center of the rock breakwater, marked with daymarkers and lights. A second breakwater inside the entrance channels traffic north and south. Guest slips are immediately south of the inner breakwater, along the bulkhead north of the fuel dock; power and water are available. Noise from the hoist just south of the fuel dock may jolt boaters out of their slumber when eager anglers begin to launch their boats just after daybreak. The Travelift and the launching facilities at the south end of the basin are for the use of boats kept in the dry storage areas.

The Port of Edmonds office, on the shore by the fuel dock, has restrooms with showers. Bait, marine supplies, groceries, and other necessities can be found in downtown Edmonds, within easy walking distance of the marina. A nice little promenade, with picnic tables, benches, and flower boxes, lies above the moorage, offering balcony views of the activity below or out across the jetty to the frosty peaks of the Olympics. From here sunset views can be exquisite.

Edmonds Underwater Park (Bracketts Landing)

Park Area: 27 acres; 1,800 feet of shoreline
Access: Land, boat
Facilities: Restrooms, changing rooms, shower, underwater reef, submarine diver trails, tidepools, informational displays
Attractions: Swimming, scuba diving, beach walking, sea lions

The underwater park north of the Edmonds ferry terminal is unquestionably the most popular dive site on Puget Sound. It began accidentally when a 500-foot-long dry dock was sunk here in 1935, long before anyone (except perhaps Jules Verne) had even dreamed of scuba diving. The wreck, with its thickly encrusted marine life, became a focal point for divers, and in 1971 the area was declared a marine preserve. Since that time, eight major structures have been added, including two large tugboats, concrete culvert stars, and a reef of earthmover tires. Floats mark the harbor line and the locations of the various underwater features, and submarine trails are marked by tethered ropes along the bottom of the cove.

Sea lions who have discovered this marine preserve move into the area

Bracketts Landing South is a great spot to watch the ferry and play in the sand.

in winter and spring. They are a fascinating sight from shore or from the decks of the ferry, but fishermen and scuba divers view them with a jaundiced eye as they deplete the fish life and pose a threat to divers. By mid-spring most have departed for breeding grounds in California and Mexico.

Boats, including canoes, kayaks, and dinghies, are not permitted within the boundaries of the park. Divers arriving by boat can anchor offshore in 30 to 35 feet of water.

Because the area is now protected, fish have become quite tame, and divers may see huge rockfish, wolf eels, lingcod, cabezon, and a wide variety of other fish, as well as octopuses. The Edmonds Parks and Recreation Department offers a brochure showing a map of the underwater area and listing regulations and safety precautions.

For nondivers the park is an interesting spot to watch the activity or, at low tide, to explore tidepools and marine life on the rock jetty; remember, this is a marine refuge and all plants, animals, and habitat are protected. Parks Department Beach Rangers are at the park during most summer afternoons on which minus tides occur, from two hours before low tide until two hours after. They will provide information about the marine and beach environment. Groups can schedule lectures by calling the Edmonds Parks Department. The beach can be walked north for some distance, but it soon narrows to a strip below the rocks of the railroad bed and at high tide disappears altogether.

A second and newer Edmonds park is Bracketts Landing South, a 2-acre flat immediately south of the ferry slip. The uplands lead to a pleasant, driftwood-rimmed sandy beach. The city intends that the park will have only minimal development. The underwater area offshore is also a marine preserve, where taking of marine life is prohibited.

Public Fishing Pier and Olympic Beach

Park Area: 4 acres; 300 feet of shoreline
Access: Land
Facilities: Fishing pier, restrooms, bait, tackle, snack bar, informational
displays, picnic tables

The Edmonds fishing pier was the first such facility on Puget Sound to be built exclusively for fishing. It has served as a model for numerous other piers constructed since then in the area. The L-shaped concrete pier begins on the northeast side of the yacht basin, inside the rock jetty, then crosses the breakwater and turns south to follow its outside edge. The pier, which is open 24 hours a day, has several bait- and fish-cleaning areas, along with informational displays and benches for watching the action.

A reef of tires has been placed 50 feet offshore from the pier to provide habitat for fish as well as for the marine life they feed on. The pilings of the pier and the rock jetty serve to divert the movement of the fish along the length of the pier to waiting fishermen's hooks. Scuba diving is not permitted in the vicinity of the fishing pier.

On the rock breakwater a school of fanciful salmon glitter and leap in the wind—they are a work of art created from recycled metal scraps such as can lids, forks, and fishing lures. If you don't see sea lions in the water, you'll find them on land, for sure—a life-size bronze sculpture of a group of sea lions, watched by a man and two children, sits at one end of the park.

Olympic Park, named for the town's athletes, is a stretch of manicured grass with picnic tables north of the fishing pier. The soft grass, or sandy beach below the bulkhead, is ideal for sunbathing or watching the ferries and feeding the city's official bird—the seagull.

Marina Beach and Union Oil Dock

Park Area: 7 acres; 978 feet of waterfront
Access: Land, boat
Facilities: Picnic tables, fireplaces, children's play structures, volleyball
net, sani-cans, drinking fountain, boat launch (hand-carry)
Attractions: Paddling, fishing, swimming, scuba diving, kite flying

At the south end of the Edmonds waterfront, Admiral Way curves around the boat storage sheds and deadends at a gem of a little park.

The Union Oil dock at Edmonds is a favorite with scuba divers.

Although the water may be chilly here, the sandy beach is so inviting one cannot help but want to wade into the waves. Above the beach is a nice assortment of driftwood to provide seats and backrests for an afternoon of lazing. Grassy mounds next to the parking lot are a favorite spot for flying kites.

The only restrooms are sani-cans in the parking lot next to the boat shed. A short road going to the south side of the park provides a spot close to the beach where car-top boats can be launched.

Scuba divers frequently put in here and swim out to explore the old pilings of the inactive Union Oil tanker pier. The bottom drops off rapidly to a depth of 100 feet, offering experienced divers an opportunity for deep dives a short distance from shore. Exercise extreme care, and stay under the dock and away from any boats in the area; jagged scraps of metal on the bottom also pose a hazard. The dock itself is off limits to public access. The beach south of the dock is park property that is maintained in a natural condition; Scotch broom and beach grass prevail.

THE SEATTLE AREA

The city of Seattle stretches along the east shore of Puget Sound for over 20 miles, filling shore, bluff, and ravine with residences and commercial enterprises. The town once fronted only on Elliott Bay, but today it has extended so far north and south that it dominates much of Middle Puget Sound, and its skyscrapers and Space Needle have become navigational landmarks from miles away.

Amid the metropolitan sprawl are an array of public facilities and accesses—some sublime, some fascinating, and some deliberately obscure. Here can be seen nearly every facet of the city—historical, natural, recreational, and scenic, as well as workaday.

THE NORTHERN SHORELINE

Richmond Beach County Park (King County)

Park Area: 40 acres; 900 feet of shoreline
Access: Land, boat
Facilities: Picnic tables, picnic shelters, fireplaces, restrooms, children's play area, changing rooms, viewpoint, water
Attractions: Beachcombing, picnicking, walking, bicycling, scuba diving, tidepools, views

For a quick getaway on a sunny afternoon from the metropolitan areas along the east shore of Middle Puget Sound, Richmond Beach is the ideal destination—however, if it is a weekend, you might find that hundreds of others had the same idea. Because this is the nicest beach north of Golden Gardens, it is heavily used; but the beach has space for a good-sized throng, and several pockets of picnic tables on the uplands provide ample spots to spread out a lunch and enjoy a broad view of the sound.

Opposite: *The public yacht basin on the Seattle waterfront lies in the shadows of skyscrapers.*

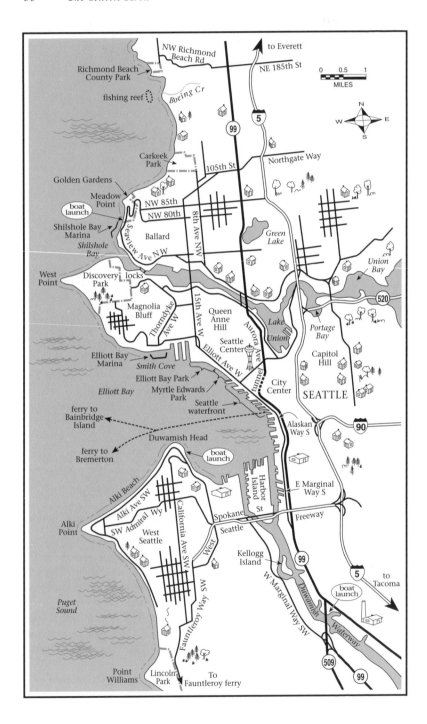

Richmond Beach County Park has a wide, sandy beach.

To reach the park by land, turn west off Aurora Avenue (Highway 99) onto North 185th Street. As 185th heads downhill it becomes Northwest Richmond Beach Road, then Northwest 195th Street. At the intersection with 20th Avenue NW, turn south and follow the road to its end at the park.

The park is divided into two sections by the shoreside railroad tracks. Upland from the tracks is a large parking lot with adjoining restrooms. Three large, concrete-walled areas are laid out on the sandy shelf between the entrance road and the main parking lot. One has an elaborate collection of children's play equipment; a second has picnic tables; and a third has a covered picnic shelter and an adjacent hemisphere of picnic tables shaded by an overhead metal lattice-work. Stairs and trails link the three areas to the entrance road. Another circular-walled picnic area is just below the road about 50 yards inside the entrance.

A small parking lot about 100 yards below the entrance has a trail leading south along the base of the upper bank to yet another picnic area rimmed by a low concrete wall. West of the park entrance, just below 195th Street, a line of benches set into a low retaining wall offer lazy viewing of the goings on in the sound south toward Meadow and West Points. On the opposite side of the entrance road, a flat gravel path winds along the top of the bank for nearly ¼ mile before arriving at a broad grass flat shaded by two stately madronas. This is one of the most magnificent view spots in Richmond Beach, overlooking the heart of Middle Sound and the entire span of the Olympic Mountains.

To reach the lower beach section of the park, follow an asphalt path

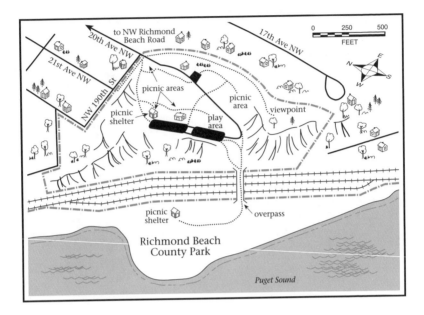

from the parking lot that wanders through a wooded glen with some picnic tables and the requisite babbling brook. Beyond, the trail reaches an overpass high above the railroad tracks, then descends to the beach. Restrooms, a picnic shelter, and nearby picnic tables perch on a bench above the steep sandy slope to the shore. The sand and gravel beach below is backed by grassy dunes and a string of driftwood. Shoal areas on either side of the point are exposed at moderate tides, extending the beach far to the north and south; at extreme low water, tidepools and the scattered remains of an old wreck lying just offshore are exposed. The most inviting beachcombing is south, below a wild 100-foot bluff.

During the 1930s many old sailing ships, reaching the end of their days, were towed to Richmond Beach and burned. Copper and brass were later salvaged from the ashes. Corroded iron fittings frequently uncovered on the beach may be from these old vessels.

The gradually sloping bottom is excellent for beginning scuba divers, who can spot sea pens, starfish, hermit crabs, and snails.

Boeing Creek Fishing Reef

About 1 mile south of Richmond Beach is the deep wooded ravine of Boeing Creek. An artificial reef, marked by buoys, has been placed offshore here to improve fishing in the area. The reef is 3½ nautical miles from the launch facilities at either Edmonds to the north or Seattle's Golden Gardens to the south. There is no upland access.

Carkeek Park (City of Seattle)

Park Area: 223 acres; 2,000 feet of shoreline
Access: Land, boat (shallow-draft boats only)
Facilities: Picnic tables, shelters, fireplaces, restrooms, sani-cans, trails, model airplane field, Environmental Education Center, children's playground
Attractions: Hiking, nature trail, picnicking, views, beachcombing, kite flying

Carkeek, the most northerly of Seattle's parks fronting on Puget Sound, combines two worlds: the saltwater and the forested. The saltwater offerings are nice enough—even though approach by boat is difficult, and the gently sloping sandy beach is ample to hold several hundred sunbathing, wading, sand castle–building, or beachcombing people.

Ah, but the forest! The park plunges deeply inland along the canyon of Pipers Creek and the side ravines of Venema and Mohlendorph Creeks and several smaller freshets. Miles of trails wander along the ravine bottoms and up hillsides in a semiwilderness with a dense cover of wild rose, berry bushes, nettles, devil's club, alder, maple, birch, and ferns. A maze of trails loop about, joining each other or the park roads; some are wide and well trod, others are scarcely more than boot paths. The ravines of Venema and Mohlendorph Creeks contain the few cedar and hemlock that survived the logging that stripped the area, and here is the park's closest approximation of an old-growth forest environment. A botanical trail in the ravines has been developed where introduced plants have been cleared out and native ones replanted in an attempt to return the area to its natural state.

In the late 1800s the ravine was the site of a sawmill that was fed by the harvest of the surrounding forest. An overgrown vestige of the skid road used to feed logs to the mill site can still be picked out on the hillside above what is now the lower picnic area of the park. A brickyard once operated here on the south side of Pipers Creek. With the

Chum salmon fry in the imprint pond at Carkeek Park

forest gone, the land was purchased in 1891 for a farm by pioneer A. W. Piper, who had lost his bakery and candy company in the great Seattle fire of 1889. Produce and flowers from Piper's garden in the ravine were carted to downtown Seattle and sold from a wagon at the Pike Place Market. His wife, Minna, planted an orchard of apple and pear trees, which can still be seen alongside the main trail up the ravine east from the Metro pump station. The property was sold for a park in 1927 and dedicated in 1929, although development did not come until some time later.

At one time great numbers of salmon swam up Pipers Creek and spawned in the gravel beds of Pipers and Venema Creeks. A salmon company trapped fish here until the 1930s, but as erosion from civilization's activities covered the gravelly spawning grounds and pollution fouled the water, the salmon runs ceased. A recent effort has been made to restore the creek to its original state and reestablish the salmon runs. Each spring since 1980, chum salmon fry from a south sound hatchery have been placed in an imprint pond at the mouth of Mohlendorph Creek and released a few weeks later to find their way downstream to the sound. Adult

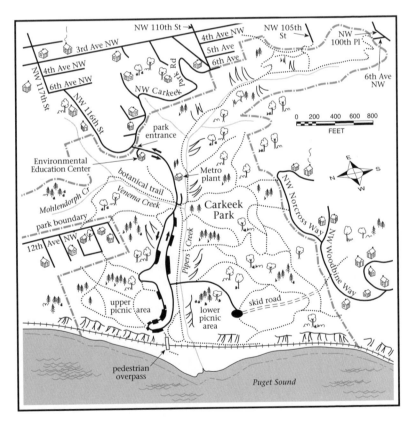

The pedestrian overpass at Carkeek Park provides high views of the beach and the Olympic Mountains beyond the sound.

salmon are now seen in ever-increasing numbers as they return to spawn.

To reach Carkeek Park by land, follow any north–south arterial to North 105th Street, then go west on 105th to its intersection with Greenwood Avenue N and Holman Road NW. To reach the park's main entrance, turn north on Greenwood, and in two blocks head west on Northwest 110th Street, which soon becomes Northwest Carkeek Park Road as it winds ¾ mile down steep, twisting curves to the park entrance. The Environmental Education Center is just above the entrance, and the trail system leaves from various spots at the park's three picnic areas. To find the upper end of the Pipers Creek trail, at the intersection of Holman Road and 3rd Avenue NW, turn north on 3rd, and in one block head west on Northwest 103rd Street, which soon becomes Northwest 100th Place. The trailhead is at the intersection of 100th Place and 6th Avenue NW, just across the street from a shopping center parking lot.

The beach is reached from a parking lot at the upper picnic area on the northwest side of the ravine; here a pedestrian overpass crosses the railroad tracks. On a day with a good breeze, it offers excellent kite flying, or maybe just a pleasant rest against the driftwood logs below the railroad tracks, enjoying the sun and salt breeze.

Habitat restoration in the Pipers Creek drainage has become a major community project, involving schools, residents, and government agencies, and a host of environmentally oriented programs are offered at the park. In 1996 the wetland at the mouth of the drainage was enhanced, and an innovative playground focused on an environmental theme was added to the park.

Shilshole Bay

Golden Gardens (City of Seattle)

Park Area: 95 acres; 3,850 feet of shoreline
Access: Land, boat
Facilities: Picnic tables, fireplaces, picnic shelters, restrooms, concession stand, bathhouse, volleyball courts, children's play equipment
Attractions: Beachcombing, swimming (no lifeguard), wading, boating, paddling, fishing, boardsailing, scuba diving, birdwatching, kite flying

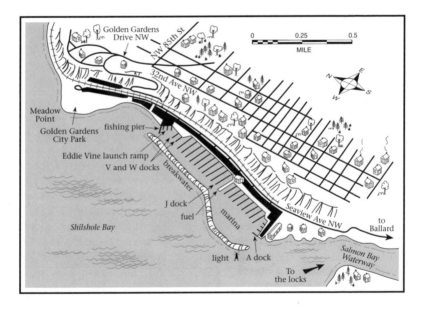

The beach at Golden Gardens attracts sunbathers on summer days.

In summer, during sunny weather, hordes of Seattle sun worshipers are lured to Golden Gardens. For over 80 years the beaches of Meadow Point, north of Shilshole Bay, have seen a succession of youths engaged in the courting rituals of the time, picnickers on family outings, and mothers tending toddlers enthralled with building fantasies in the sand.

Named in 1907 by its owners, Harry and Olive Treat, the beach was then the terminus of a trolley line that offered city dwellers a weekend salt-air retreat—surely it was only a coincidence that the route passed through adjoining areas of prime real estate huckstering. A shipyard operated here until 1913. The land was acquired by the city for a park in 1923.

The park is split by the railroad tracks; to the east is a wooded sidehill threaded by trails, while west of the tracks is the marvelous sandy beach for which Golden Gardens is so well known. The ¾-mile-long beach is an outward-curving, golden strand of sand topped by silvered driftwood. Icy Puget Sound waters, flowing over the shallow bottom, warm in summer to temperatures pleasant enough for swimming and wading.

The park has two entrances—an upper one at the top of the bluff and a lower one at the south end of the shore. To reach the upper entrance, take nearly any north–south arterial to Northwest 85th Street; turn west and follow 85th to 32nd Avenue NW. Here turn north and follow serpentine Golden Gardens Drive NW down to the park; the upper picnic area is passed along the way.

For the lower entrance, find your way to Northwest Market Street, the main east–west thoroughfare through Ballard, and follow it west past the locks, where it first becomes Northwest 54th Street, then Seaview Avenue NW. Continue on Seaview as it curves around Shilshole Bay past the Shilshole Bay Marina to terminate in the lower parking lot at Golden Gardens, just above the beach. A second parking lot is located above the railroad tracks off Golden Gardens Drive NW.

Although the beach throng in itself may be enough entertainment for the day, there's also the stream of boats in and out of the north entrance to the marina, the tug and freighter traffic on the sound, and the rugged peaks of the Olympic Mountains. Fly a kite, launch a sailboard, watch a sailboat race, or just wander to the north end of the park and hunker in the driftwood and beach grass for a tan and a semblance of solitude.

It's even a nice place to visit on a blustery winter day when the beach crowd has departed and the bite of wind across the sand brings refreshing memories of our common saltwater origin. Take along binoculars to watch for loons, black brant, and other seabirds on their migratory routes.

Eddie Vine Boat Launch

Facilities: Boat launch (ramp), bait, concession stand, fishing pier

Immediately south of Golden Gardens on Seaview Avenue NW is the Eddie Vine boat launch ramp, a 95-foot-wide asphalt ramp with boarding floats along either side and down the middle. It is busy year-round as a launch point for the hordes of anglers plying the sound. There is ample parking for about 100 cars and trailers in two large lots north of the ramp. A concession stand/bait shop is located just south of the ramp. The wavebreak at the north side of the launch area has a disabled-accessible walkway on top to allow it to be used as a fishing pier.

Shilshole Bay Marina

Facilities: Guest moorage with power and water, diesel, gas, propane, boat launch (cranes, hoist), groceries (limited), ice, fishing piers, bait, tackle, marine supplies and repairs, dry storage, marine pumpout station, restrooms, showers, laundry, snack bar, restaurant, shops

The vast boat "parking lot" on the north shore of Seattle is a certified tourist attraction, agleam with fiberglass, mahogany, teak, chrome, aluminum, and acres of bright blue canvas. It's the place to bring visitors to

Shilshole Bay Marina is one of the largest on Puget Sound.

show them a little of what boating on Puget Sound is about, or the place for locals to go to dream about their first boat—or their next one.

Shilshole Bay Marina is the second largest saltwater moorage on Puget Sound, surpassed only by the Port of Everett Marina. A multiyear waiting list for permanent moorage attests to its popularity. Permanent moorage is not the only attraction, as the marina also offers full services for visiting boaters, as well as nautical-related shops and a restaurant with spectacular views over a forest of masts in the basin to profiles of distant Olympic peaks.

The marina has provided moorage to Seattle residents and visitors for over 30 years. The U.S. Army Corps of Engineers started work on the enclosing breakwater in 1957; the marina itself was built in several stages by the Port of Seattle over a period of 20 years. Today it has nearly 1,500 permanent slips and about 75 guest moorages, plus areas for dry storage and small centerboard sailboats.

By land, Shilshole Bay is reached by following the main street through Ballard, Northwest Market Street, west past the locks. The street becomes Northwest 54th and then Seaview Avenue NW. The marina lies 1 mile beyond the locks. A huge parking lot has space for over 1,400 vehicles.

From Shilshole Bay, boat entrances to the marina are located at either end of the 4,400-foot-long rock breakwater fronting the yacht basin. The controlling depth in the channel behind the breakwater is 15 feet, and 10 feet in the area of the moorages. Guest moorage is located on J dock. Check with the marina office in the administration building regarding guest moorage.

There is also limited guest moorage at each end of the marina; at the north end, moorage is available along the north side of V and W docks, and at the south end along the head of A dock and at a small float between A and B docks. A self-registration station for boats using the south is located at building M-7 at the head of A dock. A boat repair yard with hoists is also located here. Seven small buildings with restrooms and showers are located along the parking area; the ones above J and L docks also have laundry facilities.

Most of the marina shops, restaurants, and facilities are located in the administration building near the center of the marina. Fuel, groceries, supplies, and a marine pumpout station are near the end of the central pier between I and J docks. For visitors arriving by boat, the Metro bus runs at regular intervals along Seaview Avenue. The Ballard district, with dozens of shops and services, is a few minutes' ride away; downtown Seattle is a little farther. Note that large portions of the parking are reserved for moorage tenants only, and cars without stickers will be towed.

Walk the promenade along the bulkhead at the head of the docks and choose the boat of your dreams from those tethered at the moorages below; however, except for guest docks, all dock gates are locked and accessible only by tenants. Fishing is permitted from the end section of A dock and from the pier forming the wavebreak at the far north end of the marina, south of the launch ramps.

Salmon Bay

The transition from salt- to freshwater, from tidal to nontidal, and from the outer shores to the heart of the city takes place in a 6-mile-long, east–west channel dividing Seattle in two. The canal began in 1871 as a gleam in the eye of the U.S. War Department, which conducted a search throughout the Pacific Northwest for a naval station for ship repair and resupplying. One prime candidate was Lake Washington, which had the advantages of being protected from enemy forces, close to coal supplies from mines just east of the lake, near the terminus of proposed intercontinental rail lines, and adjacent to the area's largest population center—the growing little community of Seattle.

A survey identified several possible locations for a navigable channel and set of locks that would join the nontidal waters of Lake Washington to the tidal waters of Puget Sound. One was on the lake's natural outlet via the Duwamish River to the south. Other routes proposed a cut through the narrow strip of land between Portage Bay and Union Bay in order to join Lake Washington to Lake Union. From Lake Union, canal routes were proposed either (1) at Lake Union's natural outlet through Salmon Bay to Shilshole Bay, (2) through Salmon Bay and then south to Smith Cove on Elliott Bay, or (3) from the south end of Lake Union around the southeast side of Queen Anne Hill to the north end of Elliott Bay. The last route seemed the most feasible, because the others would require major dredging in long, shallow outlet coves.

In the end, Lake Washington lost out entirely as the location of the naval station, as Port Orchard on the west side of the sound was chosen instead. City fathers had been set afire by the commercial value of such a canal, however, and continued to push for its construction. For some time little was accomplished other than the carving of a shallow flume permitting logs to be floated from Lake Washington to Lake Union and Salmon Bay. In 1894 Congress authorized funds to deepen Salmon Bay; the route of the canal was finally cast.

Progress stalled until 1910, when funds were finally authorized for construction of a set of two masonry locks. Chief among the promoters of the canal was the eloquent and convincing officer who headed the local district of the Corps of Engineers, Col. Hiram M. Chittenden, for whom the locks are now named. Construction was begun in November of 1911, and in 1916 the cut was completed between Portage Bay and Lake Washington, lowering the latter by almost 9 feet and affecting the flow of several rivers at its former drainage to the south. The locks began operating that same year and on July 4, 1917, were dedicated with proper pomp and circumstance.

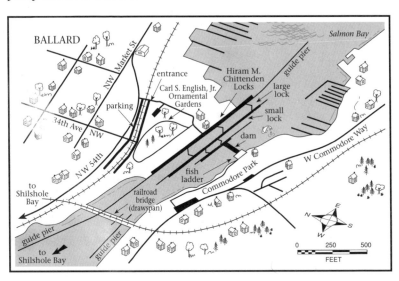

Hiram M. Chittenden Locks

Access: Land, boat
Facilities: Boat locks, restrooms, museum, gardens

The locks are the best free show in town, with every year over a million visitors watching the tos and fros of commercial tugs, barges, fishing boats, tour boats, military vessels, and hordes of recreational craft. Although there are other locks in the United States larger than these, none handle more vessel traffic. The locks are in operation continuously; however, the best boat-watching is on the weekend during good weather. To view a combination carnival and comedy-of-errors, come to watch at the end of a three-day summer weekend.

The lock complex, which is operated by the U.S. Army Corps of Engineers, consists of two parallel locks—the larger 825 feet long, and 80 feet wide and the smaller 150 feet long and 28 feet wide. Both are capable of

A fish ladder assures salmon a safe trip around the locks.

lifting boats a vertical distance of 6 to 26 feet, depending on the level of the tide on the saltwater side. To the south of the small lock is a spillway dam constructed to control the level of the water in Lake Washington and the navigational channel.

The locks are on the southwest side of Seattle's Ballard district; to reach them, follow Northwest Market Street west. As the arterial curves and becomes Northwest 54th Street, the entrance to the locks is obvious on the left. A parking lot is along some abandoned railroad tracks, just outside the gate.

At the entrance to the grounds is the Carl S. English, Jr. Ornamental Gardens, a 7-acre arboretum containing both native and exotic trees, shrubs, and flowers. In spring, the rhododendrons and azaleas add a swath of bright color to the nautical scene. A terraced lawn is designed as a spot for watching the lock traffic and perhaps enjoying a midday picnic.

A visitor center adjacent to the gardens features displays on the history and operation of the locks and the role of the Corps of Engineers in the Pacific Northwest. Visitor center hours are 11:00 A.M. to 5:00 P.M., Thursday through Monday, with guided walks conducted on weekends at 2:00 P.M. For groups, guided tours may be arranged with two weeks' advance notice. People arriving at the locks by boat are not permitted to leave their vessels to go ashore, and those on shore may not board boats.

Going Through the Locks. Taking a boat through the locks is an experience every boater should have at least once. The first time through, try to schedule your trip during midweek to avoid the confusion and mob scenes prevalent on weekends and holidays. During the latter periods lock attendants have their hands full trying to bring order out of the chaos of vessels approaching the lock, many crewed by boaters of questionable experience and sobriety. Passage time is claimed to be about 25 minutes for the large lock and 10 minutes for the small one, but additional time will be spent waiting for the locks to open, waiting for other vessels to be loaded once you are inside, and waiting for other boaters (surely not yourself!) to untangle their lines and figure how to tie up.

The following directions should make the trip through the locks less harrowing—and perhaps even fun.

Preparations: Boaters planning to go through the locks are expected to have two lock lines, each at least 50 feet long, with a 12-inch eye spliced in one end of each. These will be needed if you are directed alongside the wall in the large lock. Shorter lines will suffice for the small lock or rafting in the large lock; however, you are never sure which lock you will be entering or how you will be tied up.

As you approach the locks, ready your lines and tie ample fenders on both sides of the boat. The number of fenders needed depends on the size of your boat and how much you prize its shiny surfaces. Some skippers prefer a fenderboard if tied next to the wall in the big lock to keep

Leaving the small locks, headed for the sound

fenders from getting scuffed and slimy as they slide along the wall.

Waiting: Stay well clear of either lock when the red entry light for that lock is lit. Boats waiting for a locking may temporarily tie up to the wooden guide piers outside the locks. If not tied up, they may drift about well back from the group of boats awaiting the locking, or run the risk of dirty looks or profanity from boaters they attempt to bypass.

Locking Through: Rule Number One: PAY ATTENTION to the lock attendant! The speed limit for entering the locks is 2½ knots or slower. When the green light indicates the lock is available for entering, motor slowly and under control, in the order of your arrival, and follow the lock attendant's directions for positioning your boat. Government vessels and commercial vessels such as tour boats, tugs, or fishing boats take precedence over recreational ones; the lockmaster may direct you to hold off until they are loaded, or very large pleasure boats may be directed to come in first, out of turn, in order to be secured to the wall. Log rafts are loaded last.

The Small Lock: In the small lock, bollards, identified by number, are located on top of a floating wall that accompanies the boats up and down during the locking. Lock attendants will assist you in securing your boat when approaching from freshwater, but when approaching from saltwater, you must be prepared to pick up the numbered bollards you are directed to by yourself.

Once your lines are looped over the appropriate bollards, secure the other ends to your boat cleats and relax as the gates are closed and the lock is filled with water or emptied; however, you should stay alert, in case the floating walls hang up. When the gates are reopened, you will be given directions for casting off and leaving.

The Large Lock: In the large lock, boats are generally rafted several deep, with larger boats placed alongside the wall. Long lock lines are required for the boats against the wall. Attendants will secure the shore end of the

Entering the large locks from Shilshole Bay

lines for you. When approaching from freshwater, toss the 12-inch-eye end of each lock line to the attendants; they will put the eye around a bollard. When you are approaching from saltwater, the attendants will drop light lines to you to attach to the eye-end of your lock line so they may be hauled up. Once secure, immediately check the opposite side of your boat to assist boats directed to raft off you.

If you are rafted off another boat, you can secure your lines and enjoy the ride up or down; however, if you are against the wall with your lines attached to shore bollards, you will have to tend your lines and pay them out or take them in as necessary. In this situation, secure your lines when you first tie up, but when the gates are closed and the lock master announces the lock is going to be filled or drained, loosen the lines, leaving a single loop around the cleat. Adjust the slack in the line, using the cleat for leverage; DO NOT attempt to do this by simply holding the line in your hands, especially if you have boats rafted off you. On any but the smallest boats it is desirable to have one person available to handle each line.

Filling or Emptying the Lock: After the lock is loaded, the gates will close and water will enter or be drained. During this time there can be dangerous currents and undertows in the lock, and boats may swing around a bit. DO NOT put hands or legs over the side of the boat between the hull and the wall or between the hulls of two boats. When the gates reopen, the boats close to them will experience a bit more turbulence.

Outside the Locks: One caution for sailboats: the railroad bridge at the west end of the locks is normally open, but it closes as trains approach. Clearance under it is 43 feet at mean high tide; sailboats with taller masts will be unable to leave the area between the bridge and the locks until the train has passed and the bridge has reopened. Also, if you value your mast, do not be so intent on making a locking or heading out to the sound that you fail to notice the bridge is down.

The U.S. Army Corps of Engineers has a brochure, *Guidelines for Boaters*, that has some additional tips on negotiating the locks.

The Lake Washington Ship Canal Fish Ladder

Facilities: Viewing areas, restrooms

Because the inland freshwater lakes and streams were vital spawning grounds for over a third of a million salmon and seagoing trout, a fish ladder was incorporated into the original design of the locks. It proved only moderately successful, as the flow through it was freshwater, rather than the mixture of fresh- and saltwater that seems more attractive to fish. The ladder was replaced in 1976 with a new design that included an appropriate salty blend.

The present ladder consists of 21 steps, or weirs, that allow fish to move gradually up the grade. A viewing gallery with windows into a portion of the ladder is located along the south side; displays in the gallery identify the various species of fish and explain their migratory cycles and the operation of the ladder. Salmon can be seen from June through November, steelhead and cutthroat trout from September through February. The gallery may

Sea lions at the locks are fun to watch, even though they dine on local salmon.

be reached from the grounds of the locks by crossing the lock gates and the walkway below the dam or from adjoining Commodore Park.

In recent years a group of sea lions has turned the fish ladder into a briny delicatessen, making a substantial dent in the incoming flow of spawning fish. Concern over depleting runs has triggered an ongoing battle between the Wildlife Department and the sea lions, who are by law a protected species. So far there has been limited success in frightening or luring them away from a free lunch. Trucking the unwanted visitors out to the Washington coast met with no success, as they reappeared for an easy lunch in about a week or so. As a last ditch effort, the worst of the offenders have been trapped and deported to Florida, which should prove a more difficult swim back. Visitors (at least those who aren't anglers) enjoy watching the cavorting sea lions as much as they do viewing the salmon and trout.

Commodore Park (City of Seattle)

Park Area: 6 acres; 1,200 feet of shoreline
Access: Land, boat (small boats only)
Facilities: Restrooms, benches, fire stands, boat launch (hand-carry)
Attractions: Fishing, picnicking, viewpoint, paddling

The fish ladder and locks may be approached from the south side of the canal via Commodore Park, a pretty little park that also provides fishing, picnicking, and ready access for launching hand-carried boats into the saltwater below the locks.

To reach Commodore Park, at the south end of the Ballard Bridge head west on West Emerson Place. Pass Fishermen's Terminal and turn north on 21st Avenue W. In two blocks 21st bends west and becomes West Commodore Way. The park is on the right in ½ mile. It is open from 7:00 A.M. to 9:00 P.M.

Stairs lead down to the waterfront promenade, where there are a few benches sheltered by concrete roofs and some fire braziers in the nearby grass; concrete ramps offer easy disabled access. An expansive set of concrete steps drops down to water's edge. Hand-carried boats may be put in here. The concrete walkway heads eastward along the lock spillway to the fish ladder. Near the ladder a series of grassy tiers spill down from the park's loading area to the walkway, forming platforms for viewing the locks traffic and watching feeding sea lions; they also offer a great place for kids to roll and tumble.

Because of the proximity of the fish ladder, this area has particular fishing restrictions. Regulations are posted here and are noted in the pamphlet of sport fishing regulations published by the state Department of Fish and Wildlife.

MAGNOLIA BLUFF

Leaving the freshwater side of Seattle for another day, we return through the locks to Shilshole Bay, saltwater, and the 200-foot-high, handsome bluff that dominates the city shoreline. Although much of Magnolia Bluff is residential, the very best part of the area—the extreme tip—has become a fine, unique park, right in the heart of the city. Here, within a short bus ride from most metropolitan areas, is a grand wilderness for all to enjoy.

Discovery Park (City of Seattle)

Park Area: 534 acres; 12,000 feet of shoreline
Access: Land, boat (shallow draft)
Facilities: Visitor center, Indian cultural center, hiking trails, bicycle paths, nature trail, picnic tables, restrooms, fitness trail, sports fields (volleyball, soccer, basketball), tennis courts, museum, children's play area
Attractions: Hiking, picnicking, beachcombing, birdwatching, bicycling, historical site, lighthouse, nature programs, Seattle Mounted Police stables

Discovery Park, the largest and most choice of Seattle's city parks, is also one of its newest. For nearly 90 years the park was locked up as a military reservation, which explains why such prime real estate on Magnolia Bluff went undeveloped for residential or commercial use. Like numerous parcels of land along the sound, the property became available for public use after the government no longer needed it.

In 1894 Magnolia Bluff was one of 11 sites designated as potential military reservations for coast artillery to protect the naval station that had just been built at Port Orchard. The Army concluded that it would be wise to have troops permanently stationed close to the two population centers of Seattle and Tacoma; the proposed Magnolia Bluff reservation seemed an excellent site for an infantry garrison until it might be needed by the Coast Artillery.

From 1896 to 1898 land for the post was acquired, and in the following 10 years quarters for officers and non-coms, barracks, a hospital, stables, a quartermaster building, and other units were constructed. At this time the site was officially named Fort Lawton. Although the fort served alternatively as a post for Infantry and Coast Artillery, no artillery was ever installed here. Military activity wound down during the early years of the Depression, and the Army offered the land to Seattle for the price of one dollar; however, the city declined, feeling it could not afford the maintenance costs.

During World War II the fort sprang back to life—more than a million troops were processed here, a prison camp on the fort held 1,150 German

POWs, and another 5,000 Italian POWs passed through here en route to Hawaii. After the war, the fort remained a debarkation point for a time, then became a processing center for civil service employees and military headed to the Far East, and finally was a reserve training center. In 1970, the Army surplused 85 percent of the fort property, and the city was able to acquire it for a park (this time willingly assuming the maintenance costs). However, this was the beginning of the city's headaches. Local Native American tribes demanded the property be returned to them under the provision of early treaty rights; a compromise was reached, and 19 acres were set aside for a Native American cultural center. Special interest groups, ranging from golf buffs to hang-gliding enthusiasts, came out of the woodwork with plans and demands. The Parks Department, fortunately, maintained that the park should be a sanctuary where people could escape for quiet and solitude. Although some areas were to be developed for conventional recreational use, the bulk of the park was to remain nature oriented. In October of 1973, the land was formally dedicated as Discovery Park, named for the ship of George Vancouver, the explorer who first charted Puget Sound.

Three entrances lead into Discovery Park: one at the parking area on the south side of the park; another—the main entrance—on the east side

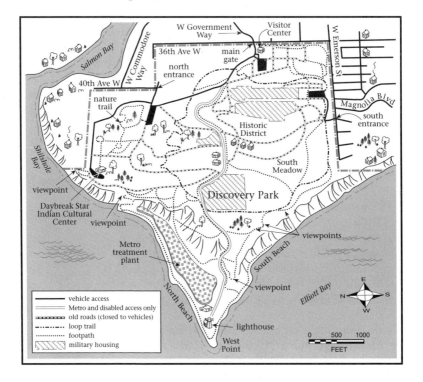

of the park, nearest the Visitor Center; and the third on the north side of the park near the Native American cultural center.

To reach the east entrance and Visitor Center, use exits from Elliott Avenue W at either the Magnolia Bridge, Dravus Street W, or West Emerson Place. From the west end of the Magnolia Bridge, turn right on Thorndyke Avenue W, which becomes 20th Avenue W, Gilman Avenue W, and then West Government Way. From the Dravus Street exit, turn north on 20th Avenue W and follow the preceding route. The West Emerson exit leads to this route at Gilman Avenue W.

The south parking lot can be reached by driving to the main park entrance, as already described, and turning south onto 36th Avenue W, then west on West Emerson, and then north into the park at 43rd Avenue W.

The north entrance is reached by turning north from West Emerson Place onto 21st Avenue W, which shortly becomes West Commodore Way. Follow West Commodore Way to 40th Avenue W, then turn south to reach the park entrance.

In keeping with the park philosophy to keep the grounds as natural as possible, nearly all the roads within the park that had been built for the fort are closed to traffic. Many of the areas must be reached by walking; trails are wide, well maintained, and (for the most part) gentle.

South Beach, at Discovery Park, is sand, driftwood, and dune grass.

Visitor Center. The informational hub of the park is the Visitor Center, newly constructed in 1996. Most classes and a regular schedule of naturalist-led tours begin here; a wide array of publications and displays are also available. The center is open daily, 8:30 A.M. to 5:00 P.M., except holidays. Tours of the U.S. Army cemetery can be arranged here. Call directly to the stables of the Seattle Mounted Police, which are located on the grounds, to arrange a visit to those facilities. A ½-mile fitness trail, combining jogging with 15 exercise stations, begins at the Visitor Center.

Discovery Park Trails. Over 7 miles of hiking trails intertwine in the forests, in the meadows, and on the beaches of the park. Some are genuine footpaths, while others follow old roads. Brochures available at the Visitor Center describe the sights along the trails—birds, plants, beach life, and points of geological interest. Take along field glasses, pause frequently, and try to identify some of the 221 species of birds that may be seen at the park.

The 2¾-mile-long Loop Trail begins at the Visitor Center, runs through grassy South Meadow (a good place to see wrens, warblers, and thrushes), skirts the crest of a cliff overlooking Elliott Bay, and then circles back to the start. It's an easy trail, with only minimal gain or loss in elevation. Side trails lead down to the beach.

The Wolf Tree Nature Trail, ½ mile long, begins at the northwest end of the north parking lot and loops through woods, a marsh, and a tiny meadow. A botanical checklist, available at the trailhead, names plants along the way. Naturalist-led tours are available by prearrangement with the Visitor Center.

North Bluff. A wide grassy field with a trail running its length tops the crest of North Bluff. One could hardly tell that only a few years ago this used to be the site of a row of barracks, so rapidly has nature reclaimed the area. Walk quietly and watch for birds or even an urban coyote. At the north end of the bluff, a wooden overlook offers sweeping views of the sound with the Olympics beyond. Watch freighter traffic, as well as sailboats racing off Shilshole Bay.

North Beach. Just beyond the North Bluff overlook, a trail heads downhill through a mostly deciduous forest—maple, elm, and alder with an undergrowth of salmonberry, ferns, and nettles. In less than ¼ mile, North Beach is reached. This is the only point along this trail where there is ready access to the shoreline.

The beach is rock and gravel—home for a wide variety of intertidal life ranging from chitons, limpets, barnacles, and mussels to sea stars, urchins, and tiny crabs. As the trail heads west along the top of a riprap bulkhead, it is sandwiched between the beach and the concrete wall of the Metro sewage plant.

After many years of controversy, Metro began work in 1991 on a secondary sewage treatment facility at North Beach in the area between the

At West Point, the lighthouse looks out to peaks of the Olympic Mountains.

shore and the bluff. Numerous environmental and esthetic compromises were made by Metro, along with a commitment for a $30 million fund to improve and expand waterfront parks. The facility, which was a major expansion of an existing sewage plant, is partially hidden by landscaping and earthen mounds, and (hopefully) not even a sensitive nose should be aware of its size or function. Restoration of the beach includes a pocket lagoon midway along the trail, a popular gathering spot for gulls, ducks, and other waterfowl.

West Point. The lighthouse at West Point, on the far western tip of Discovery Park, has one of the most scenic settings on the sound. Jumbo cargo ships lumber by, sailboats with brightly colored spinnakers race in the offshore breezes, the Olympic peaks frame the western horizon, and Mount Rainier rises above the city's skyscrapers. The lighthouse has been overseeing the passing scene since 1881, eight years before Washington became a state. It is now on the National Register of Historic Places. The lighthouse is closed to visitors.

South Beach. South Beach, stretching for more than a mile southeast from West Point, offers a marked contrast to the rocky shoreline of North Beach. Here is sand extending well out into the sound on a minus tide. Driftwood and dune grass define the high tide line at the western end. The beach supports sea pens, moon snails, sand dollars, and other sand-loving marine life.

To the east, steep cliffs rising from the beach to the bluffs above provide an interesting geology lesson on the formation of the area. Clearly defined bands show sediments from lakes and streams, topped by dark gray clay that settled out of a huge freshwater lake. Higher up, loose, yellowish sand was deposited by streams and glacial meltwater. This is topped by till—a collection of boulders, rocks, sand, silt, and clay deposited directly by the glacier that last covered this area, roughly 12,000 years ago. Scan the cliffs for the hollows of kingfishers and other birds that have made their nests in the soft sand.

Reach South Beach from the Visitor Center or south entrance by following the Loop Trail to its intersection with the South Beach Trail, then take this trail down to the beach. Alternatively, continue on the Loop Trail to its intersection with the road to the Metro plant, at the northwest corner of the Capehart Housing area, then follow the road downhill to the beach.

Daybreak Star Indian Cultural Center. The Daybreak Star Indian Cultural Center is located northwest of the north parking lot area. Here a two-story building houses a library, museum, and a gallery of Indian art (some on display, some for sale). The center also hosts touring shows by native artists, cultural heritage programs, and other special events celebrating Native American history and spiritual traditions. A wooden overlook north of the center faces expansive views north over Shilshole Bay to the distant icy cone of Mount Baker.

ELLIOTT BAY

Elliott Bay, with its deep protected waters, triggered the birth of the city of Seattle in 1852, and it has continued to nurture the city's growth over the past 150 years. The first settlers in the area landed on the shallow shore at Alki Point in West Seattle; however, it didn't take them long to recognize that a site closer to deep water was essential for creating the port city of their dreams. With a few horseshoes tied to a clothesline, they sounded the east shore of Elliott Bay and to their delight found the spot that answered all of their needs. Claims were staked out, pioneer families established homesteads, and thus (with a slight oversimplification of time and events) Seattle came to be.

The first commercial venture on the Seattle waterfront was lumber. In the 1850s Henry Yesler built a pier on the southeast end of the bay, adjoining his sawmill, to load ships with lumber for construction of the growing city of San Francisco. By the 1870s coal dug from mines southeast of Seattle had become a mainstay of the local economy, and a coal bunker wharf extended into the bay midway along its eastern shoreline.

In the rush to gain the terminus of a transcontinental railroad, most of the existing waterfront was soon relinquished to railway interests, who then declined to develop it, as it would compete with their Tacoma terminals. Resourceful Seattlites solved this problem by constructing yet another waterfront on pilings farther out over the harbor, the first of many such extensions that eventually molded the current shoreline of Elliott

Bay. By the late 1880s, waterfront access was bottled up by the railroads and a host of private piers, each concerned with their own parochial commercial interest, stifling the coordinated growth of the port as a whole.

When Washington became a state in 1889, the constitution included a declaration of state sovereignty over tidelands, with the caveat that tidelands outside harbor lines established by a state commission could be sold to private interests. Seattle harbor lines were drawn, contested, litigated, and redrawn, and eventually the harbor fell back into the hands of the waterfront monopoly. A new legislature elected in 1896 strengthened the right of public access to state harbors; however, little was accomplished in breaking the economic stranglehold of the railroads and private owners over Seattle's waterfront.

In the early 1900s the shape of the shoreline underwent major changes as the strong-willed city engineer, R. H. Thompson, decided to eliminate annoying hills and steep streets by washing them into the bay. For more than 10 years the landscape suffered a progressive regrade. Soil from the unwanted hills gradually filled the area under the plank and piling waterfront, and the land marched out to newly constructed seawalls that today define Seattle's waterfront. A decade later, when the people of King County voted to create the Port of Seattle, the elected commissioners set

Smith Cove City Park has close-up views of freighters at Pier 90/91.

about developing a master plan for the port's future and gradually were able to break the railroad-dominated monopoly on the waterfront.

In recent years, the port commissioners recognized a major change in shipping—the shift from bulk cargo to container ships. The aging piers along the downtown waterfront have neither the container loading facilities nor the large areas of waterfront storage that this type of shipping requires. As a result, the port concentrated its development in the tidal landfills along the East and West Waterways surrounding Harbor Island, at the south end of the bay, and at the Smith Cove wharves at its north end.

The world port that the original settlers envisioned has materialized, although certainly not in the form they could ever have anticipated. Today, Seattle is one of the largest container ports in the world. An average of five ocean-going vessels per day call on the commercial piers along Elliott Bay, and the annual value of goods through the port exceeds $25 billion.

Smith Cove

The giant wharves of Smith Cove lie along the northern edge of Elliott Bay. The first pier here was built by the Northern Pacific Railroad, which used it for loading coal on ships. Eight years later the railroad constructed two huge piers (now Piers 88 and 89), from which railroad-owned steamers linked transcontinental rails to trade with the Orient. Shipments of raw silk valued as high as a thousand dollars a bale were off-loaded from ships to waiting special freight trains for a high-speed, direct run to the garment factories of the East Coast.

Piers 90 and 91 were constructed at the head of the cove by the Port of Seattle. At the time of their completion in 1921, these 2,530-foot-long earth-fill piers were the longest of their kind in the world. The piers were sold to the U.S. Navy in 1942 for use as a major supply depot, but were repurchased by the Port in 1976. Today, where bales of silk once stood, now stand the latest treasures of the Orient—Toyotas, Nissans, and Subarus.

Smith Cove City Park (City of Seattle)

Park Area: 2.5 acres; 500 feet of shoreline
Access: Land, boat (shallow draft)
Facilities: Picnic tables, sani-can
Attractions: Beachcombing, viewpoint

Squeezed between Pier 91 and the Elliott Bay Marina is delightful little Smith Cove City Park. Small, a bit hard to find, and not long on amenities, the park is nonetheless a pleasant waterfront alcove from which to

The skyscrapers of Seattle accent sailboat masts at Elliott Bay Marina.

watch the shipping activities of Elliott Bay and enjoy a picnic lunch spiced with a stiff, salt-air breeze.

To reach the park, take the Magnolia Bridge from Elliott Avenue W (or 15th Avenue W, which Elliott becomes north of the bridge). A ramp leaves the bridge and drops to 21st Avenue W just north of the park. Alternatively, take 21st Avenue W south from Thorndyke Avenue W, which runs along the southeast side of Magnolia Bluff.

The park can also be reached by a bicycle path that continues north from Elliott Bay City Park on Pier 89 along the east side of the Pier 90/91 fence, then around the north end of the piers' loading area to join 21st Avenue W about ½ mile from the park entrance.

Elliott Bay Marina

Facilities: Guest moorage, power, water, cable TV, coffee shop, restaurant, groceries, fuel dock, restrooms, showers, laundry rooms, marine pumpout station, shops, hazardous waste disposal, chandlery, marine repair, observation platform

The most recent major addition to the Seattle waterfront is a 1,200-slip marina on the north side of Elliott Bay, immediately west of Smith Cove City Park. The marina is protected by a 2,700-foot-long rock breakwater along the south side of Magnolia Bluff, and a concrete wavebreak at the west end of the breakwater. Fuel, groceries, and a pumpout station

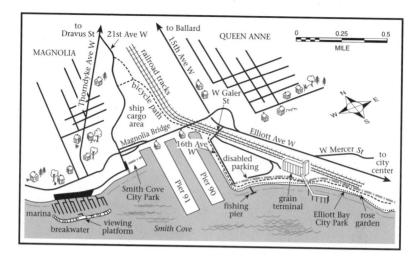

are located at the end of G dock, in the center of the marina. An observation platform that has been built atop the center of the breakwater provides views across Elliott Bay; it is accessible by boat from the channel behind the breakwater or via a shuttle boat from the end of G dock.

Guest moorage is available on A dock, the first dock inside the west side of the marina. Check with the dockmaster to register for a slip. Buildings at either end of the marina contain necessities such as laundry and showers; offices and shops are in the building near the end of G dock.

To reach it by land, take the off-ramp from the Magnolia Bridge to 21st Avenue W, and follow it south and west to the marina complex.

Elliott Bay City Park (City of Seattle)

Park Area: 10.5 acres; 4,100 feet of shoreline
Access: Land, boat (shallow draft)
Facilities: Foot and bike paths, fitness course, benches, picnic table, fishing pier, concession stand, bait, tackle, restrooms, children's play areas, rose garden
Attractions: Sightseeing, walking, jogging, skating, bicycling, fishing, picnicking, points of interest

The massive concrete silos of the Port of Seattle grain terminal mark Pier 86, between Smith Cove and downtown Seattle. From here freighters take on grain, brought from the nation's heartland, for export to foreign markets. At the base of the terminal, the narrow grass strip of Elliott Bay City Park runs along the shore for nearly a mile.

The park has two paved paths, one for pedestrians immediately above the rock-ribbed beach and another for bicycles along the fence at its inland boundary. The pedestrian path has a number of adjacent fitness exercise stations, as well as several benches from which to leisurely watch the marine traffic or a passing sea lion scouting for lunch.

Near the north end of the park, a 400-foot-long, T-shaped concrete fishing pier extends into the bay. Two orange-striped buoys 100 feet offshore mark an artificial underwater reef. Fishing near the reef must be done from the pier—angling from boats is prohibited here. Fish for surf perch, flat fish, salmon, cod, cabezon, and rockfish. The pier is open 7:00 A.M. to 11:00 P.M. daily in the winter and 6:00 A.M. to midnight in the summer. At the head of the pier are restrooms and a concession stand selling bait and snacks.

To reach Elliott Bay City Park, turn west off Elliott Avenue W at West Galer, the first intersection south of the Magnolia Bridge. In one block cross the railroad tracks; signs here point to Pier 86, Pier 89, the public fishing pier, and the bicycle path. For disabled access to the fishing pier, turn south immediately after crossing the tracks and continue to the Pier 86 grain terminal, where a small sign directs you to a narrow road between two fences leading to the concession stand. Parking is for disabled persons and concession employees only.

For all other parking, continue on Galer another block past the entrance to Pier 91, then turn left on 16th Avenue W, which runs along the west side of Pier 89. In three more blocks there is ample parking on the west side of the road north of the park entrance. A bicycle path continues

The fishing pier at Elliott Bay City Park

north from here along the east and north sides of the Pier 91 fence, eventually reaching the road leading to Smith Cove City Park. Benches in a narrow grass strip along the bank offer spots to watch the cargo transfer activity on Pier 90.

Myrtle Edwards Park (City of Seattle)

Park Area: 3.7 acres; 2,000 feet of shoreline
Access: Land
Facilities: Picnic tables, benches, sani-cans
Attractions: Picnicking, jogging, walking, bicycling, skating

The public shoreline and its bicycle and walking paths continue south from the grain terminals in an unbroken swath. The southern portion, Myrtle Edwards Park, commemorates a past city councilwoman. Benches and picnic tables along the shore offer pleasant resting spots with views to the maritime activities of Elliott Bay and, beyond, Bainbridge Island and the Olympic range.

Near the center of the park is one of Seattle's interesting sculptures, commissioned in 1976 as a part of the city's program providing 1 percent of development costs for artwork. The sculpture, entitled "Adjacent, Against, Upon," consists of three massive pairs of carved stone slabs and concrete platforms, each slab and platform related, according to the title of the work. It provides an interesting contrast of human scale versus the monumental .

Myrtle Edwards Park park can be reached by walking south through Elliott Bay City Park or by going north from the parking lot located just north of Pier 70, at the intersection of Alaskan Way and Broad Street. The metered parking lot is at the southern boundary of Myrtle Edwards Park.

The Downtown Seattle Waterfront

Access: Land, boat
Facilities: Shops, restaurants, food carts, picnic tables, parks, restrooms, aquarium, tour boats, guest moorage, viewpoints, points of interest
Attractions: Shopping, sightseeing, picnicking, touring, fishing, kayaking, parasailing, boat tours, special events

The waterfront that edges downtown Seattle is a colorful, fascinating melange of commercial and tourist-oriented facilities. On this mile-long stretch are found activities ranging from the sedate to the sensational. Visitors can sample such things as horse-drawn carriage rides, pedi-cab rides, sailing trips, cruise-boat tours, fishing trips, kayak excursions, and parasail flights. During the summer a variety of vessels that stop by, ranging from historic square riggers to modern Navy ships, are open to the public.

In early times the waterfront was a bustling center of commerce focused on shipping and fishing. As the shift to containerized cargo caused the working waterfront to move to Smith Cove and Harbor Island, warehouses on the downtown waterfront were abandoned. Several of these have been converted to complexes housing small shops and restaurants. Piers are used by cruise ships, tour boats, and the state ferries. An old railroad track alongside the Alaskan Way Viaduct has been replaced between Lenora Street and Washington Street by an asphalt footpath bordered by colorful flowers.

Alaskan Way runs the length of the downtown waterfront. The central portion of the waterfront is cut off from downtown Seattle by a steep hill and a concrete freeway viaduct. At several points sets of stairs and elevators rise from the waterfront to the upper street level. The Pike Place Hillclimb, east of Pier 59, leads up stairs and terraces to the historic Pike Place Market, one of the best-known public markets in the country. A staircase/elevator combination at Lenora Street takes visitors from the waterfront to the street level two blocks north of the market. Major attractions of the waterfront are described here, from north to south.

Visitors to the area should be aware of one problem that can be encountered on the south end of the waterfront. The south end of Alaskan Way borders Seattle's Skid Road district, where there is a concentration of homeless vagrants. Although most are harmless panhandlers, a few may become aggressive and threatening, especially if encountered in secluded spots. Use care and common sense.

The Waterfront Streetcar. In 1982 the Seattle waterfront gained a novel attraction with the arrival of four 1927-vintage electric trolleys that had been retired from service in Melbourne, Australia. From the car barns located north of Broad Street, the picturesque streetcars make their 15-minute run along the waterfront, stopping at several stations along the way. Leaving the waterfront, the streetcar

Dungeness crabs for sale at Seattle's Pike Place Market

tracks head east through Pioneer Square on South Main Street to 5th Avenue, and the end of the line at Jackson Street. Conductors on the cars enjoy the novelty of the route and frequently add their personal commentary to make the trip even more fun.

Cruise Ships. The downtown waterfront is the terminal for several cruise ships. For persons wanting a quick trip to Victoria, British Columbia, the *Victoria Clipper* ships are large high-speed jetfoils operating out of Pier 69 that provide passenger-only service year-round. The boats can also accommodate a few bicycles and kayaks. Check with Clipper Navigation, Inc., for information.

The waterfront streetcar is a 1927-vintage trolley.

The *Spirit of Puget Sound*, operating out of Pier 70, offers lunch, dinner, and moonlight cruises on the sound. Argosy Cruises, at Pier 55, provides an Elliott Bay Harbor tour package, trips through the Hiram Chittenden Locks, narrated tours of Lakes Union and Washington, and cruises to Blake Island State Park's Native American Tillicum Village. Land tours are coordinated with Gray Line buses.

In recent years, the *Lady Washington*, a reproduction of the first American vessel to explore the Pacific Coast, has spent summers on the Seattle

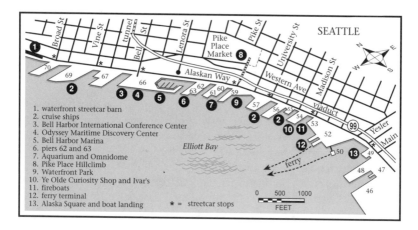

1. waterfront streetcar barn
2. cruise ships
3. Bell Harbor International Conference Center
4. Odyssey Maritime Discovery Center
5. Bell Harbor Marina
6. piers 62 and 63
7. Aquarium and Omnidome
8. Pike Place Hillclimb
9. Waterfront Park
10. Ye Olde Curiosity Shop and Ivar's
11. fireboats
12. ferry terminal
13. Alaska Square and boat landing   * = streetcar stops

The Bell Street Terminal has a fish-shaped pool and fountain where children can play.

waterfront, providing visitors an opportunity to sail for an hour or two aboard an eighteenth-century square rigger.

Pier 69: The Port of Seattle. The spiffy new headquarters for the Port of Seattle includes public shoreline viewpoints along the outside rim of the pier that offer outstanding views of nearby Pier 70, the grain loading facilities at Terminal 86, Elliott Bay, Harbor Island, and distant mountains. The lobby of the Port offices displays scale models of a tug, a fishing trawler, container cargo ships, and a gantry crane, as well as models of aircraft that fly out of the port's SeaTac International Airport. Kiosks tell of the port's activities, and an interactive computer terminal allows visitors to access more information about the port.

Pier 66: The Bell Street Terminal. Recent major reconstruction of this part of the waterfront has added a first-class marina, restaurants, an international conference center, a maritime museum, a cruise ship terminal, and docks to serve expanded cruise ship traffic. The roof of the conference center is a view plaza with benches, free telescopes, and an outstanding panorama of the Olympic Mountains, Puget Sound, Elliott Bay, the waterfront, and the Seattle cityscape.

A pedestrian bridge at the end of Bell Street links to upper city streets. At a second city access, a staircase and elevator lead up to an old street stub at the west end of Lenora Street, two blocks from the Pike Place Market, with a crow's nest view of the waterfront.

The lower level of the conference center houses a cruise ship passenger terminal, conference center, and exhibit spaces. At the Odyssey Maritime Discovery Center, an interactive nautical museum, kids or adults can play longshoreman in a container crane simulator, listen to the radio traffic of ships in the sound, ride the bridge of a fishing vessel in the stormy Pacific, enjoy a magic kayak ride, or get splashed while learning about fish.

More than 30 guest moorage slips with power and water lie in a basin protected by a huge pier designed for large cruise ship berthing. A marine pumpout station is provided, there are restrooms with showers, and the entire area is under security protection. Maximum stay is 72 hours. The deck above the marina has a restaurant and a fish-shaped fountain that invites kids to splash in it. At the entrance to the marina stands a 100-foot-high metal column that represents a lighthouse.

Piers 62 and 63. The broad wooden deck of these two piers is a city park, with picnic tables and ample space for viewing the city skyline and the bay. Concerts, community activities, and special events frequently use the incomparable venue.

Waterfront Park, between Piers 57 and 59, is a favorite with residents as well as visitors.

Piers 59 and 60: The Seattle Aquarium and the Omnidome Theater. Elliott Bay and Puget Sound are important not only for what occurs on their surfaces, but also for what exists below. The Seattle Aquarium, an outstanding attraction on the waterfront, provides a glimpse of this underwater world. One of the displays, a unique underwater dome, allows visitors to go beneath the waters of the sound and view marine life on all sides and above, much as Captain Nemo would have seen it. On view in traditional glass tanks are nearly every kind of marine life found in Puget Sound, ranging from shy octopuses, ferocious-appearing wolf eels, and technicolor nudibranchs. Displays provide information to help visitors better understand the various species and their environments.

Another feature of the aquarium is an operating fish ladder; each year salmon fry are released here to go to the sea, and one or two years later they find their way back home to spawn in the "stream" of their birth.

Probably as popular as the fish displays are the tanks containing harbor seals and sea otters. A number of the animals have bred in the aquarium and have raised their young here. The animal families are always a delight for visitors. Other displays include a "touch tank," where children can examine the crusty skin of a starfish, the squishy body of a sea cucumber, or other characteristics of fascinating marine animals.

Sharing the pier with the aquarium is the Omnidome Theater, where wrap-around screens bring viewers into the film, imparting an eerie sense of not just watching, but actually becoming a part of the scenes shown.

A basket starfish photographed at the Seattle Aquarium

The films, which use the breathtaking media technique to its full advantage, have taken viewers on underwater explorations of Australia's Great Barrier Reef, trips around erupting Mount St. Helens, and space voyages through the universe.

Piers 59 to 55: Waterfront Park. A large semicircular deck between Piers 57 and 59 forms Waterfront Park. Picnic tables along the terraced deck are favorite haunts of Seattlites who enjoy a splash of salt air as they share their lunches with scrounging pigeons and seagulls. Landscaping, a marvelously splashing fountain, and what is possibly the ugliest statue in Seattle (Christopher Columbus with a hole through his bronze head) add to the charm of the park. Distinctive, open-air viewing towers can be reached from the deck below via stairs or ramps or via walkways leading from the second level of buildings on the adjoining piers.

The Bay Pavilion, on Pier 57, houses a collection of small shops and restaurants. The open end of the pier offers a scattering of tables and benches from which to watch waterfront activity. This pier end is a public fishing area; rod holders are mounted along its perimeter fence for the convenience of anglers. Pier 56 is companion to Pier 57 that houses still more restaurants and tourist-oriented shops. One gets the impression that both residents and visitors can never get their fill of seafood and outside dining in this purportedly rainy city.

Piers 57 and 55 are the base for a variety of harbor tours, sailboat tours, parasailing flights, bicycle rentals, saltwater fishing charters, and similar adventures.

Pier 54: Ye Olde Curiosity Shop and Ivar's Acres of Clams. Two commercial enterprises on the waterfront have become Seattle institutions. Ye Olde Curiosity Shop, which has been a waterfront fixture since 1899, relocated to the north side of Pier 54 when Pier 51, its home of many years, was found structurally unsound. The store houses an eclectic assortment of artifacts, curios, and tourist kitsch— most are for sale, but some are just for display.

Pier 54 is also the home of one of the best-known waterfront restaurants, Ivar's Acres of Clams. On display in the restaurant are more than 500 historical photos of the Seattle

Pier 54 has a sculpture of Ivar Haglund feeding the gulls.

The fireboats at Pier 53 are a fascinating waterfront sight.

waterfront. In front of the restaurant, a bronze statue of the late Ivar Haglund feeding seagulls is a fitting tribute to a man who spent his life promoting the Seattle waterfront. An annual Fourth of July fireworks display in Elliott Bay, sponsored by the corporation that now operates Ivar's restaurants, also commemorates his life.

Pier 53: Fire Station #5 and Fireboats. Fire Station #5 not only provides protection for the land side of Elliott Bay; it also acts as the home base for the two fireboats posted on the bay. In addition to their primary function, the fireboats frequently participate in marine parades and other special events on Elliott Bay. They provide a breathtaking scene when their water cannons send plumes of water arching high into the air.

An historic old fire bell outside the station was originally used in the 1800s to sound alarms to all fire stations in the north end of the city. Inside the building is an antique fire engine that once answered the alarms in Seattle of the past.

Pier 52: The Colman Ferry Terminal. From this Seattle terminus of the Washington State Ferry System, ferries serve Bremerton, on the Kitsap Peninsula, and Winslow, on Bainbridge Island. From balconies in the Colman Terminal, visitors can watch the flurry of activity as the huge vessels dock, then load, unload, and depart.

The Colman dock has had a rather checkered past, perhaps because it has always played a prominent role on the Seattle waterfront. The original dock, built in 1889, was replaced in 1909 by a larger dock that sported a distinctive clock tower at its end. Three years later, a ship plowed into the wharf, severing the clock tower, which floated away in the fog. The clock was rescued the following day, and the tower was rebuilt, but it was partially destroyed by fire after only two years. Again it was rebuilt, and it stood as a waterfront landmark until 1936, when the dock was once more replaced, but without the tower. The present dock and terminal were rebuilt in 1966; extensive remodeling begun in 1991 was completed in 1997.

All automobile ferry traffic must approach the terminal from the south, along Alaskan Way. The passenger-only ferry slip is located to the south of the main terminal area at a small dock at Pier 50.

Pier 49: Alaska Square and the Washington Street Boat Landing. Prior to the construction of Pier 66, the only public boat access to the Seattle waterfront was found at Pier 49 at the foot of Washington Street. A concrete float, marked on the street side by a historic old pergola, extends about 120 feet out into the bay. The dock provides boaters a somewhat tenuous access to the waterfront, as the floats have no protection from the water side and the wakes of nearby ferries, as well as other marine traffic along the busy waterfront, make moorage rather rough. There

Cyclists at Alaska Square, Pier 49

is a 10-hour maximum time limit for use of the floats, and a 20-minute limit for one section used for loading and unloading only. Boats over 35 feet are prohibited.

Just south of the floats is tiny Alaska Square Park. Problems with vagrants led the city to replace the park's grass with concrete and asphalt slabs and a cluster of rocks around the park's signature totem pole. The resulting park is uncomfortable for inebriated snoozing but unfortunately still doesn't prevent semi-sober imbibing. Gates that are closed between 11:00 P.M. and 6:00 A.M. have helped reduce problems with transients, and the park might be closed during the winter. Although the park is more secure, it is not advisable to leave a boat unattended at the floats. Even when aboard, keep hatches secure at night.

Pier 36: The Coast Guard Museum Northwest and the Vessel Traffic Service Center. The Coast Guard Support Center at Pier 36 has a variety of attractions to interest visitors and keep children enthralled for hours. The pier is home to the United States' two largest icebreakers, which see duty in arctic seas. Three high-endurance cutters are stationed here, and when they are in port tours are sometimes offered, at the option of the captain. Visitors interested in a tour should call in advance to see if one can be scheduled. On occasion, other interesting vessels that call may be open for tours.

The Coast Guard Museum Northwest, located on the north side of the pier, houses a collection of marine memorabilia, including several models of Coast Guard vessels, historic photos and vintage uniforms. A post lantern on display was originally located at Alki Point in 1887; it was a predecessor to later lighthouses. A fourth-order Fresnel lens now in the museum was originally installed at Admiralty Head in 1903. It saw duty at New Dungeness Lighthouse from 1927 to 1976.

The museum is open Monday, Wednesday, and Friday from 9:00 A.M. to 3:00 P.M. and Saturday and Sunday from 1:00 P.M. to 5:00 P.M. Group tours at other times can be arranged by telephoning the museum or the Coast Guard Public Affairs Office.

People and gulls entertain each other at Pier 54

The Puget Sound Vessel Traffic Service Center (VTS), located in the main building on the pier, is also open to visitors from 8:00 A.M. to 8:00 P.M. daily. This center maintains radar surveillance of about 2,500 square miles of waterways in the Strait of Juan de Fuca and Puget Sound. It controls and tracks over 18,000 commercial vessel movements a month in these waters. A 10-minute slide show describes the operation of the center; personnel are available to show the vessel tracking room and answer questions about it. On screen can be seen the tracks of ships throughout the sound and strait. A visit to the VTS brings with it a much greater appreciation of the amount of traffic that travels the sound and the efficiency with which the Coast Guard controls it.

HARBOR ISLAND AND THE DUWAMISH WATERWAY

During the late 1800s, when the federal government was busily quibbling over a route for the ship canal to access Lake Washington, Seattlites grew tired of waiting and took matters into their own hands. In 1890 they obtained approval from the state legislature to construct a canal from the south end of the lake via a cut through Beacon Hill. Although the canal was never constructed, preliminary design work by the Army Corps of Engineers led, in 1895, to dredging of two channels in the Duwamish tideflats. Dredged material that was dumped between the two channels in the Duwamish tideflats formed the beginnings of Harbor Island. Augmented by rock ballast from lumber barges and from regrades at Beacon Hill, the island took the shape it has today.

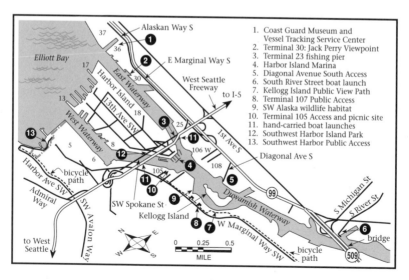

The island lay virtually unused until 1910, when local business interests, spurred by visions of burgeoning trade through the soon-to-be-completed Panama Canal, sought East Coast financing to build piers and terminals at Harbor Island. Financing attempts failed, but by the 1920s some commercial development was noticeable, mainly along the edges of the adjoining waterways. A major burst of industrial growth that started shortly before World War II has continued and turned the island into the bustling industrial area of today.

From its source at the confluence of the Black, White, and Green Rivers, the Duwamish River originally meandered 8 miles through 16 serpentine curves to the tideflats of Elliott Bay. In 1906 the White River was diverted to the south, and in 1916 the Black ceased to exist when the completion of the ship canal lowered Lake Washington, its source. Lack of flat land for industry led to extensive reshaping of the Duwamish; between 1913 and 1917 the river had 10 of its curves eliminated by the Corps of Engineers, as it was dredged to its present, relatively straight, 50-foot-deep channel.

Terminal 30: Jack Perry Memorial Viewpoint

The East Waterway is the heart of commercial activity for the Port of Seattle. The numbers associated with it are staggering: it has 10,634 linear feet of berthing space and 187 acres of adjoining marine terminal yards, it can accommodate up to 14 deep-draft vessels simultaneously, and over 4 million metric tons of cargo are transshipped yearly from its terminals.

The Port of Seattle has developed a public access and viewing site just north of Terminal 30, where the hustling activity of the port can be watched close at hand. To reach the access site, follow Alaskan Way south from the central waterfront to where it jogs southwest and then becomes East Marginal Way S. Follow the stub end of Alaskan Way straight ahead to the viewpoint; it is signed at the main road. The short road ends in a grass mini-park with a couple of trees, benches, a picnic table, and garbage cans. A sign describes the waterway activities and displays the stack insignias for the various shipping companies that call at the port.

Terminal 23 Fishing Pier

Facilities: Covered benches, fish cleaning stations, sani-can

Sandwiched between the south gate of Terminal 18 and a cold storage plant at Terminal 25, with views out to cranes and cargo ships, the public fishing pier at the end of the East Waterway puts a human perspective in this otherwise industrial area.

To reach the fishing pier westbound from the West Seattle Freeway, take the Harbor Island/11th Avenue SW exit. In about 100 yards a couple of right turns, one marked Terminal 18 South Entrance, lead into a small parking area that is just large enough for five or six cars. Look sharply, because the turns are easily missed, and there is no convenient way to backtrack once they are passed. The pier can also be reached by turning west on Southwest Spokane Street from East Marginal Way S. Additional parking is available under the freeway just after making this turn.

Benches (some covered) lining the 500-foot frontage of the pier provide pleasant spots to watch the waterway activity while waiting for a hit on the fish line. Note that bottomfish, shellfish, and crab might be unsafe to eat, due to pollution.

The fishing pier at Pier 23 has views out to the commercial shipping piers on Harbor Island.

East and West Waterways Hand-Carried Boat Launch Areas and Southwest Harbor Island Park

Although no signs advertise them as such, there are three spots amid the massive concrete footings of the West Seattle Freeway where hand-carried boats can be launched into either the East or West Waterway for a paddle tour of the Duwamish River.

As the East Waterway nears the south end of Harbor Island, a small section of it is sandwiched between Spokane Street and a low railroad trestle, both of which block water traffic for vessels of any size. The result is a calm, protected pond directly beneath the freeway, with the barriers at either end no challenge to low-slung paddlers. A paved parking lot with room for a few vehicles lies under the freeway directly across Spokane Street from the Terminal 23 Fishing Pier. Because this is also the location of on- and off-ramps for the West Seattle Freeway, it is neither feasible nor safe to turn into the parking area when traveling west. Eastbound, stay in the right-hand lane, and look sharply or you will miss the turn into the lot. A short path leads to a no-bank put-in right next to Spokane Street.

The West Waterway is navigated by vessels ranging up to huge container cargo ships. Two bridges span the channel: one a railroad drawbridge and the other a unique swing bridge for vehicle traffic. The swing bridge, in

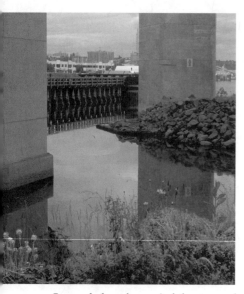

Launch hand-carried boats and paddle between the supports of the West Seattle Freeway.

which two halves rotate horizontally on two huge concrete pivots on either side of the waterway, is the only one of its kind in the country.

Northwest of the Harbor Island Marina complex, at the intersection of 13th Avenue Southwest and Southwest Klickitat Way, is tiny Southwest Harbor Island Park. This flat grassy area under the swing bridge and high-rise bridge tapers gently into the edge of the waterway. A block-long dirt road leads to the edge of the West Waterway. Hand-carried boats can be launched here, with due caution for marine traffic in the waterway.

On the opposite side of the waterway, directly under the Spokane Street bridge, is yet another hand-carry boat launch area. Here a small backwater pond around the west pivot for the swing bridge is protected from waterway traffic by a sturdy wing wall of pilings. A paved parking lot under the bridge can be reached via West Marginal Way SW; parking is available for about 40 cars. A short stub road leads to a no-bank launch site under the freeway bridge.

Harbor Island Marina

Facilities: Fuel, groceries (limited), restrooms, shower, viewing pier, guest moorage, marine pumpout station, deli (nearby)

A pleasant recreational incursion amid the commercial waterfront clamor, Harbor Island Marina is the only facility on the Duwamish Waterway for pleasure boaters. To reach it by water, head south from Elliott Bay into the West Waterway and the Duwamish River, pass under the swing bridge and the high-rise bridge, and continue past a private marina to the commercial marina on the southernmost tip of the island.

By land, turn west onto Southwest Spokane Street from East Marginal Way S, or take the Harbor Island exit from the West Seattle Freeway. Follow Southwest Spokane Street to the stoplight at 11th Avenue SW, just east of the new swing bridge. Here turn south and follow signs to the marina entrance in approximately two blocks.

The upland strip at the head of the docks has been pleasantly landscaped

The Harbor Island Marina is on the Duwamish Waterway.

and furnished with benches and a viewing platform where one can relax and enjoy the maritime activities of the waterway.

The relatively new marina has permanent moorage on four docks for about 100 boats. Fuel and some limited groceries are available at the long, outside breakwater float that T's off the end of C dock. This float has power and water and is used for guest moorage.

Diagonal Avenue South Access

Around 125 years ago the Duwamish estuary held nearly 2,500 acres of tidal marshes and swamp. Today less than 2 percent of its marshes and shallows remain. The Port of Seattle has taken a small step to restore some of this lost estuary wetland with the creation of a wildlife habitat area at the end of Diagonal Avenue S. Here fill has been removed, creating a small basin, and shore plants typical of the intertidal habitat have been reintroduced.

To reach the access, follow East Marginal Way S to Diagonal Avenue S, about ½ mile south of Spokane Street, then turn west on Diagonal, which is signed to the access.

Small greenswards surrounding the basin have a few benches and picnic tables from which to observe wildlife that is attracted by the new habitat. A 100-foot-long path runs north just above the river before ending at a fence. A gently sloping bank at the end of Diagonal Avenue permits launching of hand-carried boats into the river.

The Diagonal Avenue South Access is a small wetland.

Signs erected by the Port at the parking lot tell of the natural and human history of the estuary. One display compares the physical features and ecology of 100 years ago to those of today. It identifies major changes in the estuary's watershed that collectively reduced by about 75 percent the watershed area and the volume of water flow through the estuary and drastically decreased the rivers and streams accessible to andronomous fish (fish that spawn in freshwater but spend part of their life in saltwater).

A second sign describes the large delta island of *Tush'-Kahs,* which existed here prior to the dredging of the waterway, and tells of the Duwamish Indians who hunted, fished, and trapped waterfowl here. Several villages existed in the area up into the 1800s, and archeological digs have taken place at the site of one of them.

South River Street Boat Launch

A launch ramp for trailered boats is provided on the east side of the Duwamish River, under the abutments of the 1st Avenue S bridge. The ramp currently is a favorite launch spot for the Muckleshoot Indians, who set nets along the river to catch returning salmon runs.

To find the ramp, continue south on East Marginal Way S, and about two blocks south of the 1st Avenue S intersection turn west on South River Street. Follow this street for two blocks to the 1st Avenue S bridge. The two-lane concrete ramp drops into the turning basin on the east side of the bridge. The ramp is quite steep and tends to be slick when wet. Parking for a dozen cars and trailers can be found in a rough, muddy area under the bridge. Until the construction of the new 1st Avenue S bridge is complete, the ramp might be unusable at times.

Kellogg Island

Kellogg Island was once targeted in Port of Seattle plans as a container cargo storage area; however, the island's priority faded as the growing size of container vessels made their travel up the narrow, shallow Duwamish channel impossible. The value of the island as a nesting site for great blue heron, Canada geese, and other waterfowl was recognized by conservation groups, who lobbied to preserve this last wild environment on the lower Duwamish from encroaching commercial development. The discovery that early Native American tribes had used the island for their encampments established it as an important archeological site as well. It was finally agreed that Kellogg Island should remain in its natural state as a nature preserve in the heart of the industrial Duwamish shorelines.

Brush and brambles covering all but the very northern tip of the 600-yard-long island provide protection and nesting habitat for great blue heron and some 75 other species of birds. Because Kellogg Island itself is a wildlife preserve, it is closed to public access; however, the river bank west of the island has two public accesses, described in the following, that offer good views of it. Approach quietly on the river bank to observe and photograph; better yet, put in a canoe or small boat at one of the Duwamish access points and paddle slowly around the island. Do not go ashore.

A great blue heron takes flight near Kellogg Island.

Terminal 107 Public Accesses

The first access to views of Kellogg Island, the Terminal 107 Kellogg Island View Path created by the Port of Seattle, is a 1,500-foot-long asphalt walkway above the west river bank that parallels the island for its full length. This is a portion of a paved bicycle route that runs along West Marginal Way SW from Terminal 115 to Terminal 105. To reach the north end of the access by car or bike, follow West Marginal Way SW to Southwest Hudson Street. No parking is available in the immediate vicinity; park somewhere nearby and walk back to the signed start of the path. The south end of the path is also accessible by crossing the railroad tracks just north of the sand and gravel plant at Terminal 107; again, parking in the area is limited. This access to the path might be closed during rail switching on the spur track along West Marginal Way SW.

The island can be seen through the shoreline trees a short distance across the channel, but there is no access down the 20-foot-high bank to the river. The river bank, brush, and trees along the path are often shared by the island's avian inhabitants—walk quietly, and see how many you can spot.

A second, recently developed public access is located about two blocks farther north at Southwest Edmunds Street. Here a short road stub crosses the railroad tracks to a parking area. A path heads south from the parking lot to an overlook and continues parallel to the river bank through alder and blackberry bramble, alive with flitting, twittering birds. The path ends at a low bank above the river, where an easy scramble provides access to the river bank itself. Eventually a picnic shelter will be added. Kellogg Island lies directly across the narrow channel, in an oxbow of the Duwamish River.

Two blocks to the north, at Southwest Alaska Street, King County and the Department of Wildlife have recently developed a 400-yard section of riverfront as a wildlife habitat.

Terminal 105 Public Access, and Southwest Dakota Hand-Carried Boat Launch

Access: Land, boat
Facilities: Picnic tables, shelter, pier, sani-cans, boat launch (hand-carry)

A little park just south of the tip of Harbor Island is a nice spot to fish or just to watch the marine traffic in the busy Duwamish channel. It's especially pleasant on summer evenings when the river traffic is heavier and Mount Rainier is bathed in the glow of the setting sun.

To reach the site, follow West Marginal Way SW to a few blocks south of Southwest Spokane Street. About 150 feet north of Southwest Dakota Street turn east onto a gravel road signed "Terminal 105 Public Access." A parking area just across the railroad tracks along West Marginal Way has space for about a dozen cars. The gravel road signed "No Vehicles" continues east between a chain-link fence and a shallow channel excavated by the Port to create an intertidal habitat area. As a part of this restoration effort, all introduced vegetation has been removed from the area and replaced by native plants. A walkway leads to some picnic tables, a picnic shelter, and a 40-foot-long concrete pier. The Harbor Island Marina is directly across the river, and Mount Rainier frames the south end of the channel.

WEST SEATTLE

West Seattle has always seemed a bit apart from the rest of Seattle—partially because of its physical separation by the broad channel of the Duwamish River, and partially because it is a little bit different (and perhaps better) than the rest of the city, with its combination of extensive saltwater shoreline, outstanding beaches, and fine water-oriented views.

Although Alki Point in West Seattle was the site of the original settlement in the Seattle area in late 1851, most of the pioneers departed the following year. Their interest was in the deep water along the east shore of Elliott Bay, where they envisioned a port for ocean-going ships.

The original settlement in West Seattle languished, with little attention paid to it until 1864, when a sawmill was established on the east side of the peninsula at the new community of Freeport; the mill was soon joined by a shipyard and then a cannery. The growing town changed its name to Milton to avoid being confused with another Freeport in Washington Territory.

By 1885 Seattle was becoming congested, by the standards of the day, and the Alki area was finally platted for homesites. The one

Dad and daughter explore the beach at Duwamish Head.

Scuba divers prepare to enter the water at Seacrest Park.

problem, however, was that the area was physically isolated from Seattle by Elliott Bay and the Duwamish River. The solution was a ferry, which ran from a pier at the foot of Marion Street in Seattle to a terminal near the site of Milton. The ferry continued its 8½-minute crossing regularly between 1888 and 1913. (Try getting from downtown to West Seattle in 8½ minutes today!)

A railway trestle bridged the tideflats by 1890, and in 1902 a planked deck bridge was built at Spokane Street. Over the years bridges were continually added, enlarged, and improved; however, the access never seemed to keep up with the traffic load. The matter was brought to a head in 1978 when a freighter took out the north span of the first of two bascule bridges, precipitating construction of a new, multilane, high-rise bridge.

Southwest Harbor Project Public Access

Park Area: 5.8 acres; 4,300 feet of shoreline
Access: Land
Facilities: Restrooms with disabled access, view platforms, view tower, pier interpretive displays, children's play areas, walking paths
Attractions: Viewpoints, picnicking

For years the wedge of land between Harbor Avenue SW and the Port of Seattle's Terminal 5 has been cluttered with miscellaneous piles of junk, a hodgepodge of railroad tracks, old battered warehouses, and sagging, dilapidated piers. With the shift of the Port's emphasis from bulk to containerized cargo, space for container storage, loading and unloading, and transshipment became a premium item. When the Port decided to expand the container cargo area at Terminal 5 to use this space, part of the project package was a new shoreline park. The city of Seattle joined forces with the Port and provided improvements and landscaping along Harbor Avenue. The result is an outstanding 5.8-acre park that offers visitors a shoreside plaza at the edge of Elliott Bay, raised platforms from which to watch the industrial activities of Terminal 5, sandy, beach-like play areas for kids, and a place to picnic with an appetite whetted by the snap of salt-air breezes.

The park access road leaves Harbor Avenue SW ¼ mile north of Southwest Florida Street, near Salty's Restaurant. The road heads southwest to a parking area on the west end of the park; it then continues east and north to a smaller short-term parking area. At times this extension might be blocked by rail traffic on a spur that slices through the park to serve a barge-loading pier.

Because the park is interwoven with the working waterfront, it has pedestrian ramps and bridges across active rail spurs to connect its various sections. These raised vantage points, as well as a viewing tower, provide an

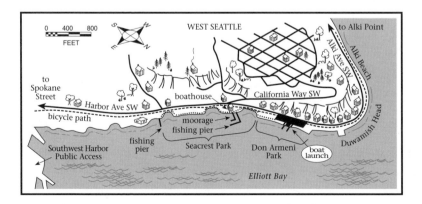

excellent spot to watch the commercial activities of the terminal and to see the Seattle skyline and Elliott Bay. A broad pier plaza holds picnic tables and interpretive signs explaining various activities of the port. A publicly accessible pier extends into Elliott Bay north from the plaza. The Port plans to restore the remainder of the north shoreline of Terminal 5 to a nature habitat.

Seacrest Park (City of Seattle)

Park Area: 4 acres, 2,200 feet of shoreline
Access: Land, boat
Facilities: Restrooms with disabled access, benches, picnic tables, bicycle path, boathouse, fishing piers, guest moorage, concession, tackle, bait, boat rental, outboard fuel
Attractions: Viewpoint, picnicking, bicycling, fishing, boating, scuba diving, skating, bicycling

In 1971 the city of Seattle acquired the property along Harbor Avenue SW, southwest of Duwamish Head, and developed imaginative plans for a premium waterfront park, complete with a 700-boat marina, a fishing pier, a boathouse, a promenade, and salmon-rearing pens. Unfortunately, plans for the marina ran afoul of Indian fishing treaty rights, and, in addition, the total package substantially outran available funding.

Plans were scaled down, but even in their final form the breathtaking views of the downtown Seattle skyline against a background of rugged

The fishing pier at Seacrest Park has fine facilities for anglers.

Cascade summits make Seacrest a gem of a park. Shoreline restoration began with the creation of a promenade along the inner rim of three small coves, with grass enclaves and benches between them on which to relax and enjoy the views. In 1989 a boathouse (a reincarnation of the old Seacrest Marina) was added. A galley, a deli, fresh bait and tackle, and kayak and small boat rentals are provided. The parking lot at the boathouse is quite small, but parallel street parking is available the length of the park. The continuation of the Spokane Street Bicycle Path runs along the edge of Harbor Avenue.

Two fishing piers extend into the bay, one at the south end of the park, and a second L-shaped one at the boathouse. Inside this latter pier is a second float for guest moorage. The jumble of decaying offshore pilings from wharves long forgotten is a favorite spot for skin diving.

To reach Seacrest Park from downtown Seattle, follow the Spokane Street viaduct west over Harbor Island, and take the Southwest Spokane Street/Delridge Way exit onto Southwest Spokane Street. In about a block take the Harbor Avenue/Avalon Way exit. At an intersection in another block, turn right onto Harbor Avenue SW, which parallels the shoreline all the way to Duwamish Head. The south end of the park is reached in about 1 mile.

Don Armeni Park (City of Seattle)

Park Area: 4.3 acres; 1,400 feet of shoreline
Access: Land, boat
Facilities: Boat launch (ramps), restrooms with disabled access, benches, picnic tables, bicycle path
Attractions: Viewpoint, picnicking, bicycling, boating, paddling, fishing, scuba diving

Don Armeni Park is a continuation of the theme of Seacrest Park, with similar fishing and beachfront attractions. The park, which lies along the shore just north of Seacrest Park, was named in 1955 for a popular deputy sheriff, active in youth fishing, who was killed in the line of duty.

Two pairs of launch ramps are in the center of the park; each pair has a loading float between them. The ramps to the south are to be used when launching, and the ones to the north when returning. The parking lots on either side of the ramps are reserved for cars with boat trailers; multiday parking rates are available. A small area at the north end of the park is available for general parking; parallel street parking can be found along Harbor Avenue.

The shoreline not occupied by launch ramps has a landscaped walkway and park benches above a bulkhead. Concrete viewing platforms are at the ends of the park and at either side of the launch ramps.

Duwamish Head

To early Seattlites, the beautiful beaches of West Seattle were a vacation getaway. As early as 1899 the Coney Island Baths opened on the beach west of Duwamish Head, and by 1905 large stretches of the beach were lined with rustic summer cottages. The Coney Island Baths were replaced in 1907 by Luna Park, an amusement site built on a deck over pilings extending into the bay, which boasted a natatorium (indoor swimming pool), a dance pavilion, carnival rides, shows, restaurants, and a tavern. In 1931 the park was torched by an arsonist and it burned to the water. Recreation shifted westward three years later when the city opened a new natatorium at Alki Beach; Luna Park was never rebuilt.

The beach north of Don Armeni Park was the site of Luna Park. In 1947 the city of Seattle acquired the property formerly occupied by Luna Park as an extension of the public beaches lying west of Duwamish Head. The former swimming pool from that park was filled with dirt and now forms a tree-rimmed grass viewpoint that extends out from the seawall. This is the only access point to the beach in this area. At extreme low tide an enormous tideflat is revealed, extending all the way to Duwamish Head and out into Elliott Bay for nearly a quarter of a mile; the stubs of the pilings that supported the park stand out above the tideflat. City

What could be greater than mucking in the mud at Duwamish Head during a low tide?

dwellers throng here to look for the few remaining shellfish in the area, to search with metal detectors for treasures, or just to squish sand between their toes.

Boaters approaching the head should be aware of the shoal, marked by a light and fog signal, which extends out for ¼ mile.

Alki Beach Park (City of Seattle)

Park Area: 154 acres; 10,000 feet of shoreline
Access: Land, boat (shallow draft)
Facilities: Restrooms, picnic shelter, fire rings, art studio, bicycle path, volleyball nets
Attractions: Swimming, wading, beachcombing, picnicking, walking, biking, sunbathing, beach sports, point of interest

In 1851 the original settlers of Alki Point gave their community the name of New York. When they were chided about this pretentious name, they would respond in Chinook jargon *al-ki,* which meant "by-and-by" or "someday." By 1853 the term had become so commonly used that the area was appropriately renamed Alki.

Alki Beach has long been a favorite Seattle saltwater playground. As early as 1905 the area had a hotel, a swimming pool, and a dance pavilion. In order to assure availability of prime saltwater beach, in 1909 the city of Seattle condemned buildings on 3,000 feet of beach-front northeast from Alki Point and erected a bathing and recreation pavilion. A natatorium, opened at the beach in 1934, was a popular spot for many years before falling into disrepair and finally being razed. Today the public beach extends along the peninsula in a continuous strip from Alki Point to the southern extremity of Seacrest Park.

A public beach is a mixed blessing

Alki Beach Park attracts all manner of sunlovers.

for the local residents, however, as recent years have found noisy, rowdy bands of youths crowding the area on summer evenings. Drastically reduced parking, increased police patrols, and an anti-cruising ordinance have materially reduced these problems. The row of salty old beach cottages that once lined the waterfront is giving way to block after block of high-priced condominiums, which forebode the future of the remaining cottages as property values (and taxes) skyrocket.

Summer crowds aside, Alki Beach Park is one of the most beautiful sand-covered expanses on Puget Sound, with exhilarating views across the sound to the Olympics and north to Whidbey Island and Admiralty Inlet. The shore tapers off gradually, and as a result the shallow waters heat enough in the summer to permit reasonably comfortable saltwater bathing. At minus tides the wide sand strip bares some distance out into the sound, exposing a menagerie of underwater life, including moon snails, starfish, anemones, and perhaps a clam or two. Because the intertidal life is now so sparse, please look but don't touch, leaving it for others to enjoy also.

A chain of beach volleyball courts at the east end of the beach attract a continuous series of pick-up games. Restrooms are found above the beach at 57th Avenue W, 60th Avenue SW, and 62nd Avenue SW. Sani-cans are placed at other beach accesses to the east. The building at 60th also houses a Seattle Parks Department art studio program. A picnic shelter is located near 62nd Avenue SW.

Alki Point Lighthouse

The prominent location of Alki Point along the main channel of Puget Sound makes it ideal for a navigational light. The first settlers to live on the point recognized this, and kept an oil lantern burning as a service to passing mariners. In due time the government also realized the value of the point and in 1887 officially authorized the placement of a lens-lantern, lit by a kerosene lantern and suspended on a wooden scaffold. This primitive but effective signal served until 1918 when the present lighthouse was commissioned.

Alki Point was the best possible duty for the lighthouse keeper stationed here. While other keepers were stuck on remote islands and far-flung beaches, the one stationed here at Alki enjoyed all of civilization's amenities, as well as the social life of the nearby city.

With the automation of lighthouses in the 1970s, one of the two lightkeeper buildings was taken over as a residence for the commandant of the 13th Coast Guard District. The lighthouse is open for public tours on weekends and holidays from noon to 4:00 P.M.

CHAPTER THREE

BAINBRIDGE ISLAND

The next best thing to living on an island is visiting one, and Bainbridge Island is especially easy to visit. Those who don't have a boat of their own need only to saunter aboard the ferry or load kayak, canoe, bicycle, or (horrors!) auto onto the ferry, and, before the hour is over, they will be soaking up island atmosphere. The Winslow ferry from downtown Seattle goes directly to Bainbridge Island, the Edmonds ferry runs to Kingston on the Kitsap Peninsula, and from there it's just a short drive south to the Agate Passage bridge and across the bridge to the island.

A sailboat leaves Eagle Harbor.

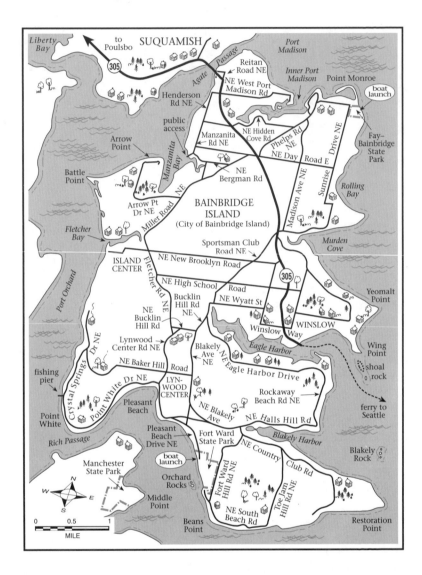

The 24-nautical-mile circumnavigation of the island by boat makes a nice leisurely day excursion, with plenty of time for side trips into Dyes Inlet, Liberty Bay, or the island's inviting harbors, as the mood strikes. Boating facilities in Port Orchard channel on the Kitsap shoreline, as well as navigational considerations in the channel and Rich Passage, are described in chapter 4.

Bainbridge Island is a favorite with bicyclers. Many roads are level, following the shoreline and offering spectacular marine views, but a few

Eagle Harbor has several marinas and yacht club moorages.

inland roads provide a real hill-climbing challenge—most notably Toe Jam Hill Road on the southeast point of the island, and Baker Hill Road, which cuts across the island's south end. Boaters or walk-on ferry passengers wanting to tour the island can rent bicycles in Winslow.

The Parks Department of the City of Bainbridge Island (which incorporates the entire island) has placed interpretive panels at various shoreline points around the island that describe the history or ecology of each site. A brochure available from the department locates each of these displays, and traveling to see the entire collection will provide visitors with a fascinating and enriching tour of the island.

THE EASTERN SHORE

Eagle Harbor and Winslow

It's hard to imagine that more diverse activities could possibly be packed into a harbor of such small size. Eagle Harbor houses a ferry terminal, ferry maintenance facilities, boat repair yards, the skeletal remains of a creosote plant, condominiums, yacht clubs, marinas, a waterfront park, and private homes with docks. Only 2 miles long (and some of that taken up by mudflat) and averaging ¼ mile in width, the harbor and the town along its north shore are the center of activity for all of the island.

Although the Agate Passage bridge on the north end ties the island to the Kitsap mainland, lives are regulated by the comings and goings of the ferry headed for Seattle and big-city jobs. Early weekday mornings may find business-suited commuters, both male and female, rowing boats from Eagledale on the south shore of the bay to Winslow on the north, stepping ashore, briefcase in hand, and dashing for the ferry.

Eagle Harbor was one of the most polluted bays in Puget Sound, with bottom sediments containing a high percentage of toxic chemicals. An underwater sill near the entrance to the harbor slows tidal flows that flush the harbor, permitting sediments and pollutants to settle out within the bay. Contributing to the problem were failed septic tanks, animal wastes, storm drain run-off, and poor industrial practices; a former creosote plant was named a major culprit. Recent cleanup efforts dumped a 3-foot-thick cap of soil over the contaminates, and many of the pollutants have broken down chemically over time, but fish, crabs, and shellfish in the bay are still considered unsafe to eat.

Winslow does its best to entice travelers to stop and enjoy the town before rushing on to distant destinations. The shopping district is uphill and to the west of Highway 305, immediately after leaving the ferry. A host of stores and businesses along Winslow Way offer opportunities to browse, buy, dine, or wet your whistle. A complete circuit of downtown is just an easy stroll, ending with the green glade of the waterfront park.

Eagle Harbor Marinas

Facilities: Guest moorage with power and water, restrooms, showers, laundry, marine pumpout stations, marine supplies and repair, groceries, ice, fishing tackle, bait (there is no boat fuel available anywhere on the island)

When entering Eagle Harbor, boaters must use care, as a shoal and rocks extend south for about 500 yards from Wing Point on the north side of the harbor. Follow the channel markers, avoiding the natural desire to head straight into the bay. Good anchorages can be found in 30 feet of water near the west end of the bay, away from the flow of traffic. Anchoring in the bay is limited to 72 hours at a time.

In lieu of mooring buoys, the city has installed an innovative spar buoy moorage system in the center of the harbor that accommodates more boats in a given space than individual mooring buoys can. Foam floats, with eyes attached, are strung along lines joining spar buoys anchored to the bottom of the bay. Visiting boats can tie to the eyes along the lines between buoys; a moorage fee is charged for use of the system. Overnight moorage is permitted at the float at Waterfront Park, but there is no power or water on the pier, and the inboard portion of the float lies on the bottom at minus tides. Winslow Wharf Marina, on the north shore west of the yacht club, has guest moorage, showers, laundry, a chandlery,

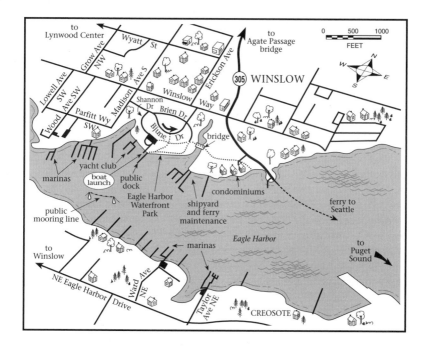

groceries, a coffee shop, and a couple of restaurants on the wharf. The
marina has no designated guest dock—all slips are permanent, and empty
ones are sublet to visitors. Reservations for guest slips are accepted, or
check with the dockmaster for available moorage on arrival.

Harbour Marina, a few docks to the west, is another tenant moorage
that offers guest slips on an "as available" basis. For open slips, check
with the moorage manager on a live-aboard at the dock. Parking and a
pub are nearby on shore.

Eagle Harbor Marina, with 150 slips, can be found on the south shore
across from the ferry terminal, at the foot of Ward Avenue NE. Facilities
include showers, laundry, exercise equipment, and a recreation room. Although the marina was originally developed as a condominium dock, there
are generally several slips that are uncommitted or available for subletting
as guest moorage. Check with the dockmaster for guest slip assignment; all
floats have power and water available. Downtown shopping is only a short
row away.

Also on the south shore of the harbor is the Bainbridge Island Marina
and Yacht Club, at the foot of Taylor Avenue NE, occupying the first
floats west of the old creosote plant at the entrance to the harbor. Both
permanent and guest moorage is available; shoreside amenities include
restrooms, showers, and a chandlery, all in buildings designed to create
an 1890s ambiance.

Eagle Harbor Waterfront Park (City of Bainbridge Island)

Park Area: 8 acres; 1,000 feet of waterfront
Access: Land, boat
Facilities: Picnic tables, fireplace, picnic shelter, restrooms, dock, boat launch (ramp), children's play equipment, tennis courts
Attractions: Walking, boating, views

The business district of Winslow is on the hillside above the bay. By some stroke of fortune a stretch of waterfront below the town remained undeveloped and now has become a pretty little park where tourists and townsfolk alike can recreate. To reach the park by foot from the ferry landing, walk down a road to the left that serves as an entrance to some condominiums; shortly it intersects a gravel path heading west, signed to Waterfront Park. A short extension of the path continues east, between Scotch broom and a yew hedge bordering the condo property, to the shore just west of the ferry landing. On the route to the west, a wooded ravine and a small backwater bay, crossed by a footbridge, lead to the east end of the park.

Madrona trees overhang the banks, and ivy-covered firs and alders reach upward. Picnic tables and benches at scenic spots provide plenty

A trail crosses a gully in Eagle Harbor Waterfront Park.

of excuses to while away some time and watch harbor activity. Kayaks and dinghies weave calmly among the yachts, ships, barges, and ferries. Ducks and gulls eye visitors, hoping for a handout, crows complain about their presence, while cormorants look on disdainfully.

The beach is gravel and mud and not inviting for walking, but paths continue along the bank and through the heart of the park to its western edge. Tennis courts, restrooms, and a picnic shelter with fireplace are a block uphill. A community center, more picnic tables, and children's play equipment are in the north portion of the park.

On the west side of the park is a single-lane concrete boat launch ramp and a 300-foot-long float. Moorage on the float is limited to 48 hours per week; rafting is not permitted. The zero-tide level is marked on the dock; check the depth and tide level before securing your boat, as a tideflat extends for some distance from the shore. Although the launch ramp is excellent, it may not be usable at an extreme low tide.

From the Winslow shopping district, almost any turn to the south leads to the waterfront park. To drive to the boat launch, turn off Bjune Drive onto Shannon Way, and drive past the Queen City Yacht Club outstation to a parking lot at the end of the road. This lot is restricted to vehicles with boat trailers; additional parking for boat trailers is permitted weekends and evenings on Brien and Bjune Drives.

Blakely Harbor

South along the Bainbridge Island shoreline, 1½ miles from Eagle Harbor, is the quiet little inlet of Blakely Harbor. It wasn't always so tranquil. The harbor once held a booming sawmill that, during the 1880s, was claimed to be the largest in the world; lumber shipped from here graced fine mansions from San Francisco to London.

In 1881, the Hall Brothers Shipyard moved their operation here from Port Ludlow when problems at the Ludlow sawmill threatened the ready supply of finished lumber at that location. The Hall Brothers' yard built 77 ships in the years they were in Port Blakely. It was a convenient cycle of events—ships were built of lumber from the mill, and then many of them carried lumber from the mill to markets throughout the world. The five-masted, 225-foot *H. K. Hall*, launched here, could hold 1.5 million board feet of fine Puget Sound lumber.

A 1907 fire devastated the mill, and it was rebuilt to only half its former size. The decline in readily available logs, combined with a depressed lumber market, finally led to the mill's closing in 1914. As the mill foundered, the Hall shipyard was moved north in 1903 to Eagle Harbor. For a time Blakely Harbor still held some importance as a ferry landing, but that too was moved to Winslow in 1937, and the harbor settled back into a quiet existence as a residential community.

Pleasure boaters today enjoy the harbor as a good overnight anchorage and an interesting cruising diversion. Private residences rim the bay—some are the remodeled buildings of the old mill and shipyard; all shore lands are private. Numerous rotted pilings and the concrete shell of an old building at the far northwest end of the bay are testimony to the previous life at Blakely Harbor.

Although the bay is exposed to winds from the east, some anchorages can be found along the south shore. The view east to Seattle is stunning, with the Space Needle and downtown skyscrapers looming large.

Blakely Rock, which is marked by a light, lies ½ mile east of the entrance to Blakely Harbor and due north of Restoration Point. A rocky shoal extends 250 yards to the north. The reef is a popular scuba diving site.

RICH PASSAGE AND PORT ORCHARD

Bainbridge Island forms the northern boundary of Rich Passage, the narrow channel the ferry must thread on its way to Bremerton. The passage is heavily traveled by pleasure boats; on rare occasions an enormous ship or other Navy vessel heading for or leaving Bremerton fills the channel. Between Point White and Point Glover, at the west end, the channel makes a sharp turn and squeezes down to less than 500 yards wide before opening up into the expanse of Port Orchard. Large vessels will sound one long blast when within ½ mile of Point Glover as a warning to approaching craft.

West of Rich Passage an arm of Port Orchard bends southwest, ending in Sinclair Inlet and the gargantuan Erector Set of the Navy shipyards. The main body of the channel sweeps steadily northward for 9 unobstructed miles between Bainbridge Island and the Kitsap Peninsula, before squeezing into Agate Passage and finally pouring into Port Madison. Navigational considerations and facilities in Rich Passage and Port Orchard are described in chapter 4.

Fort Ward State Park

Park Area: 137 acres; 4,300 feet of shoreline
Access: Land, boat
Facilities: Picnic tables, fireplaces, vault toilets, water, boat launch (ramp), hiking trail, mooring buoy, underwater park, bird blinds, Cascadia Marine Trail campsite
Attractions: Historical displays, interpretive signs, boating, fishing, birdwatching, hiking, scuba diving

It wasn't until recently, when lands on the south end of Bainbridge Island were developed as a state park, that many people even knew there had been a military fortification in the area. Visitors are now gradually discovering this history-rich corner of the island and the forested day-use state park overlooking Rich Passage.

Property at Beans Point was purchased by the U.S. Army in 1899; by 1903 construction of buildings and gun emplacements was under way and it was commissioned as Fort Ward. The post, along with the fortifications at Middle Point immediately across the channel, served for 20 years as the inner line of defense to protect the Naval shipyards at Bremerton. Three 8-inch disappearing guns and several smaller rapid-fire guns were installed in four batteries at Beans Point to protect a mine field that was to be laid across the channel. Guns were also planned for Middle Point but were never placed.

During World War I there seemed no danger of direct attack on Puget Sound, so the 8-inch guns were removed and shipped to France for use there. By 1923 all the

Ivy overhangs a rusted doorway at Battery Thornburgh, Fort Ward State Park.

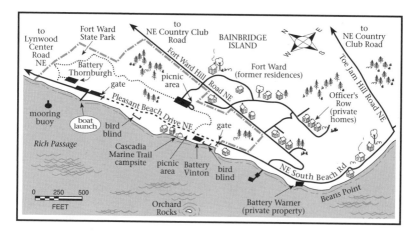

guns had been stripped from the batteries; with the "teeth" gone from the fortification, the following year the remaining troops, except for a caretaker detachment, were transferred to Fort Worden at Port Townsend.

The once vital fort was abandoned as an Army post and in 1930 was transferred to the Navy as a recreation site. It saw duty as a Navy radio school and intercept station and then as a Nike missile site before it was finally surplused. After a brief stint as a children's home, 137 acres of the 480-acre military site was acquired as a state park.

To reach the entrance at the northwest side of the park, drive west from Winslow to the head of Eagle Harbor on Wyatt Street NW, then go south on Bucklin Hill Road NE. At an intersection in ½ mile, where NE Bucklin Hill Road heads west, continue south on Blakely Avenue NE. When NE Blakely Avenue curves east, continue straight ahead on W Blakely Avenue to Pleasant Beach Drive NE. Follow it southeast to the road end in the park.

Just inside the park entrance is a large parking lot and a two-lane boat launch ramp. Launching can be difficult due to the strong tidal current and wakes from passing boats, especially ferries churning through Rich Passage. The mooring buoy offshore, just north of the ramp, is also subject to channel turbulence.

The bottom offshore is frequented by scuba divers who explore the abundance of sea life on the steep walls. To the south are Orchard Rocks, with anemone-filled grottos, and perhaps an octopus. Orchard Rocks are closed to any harvest of marine life.

At the parking lot a gate prevents driving farther along the service road. The road or the beach can be walked south to the park boundary, passing the park office and a pretty, shoreside picnic area with tables, fireplaces, water, and latrines. The brush along the beach at the picnic area screens a campsite of the Cascadia Marine Trail, the only camping available in the park. From the water the trail sign can be spotted on shore near a line of pilings with a horizontal cap south of the park buildings.

A paved side trail climbs from the picnic area through the forest to the upper park entrance. South of the picnic area along the road a few more steps lead to Battery Vinton, with an informational display and a tip-toe view over a growth of Scotch broom across Rich Passage to Middle Point.

Two unique wooden structures with benches, one midway down the road and another just south of Battery Vinton, are bird blinds for watching waterfowl in the channel. Along the shore three sets of moldering pilings topped by horizontal beams, are "cormorant parking lots," frequently holding a phalanx of these birds craning their necks to watch activity in the channel, or spreading their wings to dry.

From the launch ramp parking lot, another trail goes uphill a short distance to where a side trail leads to the ivy- and moss-encrusted Battery Thornburgh, where four 3-inch rapid fire guns were once mounted. The

Pilings at Beans Point are a favorite resting spot for seagulls and cormorants.

main trail continues up to the top of the bluff and heads south to the upper parking lot, through second-growth forest with sword fern and ivy undergrowth. From here the trail from the picnic area can be caught back down to the road. A complete loop hike, including all the sights, is about 2 miles. Do not stray off the paths, as there is poison oak in the area.

The second entrance to the park is at the top of the hill, at the southeast side of the park. To drive there, follow NE Blakely Avenue east from the West Blakely Road intersection, then turn south on NE Country Club Road, then south again at Fort Ward Hill Road NE, which leads to the state park entrance. Here is a large parking lot, picnic tables, fire pedestals, and vault toilets; there are no garbage cans, however. The trails described previously leave from either end of the parking lot.

East of the park boundary are the original buildings of the fort, in various stages of restoration or disrepair. Some carry historical signs telling what they were in an earlier life. All are now privately owned. A tour through this residential area will give an idea of the original size of the fort.

Fort Ward Hill Road NE can be followed as it continues steeply down-hill to the water and the eastern end of the gated park road; however, there is no parking at the end. The concrete remnant of another battery, Battery Warner, along the road to the south, is now on private property.

Continue south on NE South Beach Road, which follows the shoreline, and a sharp turn to the north brings one to the fabled Toe Jam Hill Road NE. The name of the hill, it is said, comes from a particularly seedy tavern that was in the area in early times. The libation served by this establishment, instead of being called Rot Gut, was given the even more derisive term of Toe Jam. The tavern burned in 1903 or 1904, but the name remained forever for the hill on which it stood.

Point White Fishing Pier

On the southwest corner of Bainbridge Island, in the small community of Crystal Springs, is a long pier that is open to the public for fishing. Even if fish are not interested in being caught some days, the dock is a nice vantage point, with miles of views up and down the channel to Port Orchard and across to Illahee State Park. The Suquamish Indians, less taken with the esthetics of the spot, called it *Tux'waxa'detc,* which translates to "goose droppings." This descriptive name came from the tideland boulders that were stained white by the birds fishing the offshore waters. The pier has no float, but the adjoining beach is quite gentle, so small boats could be beached or hand-carried ones launched. A dockhead interpretive sign tells more of the history and ecology of the spot.

To reach the Point White Pier, follow signs south to Lynwood Center, then turn east on Point White Drive NE, which curves around the point, and in 2½ miles arrives at the public pier. Parking for a few cars is on the east side of the road in a graveled pull-out. The drive or bike ride around Point White is an especially scenic one—reason enough to wander here. The road that continues north passes the junction with NE Baker Hill Road and eventually deadends. Return to civilization via NE Baker Hill Road or by backtracking to Lynwood Center.

Fletcher and Manzanita Bays

Gunkholers take note! Two small bays along the west shore of the island offer boaters a quiet overnight anchorage or a spot to drop a lunch hook. Aside from one tiny stretch, the shorelines of both bays are private. Battle Point, the tip of the triangular peninsula separating the bays, was named for a battle of long ago when the local Suquamish Indians and their chief, Kitsap, successfully fought off a band of marauding northern hostiles.

A gravel bar blocks the entrance to Fletcher Bay at midtide, and the bay itself is quite shallow, so boats should enter it only during high tide, and then with extreme care.

Paddling on quiet Manzanita Bay

Manzanita Bay, to the north, offers the best overnight stops, with good protection from southerly blows or, in good weather, placid, star-filled nights. The main body of the bay extends due south for ¾ mile; a short "thumb" trends east. Good anchorages in up to 30 feet of water can be found in either section. The only hazards are submerged pilings about halfway in from the entrance on each side of the bay.

A sliver of public access exists on the north side of Manzanita Bay at a road end, the site of a landing for a ferry that stopped here between 1895 and 1927. This is a good spot to launch hand-carried boats for exploration of the bay. To reach this access, turn west from Miller Road NE onto NE Bergman Road. In ¾ mile, where the road rounds the north shore of Manzanita Bay, watch carefully for a short spur road, Dock Street, on the left. The road stub ends in about a block at a bulkhead above the beach; parking is minimal. Property adjacent to the road and the beach on either side of the road end itself is private. Do not trespass.

AGATE PASSAGE AND PORT MADISON

The Agate Passage bridge, at the northwest tip of Bainbridge Island, is the island's only permanent tie to the mainland, freeing it from total dependence on the ferry. Since the completion of the bridge in 1950, old plans for building additional bridges have been periodically dusted off, but the increased cost of such a project, coupled with the islanders' satisfaction with the status quo, always causes plans to be shelved once again.

The call for more bridges usually comes from people on the Kitsap Peninsula, frustrated by ferry service, who want bridges to Vashon Island and the south end of Bainbridge, so they can have easier access to ferry terminals on those islands and can swear at three ferries instead of just one.

After their rapid trip through 300-yard-narrow Agate Passage, the waters of Port Orchard pour into Port Madison, a broad, round bay bounded on the south by Bainbridge Island. Point Monroe, a curving sand spit marked by a navigational light, lies at the south point of the entrance to the bay. The spit encloses a lagoon that boats can enter at its west end; however, it is quite shallow and the entrance dries at low tide. Several private homes have been built on the spit, and there are docks on the inner edge.

Reitan Road Access

This access directly under the bridge gives a unique water-level perspective on activity in Agate Passage. Traffic roars overhead, water swirls around the concrete abutments, boats sweep by grandly, given an overdrive assist by the rushing current, and an occasional black head, dripping with water, bobs to the surface. Seals? No—scuba divers!

The primitive access is on the Bainbridge Island side of the channel. Head west on Highway 305 and, just before crossing the bridge, turn north on Reitan Road NE. The narrow, paved road drops downhill and under the bridge footings. Parking for a few cars is at the side of the narrow road near a powerline tower, just northeast of the bridge.

From the powerline tower dirt steps lead to a cobble beach dropping off abruptly to the water. The beach south of the bridge is private, but about 300 feet of shorelands to the north are open to public walking.

The access is used by scuba divers who explore the bridge abutments, offshore rocks, and steep walls of the channel. Because the tidal currents can reach 6 knots, only experienced divers should use the area. Those skilled enough to handle the flow thrill to a roller coaster ride around and over rocks and past the encrusted pilings of the bridge.

West Port Madison Nature Preserve (Kitsap County)

A tiny slice of county property just west of Inner Port Madison, once maintained as a park, is now designated a nature preserve. The beach offers the only public access on the Bainbridge Island side of Port Madison, just west of some private homes.

By land the preserve can be reached by turning east off Highway 305

A ladder made of 4x4s threaded on cables descends to the beach at West Port Madison Nature Preserve.

onto NE West Port Madison Road. Follow the street as it curves north and then turns right and becomes NE County Park Road. The preserve is immediately west of the intersection of Gordon Drive NE. A signed parking lot for a dozen cars marks the head of a trail that winds north into the heavy growth of old cedar and fir. Short spurs at two points lead east to the park caretaker's house and to Gordon Drive NE.

Along the way to the beach there are two rustic picnic shelters, each with a large stone fireplace and a cedar shake roof protecting a picnic table. One wonders at the festive picnics of yesteryear that the little park must have seen.

The steep 50-foot clay bank above the beach is negotiated by a shaky ladder made of 4x4s threaded on cables lashed to an upland tree. This is *not* the spot to take small children (although they would probably enjoy it more than many adults). Remember where the trail comes out of the brush at the beach, as the spot is not easily found. At low tides the beach is gradually tapering cobble; high tide brings water right up to the tree line.

Inner Port Madison

The mile-long arm extending south from Port Madison is unquestionably one of the loveliest boating stops on Bainbridge Island and perhaps all of Middle Sound. Names around here are a little confusing—to some *this* narrow inlet is Port Madison—never mind that big chunk of water hovering to the north; to others this arm is Madison Bay. But the name by which it is known locally, and by most knowledgeable boaters, is Inner Port Madison. The community on its shore is also named Port Madison.

Port Madison (the community) was once the major commercial center on the island. Not only was it the county seat, complete with a courthouse and jail, but it also had a large sawmill, shipyards, a foundry, a fish oil rendering plant, and a population of 400 to 600 people. A geography book published at the time described Seattle as "a lumber town across the bay from Port Madison." Because this was a company town, residences were owned by the mill and rented to employees. When the company fell on hard times because of a depressed lumber market, it became heavily mortgaged by the Seattle First National Bank. Eventually the bank foreclosed and took over everything owned by the mill.

Because virtually all the property on the harbor was then in the hands of Seattle First, the bank conceived the idea of developing the property as an exclusive summer resort area. All but the best of the mill buildings were torn down, lots were sold for fashionable summer homes, and metal gates were installed on the road to keep cows from wandering through and destroying the ambiance (or depositing their own ambiance).

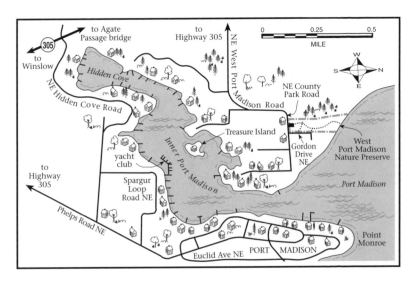

Overlooking Inner Port Madison

Over the years the summer homes gave way to the gracious permanent homes now found along the shore today. The Port Madison Yacht Club has moorages on the bay, and there is an outstation for the Seattle Yacht Club here. The small island midway along the north shore was used as a cemetery during days of the mill and so was known as Deadman's Island. When a cemetery was established elsewhere on Bainbridge Island, the human remains were moved. High society hit the bay, and the islet was renamed Treasure Island.

Boats entering the bay should hold to the middle of the channel to avoid an old ballast dump along the east shore, a reminder of the days when this was a lumber port. Ships arriving in the harbor without cargo carried a load of rock as ballast to steady them; the rock was dumped when they were ready to take on a load of lumber.

Inside the mile-long bay the only navigation hazards are shoals extending from Treasure Island and a submerged rock marked by a day beacon lying southwest of the small island. Good anchorages can be found throughout the bay, out of the way of traffic, in up to 20 feet of water.

In its last ⅓ mile the bay takes a dogleg turn to the south. This far end is known as Hidden Cove. Navigable water continues almost to the end of the bay; all shorelands are private.

Fay–Bainbridge State Park

Park Area: 16.8 acres; 1,420 feet of shoreline
Access: Land, boat
Facilities: 36 campsites, picnic tables, fireplaces, picnic shelters, restrooms, showers, 2 mooring buoys, volleyball court, horseshoe pits, children's play equipment, trailer dump, Cascadia Marine Trail campsite
Attractions: Swimming, boating, paddling, fishing, beachcombing, scuba diving, clamming, crabbing

The only campground on Bainbridge Island, aside from the Cascadia Marine Trail campsite at Fort Ward State Park, is on the island's northeast shore at popular Fay–Bainbridge State Park. The park includes some nicely wooded uplands and one of the prettiest beaches on the island. The beach faces directly on the main channel of Puget Sound, so at times wind and wave action can be severe, and even on hot summer days the water is chilly for swimming; the sandy beach, topped by a row of driftwood and tufts of seagrass, is always a delight, however. At low water the long tideflat holds promise of a few clams for the lucky. The park is heavily used by island residents and on nice summer days can get very crowded.

The historic highlight of the park is the large brass bell on display near the entrance. The bell, which was brought from San Francisco about 1883, was purchased by private subscription by the people of Port Madison and was used in the courthouse there.

For its relatively small size the park packs in a lot of activities. The

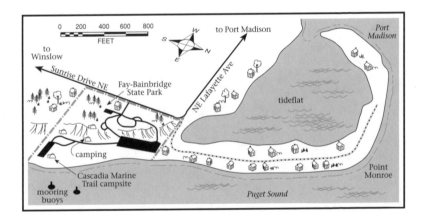

Driftwood and dune grass edge the beach at Fay–Bainbridge State Park.

upper portion of the park has a few picnic sites and some tent camping in grassy areas among the trees. Most of the camping is just above the beach at rather tightly spaced campsites for RVs along the southern side of the park. Two tent pads on the beachgrass flat at the south end of the park are Cascadia Marine Trail campsites.

On the north edge of the beach is a large parking lot. Two mooring buoys offshore are usable for a lunch stop, but lack of protection from waves and wakes could make them quite uncomfortable for an overnight stay.

By land the park is reached by turning east off Highway 305 4¼ miles north of Winslow onto NE Day Road East, which is signed to the park. When Sunrise Drive NE is reached, turn north and follow it to the park.

CHAPTER FOUR

EAST KITSAP PENINSULA

The Kitsap Peninsula has the distinction of being bounded on the west by one major waterway, Hood Canal, and on the east by a different large body of water, Puget Sound. With the exception of the major indentation of Port Gamble Bay, the western shoreline of Kitsap Peninsula rolls smoothly along the canal. The eastern edge of the peninsula, however, is heavily convoluted, with numerous bays and inlets pushing deep inland. These sheltered bays, with their miles upon miles of shoreline, lure boaters and beach walkers bent on marine diversions.

Several state and city parks along the shore offer recreation facilities, and a number of towns have marine accommodations and supplies. The shores are heavily populated—even in the parks one would be hard pressed to find a pristine beach, but the interesting villages and towns along the way compensate for this.

Land travelers usually arrive at the Kitsap Peninsula via ferry, either from Seattle to Bremerton, or from Seattle to Winslow on Bainbridge Island, and then drive or bike over the Agate Passage bridge. Either route is exquisitely scenic, with views of boating traffic on the busy marine highways, the sparkling skyline of the city, and the ethereal presence of Mount Rainier. The peninsula can also be reached from the south via Highway 16 from Tacoma or Highway 3 from Shelton.

Manchester

Facilities: Dock with float, boat launch (ramp), picnic tables and shelter, sani-can, groceries, ice, service station, bait, tackle

The only public water access between Harper and Rich Passage is at the tiny community of Manchester. Here the Port of Manchester dock, with its 150-foot-long float, is available for day use by boats and anglers; overnight moorage is not permitted. Adjacent to the dock on the north

Opposite: *The beach at Point No Point County Park*

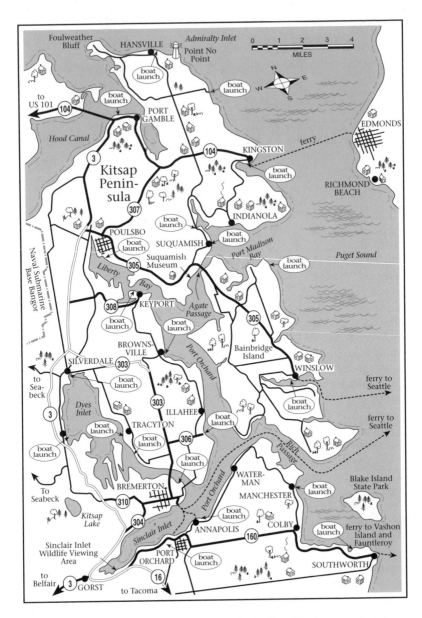

is a two-lane concrete launch ramp. The dock also affords expansive views west to the Seattle cityscape, the West Seattle shoreline, and nearby Blake Island and south to Mount Rainier.

Just south of the dock is tiny Pomeroy Park, which consists of a patch of grass above the beach with a few benches, picnic tables, and a small

On the beach at Manchester

picnic shelter. Car parking at the dock itself is limited to two spaces for disabled persons. The closest general parking area is 1½ blocks up the street, north of the Colchester/East Main intersection. The heart of Manchester is a cluster of stores around this intersection.

Manchester is most easily reached from the east via the Southworth ferry. From the ferry landing follow State Highway 160 north for 3¾ miles, then turn east on Southeast Colchester Drive, signed to Manchester and Manchester State Park. The intersection above the dock is reached in another 1¾ miles.

RICH PASSAGE

Rich Passage is one of the most scenic spots along the route of the Bremerton ferry. Here the channel squeezes at its most slender point to a mere 500 yards wide, and passengers are treated to close-up views of salty beachfront homes tucked into green-clad shoreline.

Pleasure boaters should be wary of stiff tidal currents that can be encountered in the channel, especially at the west end. Several rocks lying just offshore are well marked with lights or daymarkers. The largest of the obstacles, Orchard Rocks, lying on the north side of the channel just inside the east entrance, are partially exposed at low tide. Boaters will encounter no problems if they stay in the marked channel but should keep an eye over their shoulders for ferries bearing down on them.

Manchester State Park

Park area: 111 acres; 3,400 feet of shoreline
Access: Land, boat (limited winter hours)
Facilities: 50 standard campsites, 3 hiker/biker primitive sites, group
camp, picnic tables, fireplaces, picnic shelters, water, restrooms,
showers, bathhouse, hiking trails, nature trail, historic fortifications,
trailer dump station, Cascadia Marine Trail campsites
Attractions: Historical displays, hiking, fishing, boating, paddling, scuba
diving

At the turn of the century, although the United States was not at war,
the Army feared foreign ships could sneak into Puget Sound and attack
the vital naval shipyards at Bremerton. A military station was built at
Middle Point on the south shore of Rich Passage to operate a mine field
that was to be laid across the channel. By 1910, even before World War I
broke out, the technology of the type of mine installed here became ob-
solete and, because there was no dire threat of attack, the fort was deac-
tivated; the site was then for a time used for testing mines (or torpedos,
as they were then called).

During World War II anti-submarine nets were stretched from here
across the channel to Fort Ward. The nets were lowered whenever ferries
passed. After the installation was no longer needed, part of the military
land was taken by the Navy for a supply depot; the balance of the property was eventually surplused, and the public got lucky and gained another prime beachfront state park.

To reach Manchester State Park from Bremerton, follow the road
paralleling the shoreline around Sinclair Inlet. After going through the

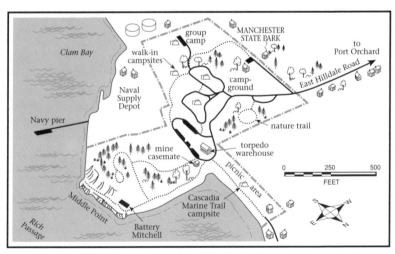

The torpedo warehouse at Manchester State Park now serves as a picnic shelter.

small community of Waterman, the road leaves the shore and turns due south. In ½ mile turn west on East Hilldale Road, which is signed to the park.

From Southworth, the terminus of the Vashon ferry from Fauntleroy, the park can be reached by heading west on Highway 160; in 3¾ miles turn right on Southeast Colchester Drive and follow signs to the park, a total distance of 8 miles from the ferry terminal. When going through Manchester, be sure to take the first right, a short ½ block west of the Colchester/East Main intersection, onto Beach Drive E.

By boat, the park is 10½ miles from Seattle's Shilshole Bay and 5½ miles from downtown Bremerton or Port Orchard.

The park fronts on a small, shallow cove—not especially good for swimming, but an adequate spot to launch hand-carried boats. Underwater rocks off Middle Point are an attractive scuba diving site. The campground, on the hillside above the cove, lies in tall cedar, fir, alder, and maple with an undergrowth of sword fern and salal. Two Cascadia Marine Trail campsites are tucked in the brush just above the picnic area.

Especially interesting are two old remaining structures of the fortification, a torpedo (mine) warehouse, and mining casemate. Informational displays describe the system of placing and detonating the mines and the tracking of ships in the channel. The huge brick torpedo warehouse, with gracefully arched windows and doorways, is now a mind-blowing picnic shelter.

Several trails lace the park, connecting the campground with the picnic area and beach; most follow old service roads. A short loop interpretive nature trail is immediately north of the park entrance. Signs advise hikers to stay on trails and avoid brush near the shore because the area contains a heavy growth of poison oak.

A trail leads west from the beach and picnic area to the concrete pit of Battery Mitchell. The Army had planned for the Middle Point fortification to have two 3-inch guns to protect the mine field, but the four batteries at Fort Ward on Bainbridge Island, immediately across Rich Passage, offered ample protection, so the guns were never installed.

PORT ORCHARD AND SINCLAIR INLET

The purpose of geographical names is supposed to be to clarify locations. Unfortunately this is not the case with Port Orchard, as the name refers to (1) the 9-mile north-south-flowing channel separating Bainbridge Island and the Kitsap Peninsula, (2) the baylike continuation of that channel that runs southwest to Bremerton, and (3) the small town on the shore of, not Port Orchard, but Sinclair Inlet.

Beach Drive E, paralleling the water along the south side from Rich Passage to the town of Port Orchard, is an ideal bicycle or Sunday-drive route with plenty of places to stop and picnic, birdwatch, fish, or photograph. Monster ferries lumber by, sailboats blow in the breeze, the naval shipyards look like some enormous Erector Set construction, and above it rise the crystal peaks of the Olympics.

At minus tides the baring shoreline shows interesting lines of parallel rock strata extending diagonally outward from the beach. These are the edges of tilted layers of hard rock that were ground off by an ancient glacier.

Waterman

Facilities: Public fishing pier, sani-can

In the late 1800s steamers of the Mosquito Fleet stopped regularly at Waterman, on the south shore of Port Orchard, to load bricks from the local brickyard and pick up and discharge passengers. The brickyard closed in 1889; in time the steamers ceased calling here and the old piers of the brickyard rotted away. Today the only reminder of the once-busy town is a pier rebuilt on the pilings of the former ferry dock.

The 200-foot-long pier, maintained by the Port of Port Orchard, has a fishing platform at its end. At the head of the dock, a wooden deck with

The Waterman fishing pier is located on the site of a former Mosquito Fleet dock.

a pair of benches and a sani-can fronts a paved narrow parking area. Next to the shore, wooden stairs give access to the beach; however, the beach is public only immediately under the pier.

Annapolis Recreation Area

This Department of Fish and Wildlife boat-launching area is a 200-foot strip of beachfront at the east city limits of Port Orchard immediately next to the Annapolis–Bremerton passenger ferry dock. The only facilities are a single-lane, surfaced launch ramp and a large parking lot for vehicles with boat trailers. The gravel and mud beach slopes outward quite gradually, and the ramp is not in the best of shape. There are no restrooms near the ramp area, but there is an RV holding tank disposal station about 200 feet east on the south side of the road.

Just west of the recreation area is the Port of Bremerton Annapolis Dock, used by a small passenger ferry that takes commuters to Bremerton. The 300-foot-long dock has a float that can be used for fishing when the ferry is not in. The parking lot at the head of the dock is reserved for cars with permits.

Inspired by the prospects of the naval shipyards about to be built on Sinclair Inlet, the founders of Annapolis named their town after the site of the U.S. Naval Academy in Maryland and gave the streets names of naval heroes such as Farragut and Perry. The former business center has been annexed by Port Orchard and is now part of that town.

Port Orchard

Port Orchard (the town) is frequently the prime destination for people boating in Port Orchard (the waterway). The town is the antithesis of industrial Bremerton, facing it across the inlet—here life is slow-paced, except briefly during shift change at the Navy shipyards, when commuter traffic pours through. The town caters to tourists; its main street, with wooden-canopied walkways reminiscent of the Old West, has an assortment of interesting shops to browse and eateries to try.

Three blocks straight up the hill on Sidney Avenue at the intersection of Dekalb Street is the town's Log Cabin Museum—a case where the building is every bit as fascinating and historic as its contents. The two-story log structure, which dates from 1913 to 1914, houses a collection of memorabilia and authentic furnishings. Hours are Sunday 1:00 P.M. to 4:00 P.M. and Monday 10:00 A.M. to noon.

Port Orchard began its history in 1866 as Sidney, named after the father of town founder Frederick Stevens. In 1903, after 10 years of political arm wrestling with the town fathers of Charleston, on the opposite side of the inlet, who decided they wanted the name Port Orchard too, the name was changed. At that time the shipyard mail was addressed to Port Orchard (the waterway), and everyone was trying to capitalize on it.

From the beginning, Mosquito Fleet boats were vital to the existence of businesses in Sidney (Port Orchard), but once the shipyards became

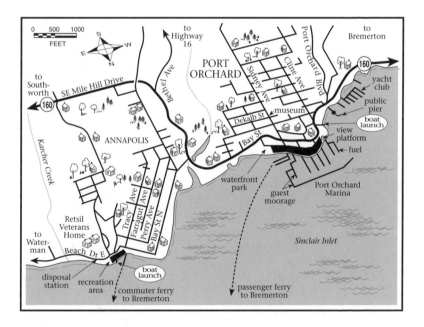

active the steamers also served to transport workers from their homes on the south side of the bay. The historic Mosquito Fleet is now just a fond memory, but it is possible to recapture some of the feeling of that era by hopping the little passenger ferry still running to Bremerton. The boat departs from the terminal immediately east of the marina about every half hour; crossing time is about 15 minutes. Take advantage of the trip and linger to walk around Bremerton, avoiding parking or mooring woes. A second passenger ferry leaves from Annapolis, on the east side of town, but that boat is primarily used by shipyard workers and operates only during commuting hours.

Port Orchard Marina and Waterfront Park

Facilities: Guest moorage with power and water, diesel, gas, restrooms, showers, marine pumpout station, picnic tables, picnic shelter, viewing platform

The centerpiece of the town of Port Orchard is the large modern marina operated by the Port of Bremerton. Nearly half of the 600-plus slips in the marina are allocated for guest moorage—which soundly attests to the popularity of the town and its facilities as a cruising destination. A long, concrete float cups around the moorage area; the entrance is at the

A waterfront promenade overlooks the Port Orchard Marina.

west end. The fuel dock and a short guest moorage dock are at gate 1, immediately inside the marina. Gates 2 and 3, the covered moorages in the center, are all permanent tie-ups. The main guest area is along the breakwater and at its western end, adjoining gate 4. In summer late-arriving boaters may have to tie up on the outside of the breakwater, where waves and wakes can make for an uncomfortable stay.

At night the dock gates and the doors of the on-shore restrooms by the harbormaster's office are opened by a keycard, which guests can obtain from the harbormaster. A restroom open to the public without the use of a keycard is at the west end of the parking lot. Near the west end of the marina parking lot is a one-story viewing platform. The unique, cylindrical concrete structure provides an outstanding overlook of the Port Orchard Marina and the mothballed Navy fleet across the inlet. Grocery stores, restaurants, marine supplies, and other shopping are only a block's walk away.

Immediately east of the marina are a three-block-long promenade and a waterfront park. Benches along the promenade overlook nautical activities. At the park is a small pavilion with bleachers that also serves as a picnic shelter when not used by entertainment playing to the bleachers. A wide set of concrete steps leads down to the sand and gravel beach. Take along a sandwich and make use of the picnic tables or shelter at this end of the park.

Port Orchard Boat Launch and Public Pier

Continue west along the waterfront drive to find the city's public boat ramp, immediately across the street from the white concrete block Port Orchard municipal building, at the intersection of Bay Street (Highway 160) and Cline Avenue. The two surfaced launch ramps are separated by a 50-foot finger pier for loading. The adjacent parking lot has space for eight or nine vehicles and trailers.

A commercial boathouse lies to the west of the launch ramps, and beyond that, at the intersection of Bay Street and Port Orchard Boulevard, the City of Port Orchard Pedestrian Pier juts into Rich Passage. The 150-foot-long float, reached by a ramp, nearly rests on the bottom at low tide. Take advantage of the pier and float for fishing or just dawdling.

Sinclair Inlet Wildlife Viewing Area

A variety of waterfowl gather at the head of Sinclair Inlet—cormorants perch on old pilings, scanning the water's surface for an unwary fish, migratory ducks paddle in flocks along the protected shoreline, resting and refueling before continuing on their journey. On the south shore of the inlet 24 acres of tidelands have been set aside by Kitsap County and the U.S. Fish and Wildlife Service as a fish and waterfowl refuge.

The preserve is immediately west of the interchange where Highway 160 joins Highway 16. A large dirt parking lot on the north side of the road has a log-framed sign at the edge of the wooded shoreline, but there are no signs along the highway to identify the lot, so you must watch carefully for it. The preserve lies immediately west of a large garden nursery on the north side of the road. A concrete median in the highway blocks access to the lot by eastbound traffic, but there is a turnaround loop just after Highway 160 E leaves Highway 16.

The shoreline is soggy and densely overgrown—not much for walking—and the offshore tideflat is a wide, mucky mess at minus tides. However, the area was meant

Migrating waterfowl can be seen at the end of Sinclair Inlet.

as a habitat for wildlife, not people, and it serves that function nicely. The best way to appreciate the extensive wetlands and possibly view some of the waterfowl is from a kayak or canoe. They can be launched at the parking lot at high tide.

BREMERTON

Bremerton is a one-industry town, and life here revolves around its blue-collar job of maintaining Navy ships. The town waterfront has some allure from a distance, with the latticework of the enormous hammerhead crane silhouetted against the pale outline of the Olympic Mountains and the mothballed ships lying in the harbor like snoozing dinosaurs. Up close, however, the oppressive barrier of cyclone fencing and the gritty industrialism of the shipyard sink in; with the exception of the Waterfront Boardwalk and two small museums, there is precious little in the downtown to cause arriving ferry passengers to tarry here. Civic boosters periodically develop grand plans for sprucing up the area to attract more tourists, and a few of these dreams, such as the Waterfront Boardwalk, have actually become reality.

The local residents are pretty defensive about the shipyard—they know that either directly or indirectly it puts food on the table for nearly everyone in town. In fact, if it weren't for the shipyard, Bremerton might not exist. There were several other well-established towns in the vicinity when Lt. Ambrose Barkley Wyckoff selected a site on the north shore of Sinclair Inlet as the best possible location for a new Navy shipyard. In 1891 he purchased 190 acres of land from several property owners, including 86 acres owned by William Bremer. The Bremer property was part of a 168-acre parcel he had previously acquired from his brother-in-law, Henry Hensel. Bremer sold the land to the Navy for less than he had paid for it, feeling the presence of the shipyard would increase the value of his remaining holdings. He built a wharf on the water near the shipyard, cleared and platted 40 acres, and named it Bremerton. A town was born.

The Navy yard had its beginnings in 1888 when a commission was appointed to find a site somewhere north of San Francisco for a naval station. Several potential sites in the Puget Sound region were located, but the most favored candidates were Port Orchard and Lake Washington. Because the latter site would involve construction of elaborate, expensive, and militarily vulnerable channels and locks, the site on the shore of Port Orchard was selected, and in September of 1891 construction began.

For its first five years the naval station consisted of a wooden Civil War gunboat, the USS *Nipsic*, anchored offshore, which served as offices and quarters for the commandant, Lieutenant A. B. Wycoff. By 1896 an office building, officers' quarters, and the first drydock were complete; however, in 1899 development came to a standstill when the admiral in charge of the Bureau of Yards and Docks decided the station was poorly located and should be closed. The hue and cry of

The USS Turner Joy *is typical of navy ships built and repaired at Bremerton.*

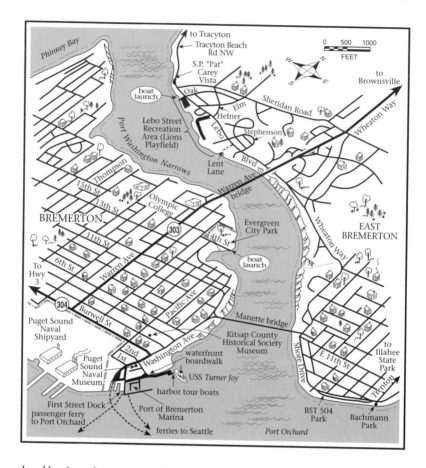

local business interests was felt in Congress, and construction was resumed.

In 1904 land was acquired on Dyes Inlet at Ostrich Bay for construction of a Naval Ammunition Depot to assemble explosives and ammunition components into shells for the Navy and Coast Guard and overhaul ammunition carried by vessels calling at Bremerton for maintenance.

By 1906 a second drydock was needed, and construction of Dock II, the Navy's largest drydock, was completed in 1913. Over the next 10 years a marine reservation, a hospital, a wireless station, several machine and repair shops, and additional quarters and barracks were added. With the outbreak of World War I, the Navy added shipbuilding to the maintenance role of the yard, and a third drydock was constructed. The yard was also designated a training site for naval and marine recruits. Regrading out into Sinclair Inlet (no environmental impact statements required in those days) of a large portion of the hillside to the west added 34 acres to the installation in 1920.

With the end of the war work, the yard force rapidly dropped from 6,500 to 2,700. Some of the limited shipbuilding continued, but it wasn't until 1932 that federal spending to relieve unemployment during the Depression funneled money into shore construction. Drydocks were expanded to accommodate the new aircraft carriers, and the hammerhead crane that identifies the yard today was added to handle battleship guns and turrets.

The invasion of Poland by Germany in 1939 triggered a flurry of defense activities, including the addition of a fourth drydock to the yard. Three years later the Japanese attack on Pearl Harbor brought the yard to full round-the-clock operation to meet the immediate demand for naval vessels. With increased ammunition shipments to Alaska and the Pacific, additional ammunition-handling stations with easy rail access became critical, and the Navy acquired the Hood Canal site at Bangor for a naval magazine.

With the end of World War II, the yard began another series of boom-or-bust cycles, dependent on naval maintenance requirements and appropriations. Today the yard is the home of a dozen or so mothballed ships. Active fleet ships still call at the yard for maintenance and upgrades, but shipbuilding here is now nonexistent. The ammunition station at Ostrich Bay has since been converted to the Jackson Park naval housing area.

Currently, the nearby town of Keyport has an expanded role as the Naval Undersea Warfare Center; torpedo testing areas were expanded from Port Orchard to include most of Dabob Bay on Hood Canal. The Bangor facility went through several cycles of activity, with highs during the conflicts in Korea and Viet Nam and lulls in intervening periods. The conversion of Bangor to a home port for Trident submarines brought this area to its present-day mission and condition.

Today many downtown stores are linked to the needs and tastes of shipyard workers and the Navy. Scattered among the blue-collar taverns, bars, and cafes are such Navy-specific enterprises as a uniform supply. The downtown shopping district lies along Pacific Avenue, two blocks from the ferry terminal.

Port of Bremerton Marina

Facilities: Guest moorage with power and water, restrooms, showers, laundry, marine pumpout station

North of the ferry terminal is the First Street Dock, a pretty waterfront facility with a distinctive clock tower and park benches under a broad-roofed pavilion. A breakwater that runs north from the end of the dock serves both as a loading platform for passenger ferries to Seattle and

A historical display interests youngsters at the Bremerton Waterfront Boardwalk.

Annapolis and as protection for the waterfront moorage basin. Behind the breakwater are floats with room for 50 to 60 guest boats. Access to all but the breakwater floats is secured by a keypad gate; the code is provided by the harbormaster upon payment of moorage fees.

Bremerton Waterfront Boardwalk

Pilings support an over-water concrete boardwalk that runs along the waterfront between First and Burwell Streets. Benches, tables, and planters create a pleasant park and provide places for a picnic lunch or to watch seagulls supervising waterfront activities. A huge, bronze, shaft-mounted propeller (approximately the size of those that drove the nearby destroyer) has been etched with a montage of historical photos of the Navy Shipyard.

At the foot of 2nd Street a small, one-story building has a circular staircase winding up its side to an observation platform topped by a tall flagpole. Views are south and east across the marina and the boardwalk to Dyes and Sinclair Inlets.

USS *Turner Joy*

Although the USS *Missouri,* formerly berthed in Bremerton, has gone to Hawaii, the city does have its ship. The revitalized waterfront features the 418-foot destroyer USS *Turner Joy,* which is open for public tours.

The bridge on the USS Turner Joy

Tickets for self-guided tours can be purchased at a gift shop on 4th Street at the end of the boardwalk. Boat tours of the harbor are also offered.

The self-guided tour of DD-951, the *Turner Joy,* is in itself well worth the trip to Bremerton. Kids (and/or accompanying adults) will quickly get lost in the rabbit warren of companionways on the ship's five decks. The narrow corridors lead past wardrooms and elbow-tight berthing areas, with intervening peeks into the Combat Information Center, the Captain's Quarters, the Electronic Countermeasures Room, and the engine room. A memorial replica of a POW prison cell in Viet Nam is a sobering note.

Everyone will want to command the ship from the bridge and pilot house, and the more agile will revel in climbing into the gunner's position in one of the aft 5-inch-gun mounts. A tour ticket is good for all day, so you can make a quick pass through, go ashore for lunch, and return for continued exploration. The ship is open for tours daily from Memorial Day through Labor Day from 10:00 A.M. to dusk. Winter hours may vary from year to year. Call the number listed in appendix A for current information.

A ship model at the Puget Sound Naval Museum

Puget Sound Naval Museum

For many years a corner of the ferry terminal housed the rather dusty relics of the Puget Sound Naval Museum. In 1986 the museum moved up the hill one block to a brighter, more spacious new location at 130 Washington Avenue. It is open from 10:00 A.M. to 5:00 P.M. Monday through Saturday and 1:00 P.M. to 5:00 P.M. on Sunday.

The museum focuses on the history of the Navy Yard and ships built there, but it also has displays of ship memorabilia, swords, cutlasses, armaments, mines, and other interesting nautical paraphernalia. There are numerous minutely detailed 15-foot-long replicas of battleships, cruisers, destroyers, and aircraft carriers, and some plastic see-through builder's models that reveal all the interior plans. Other attractions include maps of Pearl Harbor showing locations of ships and military facilities before and after the Japanese Navy attack in 1941.

Kitsap County Historical Society Museum

For many years the Kitsap County Historical Society was located in an historic old bank building at the northeast corner of the Silverdale Waterfront Park. The bank was referred to in the book *Kitsap County: A History,* where Fredi Perry writes succinctly: "Nothing much ever happened in Silverdale. Folks made a comfortable living raising cows and chickens and turkeys while others commuted to PSNS. Once the bank was held up" (and the robbers' escape vehicle was a rowboat). The museum eventually outgrew the old bank and in 1997 moved to expanded quarters in (what else?) a remodeled bank building in Bremerton at 280 4th Street.

The early history of the county centered on logging and farming, but eventually was influenced by the local military installations in Bremerton, Keyport, and Bangor. The Historical Museum does an exceptionally nice job of depicting an illustrated time line of the growth of the county. It covers time from its original pioneer days, through its agricultural period, on through the build-up of the Navy Yard, and finally ending with the development of the Naval Undersea Warfare Center at Keyport and the Naval Submarine Base at Bangor. In addition to the main time-line displays, both the main floor and the mezzanine area have rotating displays of various other facets of the county's history.

PORT WASHINGTON NARROWS

The city of Bremerton straddles the ¼-mile-wide trough of the Port Washington Narrows. Two bridges span the channel: near the mouth, Highway 304 crosses on the Manette bridge; midway up the channel the Warren Avenue bridge carries Highway 303. The 3½-mile-long Port Washington Narrows runs between 80-foot bluffs that gentle out midway up the channel. The deep channel has no navigational hazards; however, tidal currents, which can run in excess of 4 knots, might noticeably affect boat speed and can cause problems for paddle-powered craft.

Bremerton's Manette bridge crosses the Port Washington Narrows.

Aside from the yacht club on the west shore of Phinney Bay, the only commercial marine facility on the Port Washington Narrows or in Dyes Inlet is the Port Washington Marina, located on the south shore of the narrows, west of the Warren Avenue bridge. The marina is difficult to find by land. It is off 15th Street at the end of Thompson Drive. The facility has marine supplies, repair services, some guest moorage, restrooms, and a laundry, but it does not have fuel. Some limited groceries are available nearby.

BST 504 Park (City of Bremerton)

Boy Scout Troop 504 created this minuscule city park, maybe 40 feet wide and 50 feet deep, as a troop project. Parking space for a few cars fronts a small patch of grass with a children's gym, a picnic table, and a scramble access over a jumbled concrete block bulkhead to a cobble and gravel beach. Beaches on both sides are private; the view is southwest to the USS *Turner Joy*. The park lies alongside the east-directed one-way section of Shore Drive at the south tip of the East Bremerton peninsula.

Bachmann Park (City of Bremerton)

On the east side of the entrance to the Port Washington Narrows, at the tip of Point Herron, a tiny park offers an excellent view of traffic shuttling to and fro in the bay and entering the narrows. To reach the park from the ferry terminal, turn right after leaving the unloading area and follow Washington Avenue to the Manette bridge. Immediately after crossing the bridge, turn right and follow the arterial (11th Street) to Trenton Avenue. The park is two blocks to the right, at the end of Trenton.

The park's small wooden gazebo with benches sits on pilings over the water; another bench and a pair of picnic tables are in grass patches onshore. A breach in the concrete bulkhead allows visitors to reach the water and walk the cobblestone beach or launch hand-carried boats.

Evergreen City Park (City of Bremerton)

Park Area: 6 acres; 300 feet of shoreline
Facilities: Boat launch (ramps) with boarding float, restrooms, benches,
    picnic tables, picnic shelters, water, fireplaces, children's play equipment
Attractions: Boating, fishing

This park is located on the west shore of the Narrows, between the two Bremerton bridges, at the intersection of Park Avenue and 14th Street. A large parking lot adjoins the two-lane, concrete launch ramp with a centered boarding float.

The level, grassy park has numerous benches and a picnic shelter for family picnics. Play equipment is available for energetic youngsters and a pair of World War II–vintage 3-inch rapid-fire guns sit astride a flagpole at the head of the launch ramp. The gravelly beach is not inviting for swimming but is a good spot to try your hand at shore fishing.

Lebo Street Recreation Area (Lions Playfield) (City of Bremerton)

Park Area: 15 acres; 1,700 feet of shoreline
Facilities: Float, fishing pier, boat launch (ramp) with boarding float, picnic tables, fireplaces, children's play equipment, concession stand, baseball diamonds, restrooms, jogging track
Attractions: Fishing, boating, swimming, team sports, beach walking

The city of Bremerton and the local Lions Club have put a five-block-long stretch of waterfront to its best possible use—a multipurpose recreation complex, appealing to interests ranging from baseball to boating. The park is located on the north shore, near the western edge of the Port Washington Narrows. From land, the park is on Lebo Boulevard, which

The boarding float at Lebo Street Recreation Area

parallels the shore west of the Warren Avenue bridge. Entrances are in the middle of the park at Hefner Road and at the west end at Oak Street. A third access is at the east end of the park at Lent Lane; here there is only a rough gravel parking lot, a large open lawn, and a gated road to a low bank access to the water. Beach walks west from here can continue past the park along the shore below Tracyton Beach Road NW for a distance of 3 miles. The central section of the park fronts on sandy beach, perfect for sunbathing or courageously swimming in the chilly waters of the narrows.

Boating facilities at the west end of the park by the Oak Street entrance include a three-lane, surfaced launch ramp with a short concrete float (aground at low tide) for loading boats or for passing boats to stop and enjoy the facilities. A long, concrete fishing pier parallels the shore. Benches in a pretty wooden gazebo at the head of the boarding float provide a spot to relax and enjoy the stunning view up Dyes Inlet to the rugged Olympic peaks.

S.P. "Pat" Carey Vista (City of Bremerton)

The road continuing north from Lebo Street Recreation Area, Tracyton Beach Road NW, follows the shoreline, with numerous spots providing access to the beach. The level, blacktop road, which is marked as a bicycle route, is ideal for cycle touring, but it is narrow and has no shoulder. A few blocks north of the Lebo Street Recreation Area is a tiny Bremerton city park consisting of landscaping, a few benches, and a picnic table overlooking the stretch of the narrows between Phinney Bay and the Warren Avenue bridge. Here is a nice spot for a leisurely snack while watching boats headed to and from Phinney Bay and Dyes Inlet. Hand-carried boats can be launched over the low jumble of concrete that forms a bulkhead.

Dyes Inlet

Dyes Inlet is a cruising delight, with fascinating little bays and coves, scenic shorelines, and quiet anchorages. Once past Port Washington Narrows, the waterway suddenly opens to the 1½-mile-wide inlet, resembling a large protected lake rather than the open reaches boaters are accustomed to on Puget Sound. The sheltered waters are ideal for kayak and small boat exploration, as well as cruising in bigger boats. Much of the waterfront on Dyes Inlet is private; do not trespass.

Several deep bays penetrate the south shore of the inlet. Phinney Bay, at the northern end of the narrows, hosts moorages of the Bremerton Yacht Club. The next cove to the west, slender Mud Bay, is well named—it is a tideflat, navigable only at high tide by kayaks or dinghies.

Ostrich Bay, the largest cove on Dyes Inlet, is on the southwest corner. Adventuresome boaters will want to follow the narrow slot on the

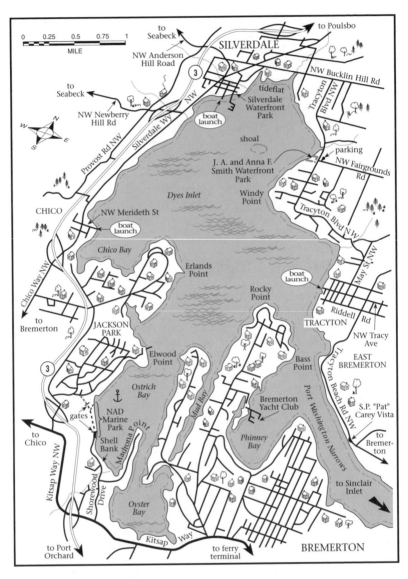

west shore of Ostrich Bay leading into the tiny pocket of Oyster Bay; at extreme low tide there is 6 feet of water midchannel. Good anchorage can be found in either bay. A large rock lies near the west shore, about 250 yards north of the large abandoned Navy wharf. A ¼-mile section of shore along the southwest side of Ostrich Bay is a Bremerton city park, and a short segment near the end of the bay is owned by the Washington State Historical Society. All other shore land is either private or part of the Naval Ammunition Depot and the Jackson Park housing for Navy families.

We readily decided there are no ostriches on Ostrich Bay, but oysters on Oyster Bay? Perhaps. Japanese oysters were introduced in the early 1940s by Japanese-American entrepreneurs who established an oyster farm on the east side of Dyes Inlet. The business thrived, but unfortunately, with the outbreak of World War II, the owners were confined in an internment camp, and the operation closed. The oysters remained to fend for themselves in the inlet, wherever they could find a suitable environment.

It is believed that ancestors of Manila clams found today in Dyes Inlet hitchhiked here on barges that brought in Japanese oysters. Today, however, the encroaching housing developments along the shoreline have raised pollution levels in the inlet to the point that all shellfish gathering has been declared hazardous by the Department of Health.

Shell Bank

In 1906 the Kean brothers built a rustic summer resort at the head of then remote Ostrich Bay. The property and the large log building that served as the resort's focal point were donated to the Washington State Historical Society by Ruth Entz and for many years sat moldering and unnoticed as suburban Bremerton grew to envelop the site. In 1995 an Americorp project cleaned up the property and boarded up the building to prevent further deterioration from vandalism. Today the wonderful old log structure, with its dormers and elaborately decorated stone chimney sits solemnly amid a stand of good-sized trees. The shell-spattered gravel beach below tapers gradually into the end of Ostrich Bay. The site is on Shorewood Drive, about ½ mile north of Kitsap Way; parking is very limited.

Naval Ammunition Depot Marine Park (City of Bremerton)

An old road end along the west shore of Ostrich Bay offers a rare treat—public access among the prized waterfront properties. The undeveloped city park lies at the end of Shorewood Drive. To reach it, follow Kitsap Way west out of Bremerton; just before reaching Highway 3, turn right onto Shorewood Drive, and follow it to its gated end and a small parking area.

The abandoned road can be walked all the way to the Jackson Park navy housing development. Enjoy nice views of the bay through a light screen of trees, or shiver in the reflection of the dense forest above, which reminds one of the haunted forest en route to the castle of the wicked witch in the *Wizard of Oz*. Woodpecker-chopped holes in tree snags and a crescendo of chirping in the woods portend good birdwatching for an observant visitor.

A boot path leads down the 30-foot-high bank near the parking lot to the rocky beach. The beach can be walked to the north end of the park, where a short stub road to a utility building reaches a low rock bank near the beach level.

Chico Launch Ramp

Forsaking Highway 3 and following Chico Way NW, the scenic shoreline route around the west side of Dyes Inlet, one encounters the community of Chico. In spite of its Spanish sound and the fact that many nearby streets have Spanish names, the community was named for William Chico (or Chaco), a friendly Native American chief who lived nearby.

Chico was a point of commerce for boats of the Mosquito Fleet and settlers who lived inland on the Kitsap Peninsula; one of the first roads in the area led from Chico to Crosby. Many of the early steamers were shallow-draft and could be beached. Passengers disembarked via a gangplank dropped from the deck to shore; cows and horses destined for pioneer farms were simply booted overboard to swim the short distance to the beach. It wasn't until 1905 that a dock (a raft of cedar logs) was built.

The only public facility at Chico today is a surfaced launch ramp just off Chico Way NW at the end of Northwest Merideth Street operated by the Port of Bremerton. The ramp, whose location is unmarked along Chico Way NW, has parking space for five or six cars along the wide shoulders of the road above (take care not to block private driveways). To locate the ramp, watch for a small commercial building, in its latest reincarnation a cabinet shop, on the west side of the road.

Silverdale Waterfront Park (City of Silverdale)

Park Area: 4 acres; 600 feet of shoreline
Facilities: Picnic tables, group picnic shelter, fireplaces, benches, restrooms, water, children's play area, gazebo, fishing pier, floats, guest moorage, boat launch (ramp)
Attractions: Fishing, swimming, boating, beach walking, picnicking, paddling

The major boating attraction on Dyes Inlet is the superb little beachfront park at Silverdale, at the north end of the waterway. A 300-foot-long fishing pier has floats at the end with a capacity for 40 to 50 boats. Guest moorage is available, with a three-day limit; moorage fees

The floats at Silverdale Waterfront Park are good for sunbathing as well as mooring boats.

are deposited in envelopes in a box at the head of the dock. Although the end of the bay is quite shallow, the dock extends out far enough to provide 35 feet of water under the floats at zero tide. To the north, the extreme head of the bay is a 300-yard-long tideflat.

The remainder of the park is grassy hillocks and a scattering of picnic tables with beachfront views. A low concrete bulkhead, breached by staircases, rims the beach; at high tide the water comes right up to the bulkhead. Low tide reveals some cobbles and rocks at the high water level, with a sandy swimming beach below. A children's play area, a large group picnic shelter, and a small wooden pavilion line the east side of the park.

To reach Silverdale by land, follow Highway 3 north out of Bremerton to the marked Silverdale exit. The modern part of town is spread north along Silverdale Way NW; the original settlement, Old Town Silverdale, with its interesting buildings and waterfront park, is on a point of land on the northwest shore of the inlet. The park is at the end of Washington Avenue. By water, the park is 5½ nautical miles from the eastern entrance to the Port Washington Narrows.

A block west of the dock, at the end of McConnell Avenue, is a two-

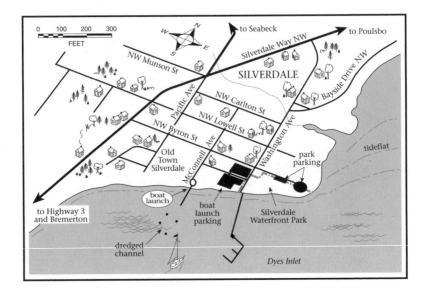

lane concrete launch ramp with a boarding float between lanes. The ramp extends well out into the bay, so there is no problem launching, even at low tide. A 30-foot-deep channel, marked by offshore pilings, has been dredged in the tideflat outboard from the end of the launch ramp. Two large parking areas in the block between the park and the launch ramp are reserved for vehicles and trailers using the ramp. Parking for park visitors can be found at the east end of Byron Street.

J. A. and Anna F. Smith Children's Park (Kitsap County)

Facilities: Benches, picnic tables, restrooms, water, Master Gardener demonstration garden, amphitheater, disabled access, Cascadia Marine Trail campsite
Attractions: Picnicking, gardens, paddling

The focal point of this small county park on the east side of Dyes Inlet is the garden area in the upland portion; however, a trail also leads down the high bank, past a tiny primitive amphitheater overlooking Dyes Inlet, to a gently sloping gravel and boulder beach.

The upland area has a tidily mowed lawn with a few benches and picnic tables around the edge of a pretty little cattail-fringed pond. At the south end of the lawn is the Master Gardener demonstration garden, a collection of 25 to 30 little beds, holding an amazing variety of flowers, fruits, and vegetables that are carefully nurtured here.

The narrow grass strip above the beach bulkhead has been designated a Cascadia Marine Trail campsite. From the water it can be identified by a sinuous 4-foot-high concrete bulkhead directly southeast across Dyes Inlet from Silverdale Waterfront Park.

By land, the park is located at the intersection of Tracyton Boulevard NW and Northwest Fairgrounds Road. A marked footpath leads downhill into the park about 100 feet north of the intersection. There is no parking available on Tracyton Boulevard at the entrance path; however, there is a large dirt lot off Fairgrounds Road just east of the intersection. Two disabled-accessible parking spots are located off a private road spur about 50 feet north of the park entrance.

Mom and the kids out for a stroll at the children's park

Tracyton Launch Ramp

The village of Tracyton on the east shore of the inlet has a small waterfront access at a boat launch ramp. The single-lane concrete ramp is just off the main road (May Street NW), at the end of Northwest Tracy Avenue. The upper portion is quite steep, but the ramp is usable at most tide levels. There is parking for a dozen or so cars along the side of Tracy Avenue. Boats launched here have ready access to the network of bays at the south end of the inlet. A group of pilings offshore just south of the ramp should help to identify it from the water.

PORT ORCHARD CHANNEL AND LIBERTY BAY

Leaving Dyes Inlet, you return to Port Orchard, the long channel flowing north along the back of Bainbridge Island. Superlative boating country, this, with a wide, unobstructed channel enclosed by forested shores and graced at its farthest point with the queen of tourist towns, Poulsbo.

A torpedo testing area is located along the west side of the channel, from Keyport south to Brownsville. Such testing is quite rare, but when it does occur red lights on Navy range vessels and on top of one of the buildings at Keyport flash a warning. Boaters should not enter the area at that time. Those remaining nearby should shut off boat engines, depth sounders, or any other equipment generating underwater noise, because some torpedoes are guided by sound.

The entrance to Liberty Bay is twisting and becomes narrow as it rounds Lemolo Peninsula, but there are no navigational hazards. Once past Keyport the channel spreads to ½ mile in width and heads north to Poulsbo, at the end of the bay. Excellent anchorages can be found in muddy bottom in several small coves; those near Keyport and Lemolo offer the quiet protection of the beautiful little bay without the summertime bustle of the Poulsbo docks; these snug coves, however, do not have any shore access.

Accesses and anchorages in the Port Orchard channel along the Bainbridge Island shoreline are described in chapter 3.

Illahee State Park

Park Area: 74.5 acres; 1,785 feet of shoreline
Facilities: 23 standard campsites, 1 disabled-accessible campsite, 8 primitive campsites, picnic tables, fireplaces, kitchen shelters, primitive group camp, 2 group day-use areas, restrooms, showers, water, RV pumpout, ballfield, children's play equipment, horseshoe pits, hiking trails, boat launch (ramp), dock with float, 5 mooring buoys, fishing pier
Attractions: Boating, fishing, clam digging, swimming, scuba diving, beachcombing, hiking, historical naval gun display

A 250-foot bluff above the channel of Port Orchard may seem an unlikely location for a marine-oriented park, but Illahee State Park manages to blend its wooded uplands nicely with its waterfront attractions. The upland portion of the park—campground, group camp, and picnic area—is in timber, with no view of the water. The beauty of the old-growth forest of maple, cedar, and fir more than makes up for the lack of marine vistas. Two 5-inch naval guns mounted on grassy platforms near the park entrance recall the military heritage of the area.

The beach portion of the park is reached via a steeply switchbacking road or a steeply switchbacking trail—take your pick. Trailered boats that have made it down the hairpin turns of the road will find a single-lane launch ramp adjacent to the parking lot. A float at the end of a 380-foot fishing pier provides about 200 feet of tie-up space for boats; a second float to the north serves as a breakwater. Five mooring buoys are strung along the shore to the south.

Tidelands south of the pier flare out gently into sandy beach, delightful for sun-snoozing or wading. A lucky digger may find a clam or two,

Kids love climbing on the guns at Illahee State Park.

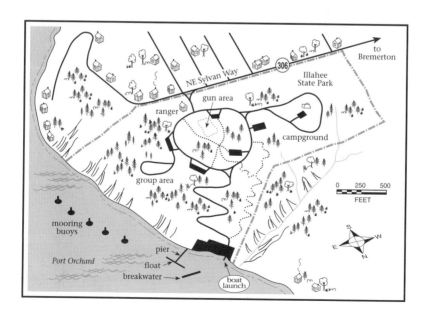

although the area is heavily harvested. At high tide, water laps the foot of the bluff.

The park, lying on the north outskirts of Bremerton, is loved by local residents, who use it heavily. To reach the park, drive north out of Bremerton on Highway 303 (Warren Avenue) and turn east at a signed intersection onto Northeast Sylvan Way (Highway 306), which leads to the park. Highway 304 (Trenton Avenue) can also be taken north to Northeast Sylvan Way.

Illahee

Facilities: Floats, groceries, gas (at service station), fishing pier, artificial reef
Attractions: Fishing, boating, scuba diving

To reach the road following the shoreline north along Port Orchard, continue on Trenton Avenue north from the Northeast Sylvan Way intersection, and in a few hundred feet, at a Y-intersection, turn right onto Illahee Road NE, which drops down to the water and the small community of Illahee.

Here a pier with two short floats provides a spot for boaters to stop and pick up supplies. Large boats should approach with care, as the surrounding water is shallow, but small boats should have no problems except during low tides. The dock and floats are closed to the public between 10:00 P.M. and daylight, and there is a three-day mooring limit. A grocery store and service station are a short block up the street. The end of the pier spreads out into a broad platform for fishing.

Pilings of the old dock are coated with a forest of fluffy, pastel-colored sea anemones and purple tube worms—paradise for scuba divers who explore the seawalls south from here to the state park, a mile away. Fishing and diving in the area are greatly enhanced by a 300-foot-long artificial reef, marked by buoys, lying 140 feet off the end of the pier. The old tires forming the reef create a habitat for invertebrates that in turn serve as food for a variety of fish, including cod, flounder, rockfish, and salmon. The fish population in the area has more than doubled since the construction of the reef.

Brownsville Marina

Facilities: Guest moorage with power and water, boat launch (ramp), groceries, deli, ice, bait, fuel, boat rentals, marine repair, tidal grid, restrooms, showers, laundromat, picnic tables, fireplaces

The narrow slot of Burke Bay, penetrating the Kitsap shoreline for nearly ½ mile, is too shallow to be attractive to boaters; however, the excellent,

The Brownsville Marina faces Port Orchard channel.

full-service marina on the north shore at the entrance to the bay, operated by the Port of Brownsville, makes a nice layover for boaters cruising in Port Orchard channel. The modern, 325-slip facility is a surprise from either land or water, because the community of Brownsville is just a smattering of homes along the shore. The marina is just off Brownsville Highway NE, midway between Bremerton and Keyport.

Two breakwaters protect the extensive moorage. Visiting boaters can reach the fuel dock by entering the marina float area at the south end of the east breakwater. From here they are directed to available guest slips. An excellent two-lane concrete boat launch ramp with a boarding float runs steeply into the water north of the fuel dock. A huge parking lot for boat trailers is just west of the marina.

The marina is a pleasant stop, even for nonboaters. The north breakwater serves as both guest moorage and a fishing pier and provides nice views up to Agate Passage and across the busy water highway to Bainbridge Island. On the high bank above the marina is a small park with a picnic shelter, picnic tables, and fireplaces. More picnic tables line a grass strip along the north shore of Burke Bay.

As a part of the development of Everett as a carrier home port, the Navy arranged a swap of tidelands with the state. Included in this swap was the 2-mile stretch of tidelands between Brownsville and the Keyport Naval Reservation. Although the uplands are private, and the beach involved is mostly mud, these new public tidelands open additional beaches for shellfish harvesting.

Naval Undersea Museum

Since 1910, when the Navy put Keyport on the map by selecting it as the site for the storage, repair, and testing of torpedoes, most of the activity on this tiny peninsula has been hidden behind chain-link security fences. An impressive new Naval Undersea Museum is located just inside the gate of the Naval Undersea Warfare Center—the first place where tourists have been invited to share the mysteries behind the fences. Attractions begin at the edges of the parking lot. Most interesting here is the *Trieste II,* a huge submersible that set the world's record for undersea descent when it dove to 35,800 feet off the Guam Trench.

At the entrance to the museum a large hydrospheric globe serves to introduce the museum's theme of the earth as a water planet. Exhibits, some of which are interactive, tell of the sea and the undersea technology that helps us explore and better understand it. A simulated rock grotto shows the evolution of undersea technology and an historical tracing of man's efforts to conquer the undersea realm, from the first Sumerian divers in 650 B.C., to the first submarine in 1620, the first hose-free diving in 1865, and finally the landing of the submersible *Alvin* on the deck of the sunken *Titanic* in 1989. A portion of the museum shows undersea weapons and the history of their development and the contributions of the submarine service during World War II.

To reach the Naval Undersea Museum, take Highway 3 north from Bremerton to Highway 308, then follow it east to Keyport, where signs will lead the way.

The submersibles Trieste II *(left) and* Deep Quest *(right) at the Naval Undersea Museum*

Port of Keyport Marina

Facilities: Guest moorage, boat launch (ramp), restrooms, gas (at service station), groceries and ice (nearby)

The acres of stern gray buildings and warning signs visible from the water at the Keyport Undersea Warfare Engineering Station are a rather intimidating introduction to Liberty Bay. By land, a sign at the outskirts of town announces, "Welcome to Keyport, Torpedo Town USA," and visitors have the feeling they should step ver-r-ry carefully.

Up until the time that the town became the site of the Navy facility, it had been just another of the struggling little villages along the Kitsap shoreline. When early settlers gave the town its name because they expected it to become the key port on Liberty Bay, they certainly could never have envisioned its future.

A small marina offering some limited boating facilities lies just west of the Navy installation at Keyport. A small amount of guest moorage space is available on the floats, with the stay limited to six hours. A single-lane surfaced launch ramp is tucked behind the float—its location makes it difficult to spot from the water. To reach the marina from land, turn north at the junction of Highway 308 and Brownsville Highway NE onto the road signed to Keyport. Drive to the cross street just outside the Naval Station gate, Washington Avenue, and follow it two blocks north to its end. The quiet little marina seems a world away from the bustle of the moorages at Poulsbo, just across the bay.

POULSBO

Even that shrewd old Norseman, Leif Eriksson, would think he had set foot on his native country rather than on some foreign shore if he landed his ship in Poulsbo. Streets above the waterfront are named King Olaf V Vei and Queen Sonja Vei, "Velkommen til Poulsbo" a sign proclaims, and storefronts decorated with peasant designs echo the greeting. The historic town is not ersatz Scandinavian—it has a deeply rooted Nordic heritage, from the graceful spire of the First Lutheran Church overlooking the town to the fishing fleet moored in its harbor.

The town was settled in the 1880s by Norwegians from the Midwest, who were drawn here by tales of thickly forested hills and fish-filled bays, so much like their homeland. The first postmaster named the town Paulsbo or "Pauls Place," after his home village in Norway, but the U.S. Postal Service, whose early errors have had a hand in changing a number of Washington names, misspelled it as Poulsbo, and thus it has remained.

These first settlers were tough farmers and fishermen, well prepared to deal with the rigors of pioneer life. Before the advent of the Mosquito

Pastries at a Poulsbo bakery

Fleet, it was necessary to row 20 miles to Seattle, the growing metropolis on Elliott Bay, in order to get provisions. After such a round-trip, an oarsman's hands were frequently so cramped he could not uncurl his fingers for several days. It is claimed that one sturdy pioneer, after crossing the roadless wilderness of the Cascade Mountains with a covered wagon and horses, loaded wagon and team onto a boat in Seattle and rowed them to Poulsbo (oh, for an Evinrude!).

One of the earliest waterfront industries gave the bay its name—a dogfish rendering plant produced the odoriferous oil that was used to grease logging skid roads, and the waterway was officially known as Dog Fish Bay. In the 1890s townsfolk petitioned that the name be changed to the more attractive name of Liberty Bay. When the legislature refused,

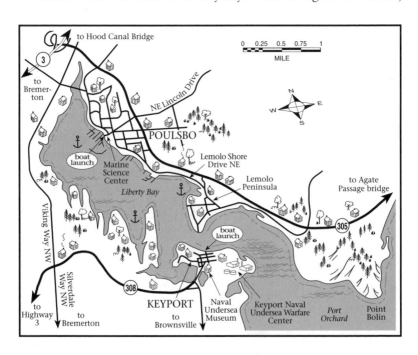

Kayaks make a colorful pattern at the Poulsbo Marina.

stubborn Norwegians proceeded to use their preferred name anyway, and common usage finally won out. Today, only a small cove near Keyport bears the original name.

By land the town can be reached either by taking the Winslow ferry to Bainbridge Island and following Highway 305 across the island and the Agate Passage bridge to Poulsbo or by driving Highway 3 north from Bremerton and turning south onto Highway 305 to reach Poulsbo.

By water, Poulsbo lies 13 nautical miles from Shilshole Bay in Seattle, via Agate Passage, or 12 nautical miles from the Bremerton or Port Orchard waterfront. For boat crews the supreme attraction of the town is the opportunity to browse the shops and haul off bags full of mouth-watering booty from the Scandinavian bakery. Several fine restaurants offer a welcome break to galley slaves.

Poulsbo townsfolk love their celebrations and have plenty of them—Viking Fest, celebrating Norwegian Independence Day, is in mid-May; in summer, Midsommer Fest, the Strawberry Festival, the 4th of July (celebrated with nautical events), and a Boat Rendezvous are scheduled; for the strong-of-stomach there's the Lutefisk Dinner in October. All of these festivals (with the possible exception of the Lutefisk Dinner) attract huge numbers of visitors, both by land and by water. Scandinavian and Northwest food, crafts, and art are offered for sale, and ethnic musicians and dancers entertain. At such times boating facilities usually are filled, and boats are anchored hull-to-hull at the head of Liberty Bay.

Marine Science Center

Facilities: Marine displays, gift shop

This interesting facility, located just east of the marina boat launch ramp, provides teacher training programs and curricula for the school districts on the Kitsap Peninsula and offers an extensive selection of classes for adults and families with children. The building houses about a dozen saltwater tanks with marine creatures for touch-and-feel experiences, interactive workstations, and displays of marine mammals and shellfish. The center is open for public visits from 10:00 A.M. to 4:00 P.M. Tuesday through Sunday and noon to 4:00 P.M. on Monday.

Port of Poulsbo Marina

Facilities: Guest moorage with power and water, gasoline and diesel, boat launch (ramp), kayak rentals, restrooms, showers, laundry, marine pumpout station, tidal grid

Among boaters Poulsbo's reputation lies in its fine waterfront facilities. The marina, operated by the Port of Poulsbo, provides guest moorage at the downtown docks. Excellent guest slips on the north side of the moorage accommodate over 100 boats. Boaters must get a key code from the harbormaster to use the onshore restrooms and showers. A plank and piling breakwater shelters the yacht basin. The south side of the moorage is filled with boats of the commercial fishing fleet, and beyond that, next to the harbormaster's office, is a single-lane surfaced launch ramp with a boarding float.

American Legion Park and Liberty Bay Park

Park Area: 6 acres; 2,500 feet of shoreline
Facilities: Picnic tables, fire rings, restrooms, pavilion, children's play area, walking trail, overwater causeway
Attractions: Walking, viewpoints, bicycling

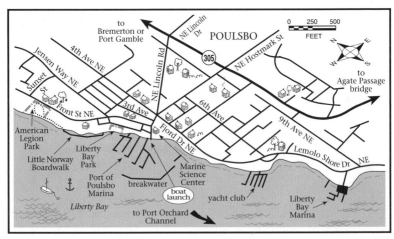

The boardwalk at Liberty Bay Park meanders along the waterfront.

If trolls indeed live under bridges (as claimed in old nursery tales), this is certainly the place to find one. Two waterfront parks are linked by the Little Norway Boardwalk, an 800-foot-long wooden walkway elevated on piers above the shore. Two sets of stairs at its north end provide beach access. Look quickly over the edge and you might catch a glimpse of a grizzled troll scurrying out of sight.

Liberty Bay Park is on the downtown waterfront, by the marina. The beautifully groomed and landscaped park has restrooms, picnic tables, fire rings, and large rock erratics for small children to play king-of-the-mountain on. This is the favorite stop (aside from the bakeries) for bicycle tourers, who rest on the manicured grass and soak in the atmosphere. Centerpiece of the park is the Rangvald Kvelstad Pavilion, which provides a nice view of bay activity and is also used for concerts, folk dances, and social functions. A statue of a Viking (Leif Eriksson himself, perhaps?) stands guard over it all.

From the north end of the park, the wooden boardwalk rounds a bluff above the tide and below hillside homes, eventually joining an asphalt path continuing along the bank. Side trails lead down to the mud and rock beach. Shortly, the children's play apparatus and picnic tables of American Legion Park are reached. Here the path turns uphill to a concrete platform (restrooms) overlooking the bay. Return via the beach if the tide is out, or via the road; round trip walk is about ½ mile.

AGATE PASSAGE AND PORT MADISON

Agate Passage, with its lofty bridge linking Bainbridge Island and the Kitsap Peninsula, marks the northern entrance to Port Orchard. The tidal current here can reach a velocity of 6 knots where the channel is squeezed between the rocky walls to a mere 300 yards wide. A shoal near the middle of the north end is marked by a buoy. Kelp covers rocks lying near the shore. The passage is frequently used by skilled scuba divers who "drift"

Agate Passage, seen here from the Bainbridge Island side, is a favorite scuba diving site.

dive here—floating and tumbling along the channel as the current provides an exhilarating roller-coaster ride.

The corridor was named, not for the rock hound's prize, although agates can be found along the shore, but for Alfred T. Agate, the artist who accompanied Lt. Charles Wilkes on his surveying expedition of 1841.

In 1905 the U.S. government purchased a section of land on Agate Passage north of where the bridge now stands. The plan was to build a mine control center here and lay mines across the channel, as was done in Rich Passage, in order to protect the Bremerton shipyards from enemy attack. No construction ever took place.

The north end of Agate Passage opens into the lovely round bay of Port Madison, rimmed by bluffs and a scattering of homes. All of the Kitsap shoreline facing on Agate Passage and Port Madison, with the exception of part of Miller Bay, was a part of the Port Madison Indian Reservation, assigned to the Suquamish and Duwamish tribes in the 1855 Treaty of Point Elliot. Over the years much of the land, especially the waterfront, was sold off, sometimes by federal agents who were empowered to act for the individuals they considered "incompetent." Suquamish holdings are now about half of the original reservation and are largely inland.

Suquamish Museum

Park Area: 10 acres; 1,000 feet of shoreline
Access: Land
Facilities: Museum, restrooms, gift shop, picnic tables, nature trail

Photos, recorded words, and artifacts serve to tell the story of the Suquamish Indians from the time of the arrival of European explorers through pioneer days. In its major exhibit, "The Eyes of Chief Seattle," the Suquamish Museum uses the words of tribal elders to eloquently evoke not only a time gone by, but a culture nearly lost.

The museum was built by the Suquamish tribe to house and display artifacts discovered by a 1975 archeological excavation at Old Man House. The exhibit also includes items on loan from individuals and other museums and over 2,000 historic photos that have been copied for tribal archives. Hours are 10:00 A.M. to 5:00 P.M. daily, May through September, and 11:00 A.M. to 4:00 P.M. Wednesday through Sunday, for the rest of the year. Guided tours are available by appointment.

The museum is on the top floor of the tribal center, located on a timbered hillside overlooking Agate Passage. Signs on Highway 305 direct visitors to a turn-off at Sandy Hook Road, which leads to the parking area. A short nature trail departs from near the museum, looping south in the cedar-scented forest for ¼ mile. A few picnic tables on a grassy platform below the building have views of the water.

Old Man House State Park

Park area: 0.7 acre; 210 feet of shoreline
Access: Land, boat
Facilities: Fireplaces, picnic tables, vault toilet, water, interpretive displays, boat launch (hand-carry)
Attractions: Historical displays, picnicking, scuba diving, swimming

Enrich a visit to the Suquamish Museum with a stop at the site of Old Man House, now a State Park Heritage Area. It is believed that Chief Sealth, who befriended the white settlers, was born in the longhouse that stretched along the shore, although Blake Island also claims that distinction. An informational display at the park tells the history of the longhouse, said to be the largest such structure ever to have been built, and shows methods used in its construction. Exact dimensions of the building are uncertain, but it is known to have been at least 500 feet long, and possibly close to 900 feet. It extended far beyond the boundaries of the present-day park, onto what is now private property.

The longhouse was burned sometime after 1870 by federal agents who wanted to discourage communal living and force the Indians to lead a "civilized" life. Some of the large framing posts remained standing for many years; the last is reported to have rotted off and fallen in 1906. Archeological digs show that Indians lived on the site even before the longhouse was built.

Chief Sealth's grave at Suquamish

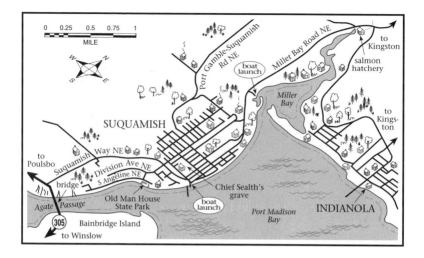

The state park is on the outskirts of the town of Suquamish. To reach it, just west of the Agate Passage bridge turn north off Highway 305 onto Suquamish Way NE. In just over a mile turn south on Division Avenue NE and follow signs to the park. Parking is on the road end of Northeast McKinstry Street and just off South Angeline Avenue NE.

The park faces on a beautiful beach with sand at the high tide level and gravel below (no wonder the Indians chose this spot). There are a couple of picnic tables, a fire ring, a vault toilet, and a water faucet; a broad, grassy expanse provides plenty of spots to spread a picnic cloth. There are no garbage cans or collection at the park; pack it in, pack it out. Scuba divers frequently use the park as a put-in for dives along Agate Passage. Boats can easily be beached or hand-carried on the sloping beach, as the Native Americans did for several centuries. From the water the park can be located by the daymarker on its northern boundary and a "cable crossing" sign on the beach.

Suquamish

Facilities: Fishing pier, boat launch (ramp), groceries, gas, shopping, historic cemetery
Attractions: Historic site, fishing

Suquamish has had a checkered past with regard to the community name. The tiny hamlet was originally named Bartow, for an early Indian agent. This name didn't last, however, and it was renamed to its original Indian *Suk-wa-bish*. Real estate entrepreneur Ole Hansen purchased the Suquamish waterfront in 1909 from its Indian owner. Hansen renamed the area Silverstrand, subdivided it, and hyped his lots to Seattlites looking to invest in view property. Locals objected to the new name, and one day, as he was arriving with a boatload of prospective buyers, Hansen was startled to find his new, neatly lettered town sign floating in the bay. Suquamish it has been ever since.

The difficulties of early transportation slowed growth of the area, so Hansen did not realize the fortune he had hoped for from the property. He went on to fame as a flamboyant mayor of Seattle, and even hoped to run for president on his ability to see a Bolshevik behind every bush in those Socialist-paranoid times.

A 450-foot-long fishing pier on the Suquamish waterfront offers dynamite views down the throat of Agate Passage, across Port Madison, and up to Indianola. The pier has no float, so boat tie-up would be difficult. To reach it by land, follow Suquamish Way NE to its end on the south side of town. The path to the pier is adjacent to the launch ramp and is marked with a sign quoting Chief Sealth's admonition to "love this beautiful land"; the parking area is across the street from the town's two taverns. The single-lane surfaced ramp drops down steeply from the parking lot.

Just 1½ blocks up the hill on South Street is St. Peter's Catholic church and cemetery, where Chief Sealth is buried. The structure surrounding the grave site—four cedar poles topped by canoelike carvings—is representational of the traditional Native American burial method of putting the deceased in a canoe tied high in a tree. Other interesting old gravestones in the cemetery give insight into life on the reservation. A remarkable number of graves are marked with simple flat stones marked "Unknown." John Kettle, whose grave is located here, is the native from whom Ole Hansen purchased Suquamish.

St. Peter's, was originally an Indian mission, built in the early 1860s. The first building stood about a mile to the south when the government purchased the land as a military reservation; the church was rebuilt at its present location.

Miller Bay

Facilities: Marina, boat launch (ramp), gas, guest moorage, fishing tackle, marine repair

The only marine facility on Port Madison is north of Suquamish in Miller Bay. A small marina on the west shore, just off Miller Bay Road NE, has a single-lane concrete launch ramp and boating facilities. A long sand spit extends from the east side of the bay, nearly blocking the entrance. Do not enter at low tide, as the channel and much of the bay hold a foot of water or less at low water. A good anchorage in 6 feet of water can be found just north of the second buoy.

Boaters who enjoy exploring out-of-the-way corners will delight in the

The Northern Tip

Beyond Indianola the Kitsap shoreline takes on a different look. Gone are the sheltered beaches and forest-edged channels, as the peninsula sweeps north to its climax at Foulweather Bluff. Beaches here are wild and wind torn, with mounds of ragged beach grass and a strand of silvered driftwood deposited by the waves of Puget Sound.

Kingston

Facilities: Guest moorage with power and water, diesel, gas, boat launch (sling), restrooms, showers, laundromat, portable toilet dump, marine pumpout station, fishing pier, marine supplies and repairs, groceries, tackle, bait, tidal grid, stores, restaurants, picnic tables

The one bit of shelter offered along the northeast side of the Kitsap Peninsula is at Kingston on Appletree Cove. A dredged yacht basin behind a rock breakwater has full facilities for boaters. The 40-slip visitor float is located just behind the rock breakwater. The cove itself is an extremely shallow tideflat; do not stray out of the channel. Self-register at the head of the dock above the fuel float or at the marina office.

Half a block from the head of the dock is a building with the marina office, restrooms, a laundromat, and a portable toilet dump. All but the latter are key-coded, with access restricted to registered guests

A Washington State ferry lands at Kingston.

Quiet little Miller Bay is a nice spot for boaters to drop an anchor for lu

quiet little bay ringed by homes. All shore land is private. A Suquam tribe salmon hatchery is located on Grovers Creek at the north end of t bay. Visitors are welcome, and displays answer several frequent questio about salmon and hatchery activity.

Indianola

The community of Indianola was developed in 1916 as a summer and weekend getaway, but because it was only an hour's steamer ride to Seattle, it didn't take long before property owners who wanted to live here year-round and commute to Seattle demanded regular ferry service. Boats were soon shuttling back and forth on regular passenger runs, and eventually even an auto ferry was put in service. Landing or loading could be a real adventure when winter storms whipped the long pier. The ferry service was discontinued in 1951 after the bridge across Agate Passage was built.

The 300-yard-long dock used by the ferries was rebuilt in 1972 by the Indianola community and the Interagency for Outdoor Recreation. It serves as a fishing pier and view platform, with views down Agate Passage and across to Seattle. Pause to imagine a doughty little ferry chugging up to the dock to transport a waiting flapper-era crowd.

In summer a short float at the end of the pier serves for loading or unloading, but overnight moorage is not permitted. The beach at the head of the pier is for use of residents only. A small grocery store and the post office are on shore nearby. The dock is located at the end of Indianola Road NE.

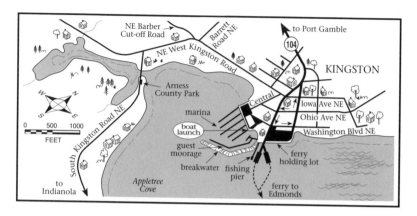

only. A sling launch extends into the basin between D and E docks of the permanent moorages. The marine pumpout station is located on a wing of the fuel float.

Picnic tables in a little park above the marina provide a nice overlook of boating activities. There is ample parking for cars and trailers in a large fee lot at the west end of the marina, but free visitor parking alongside the grass picnic area is strictly limited to two hours.

Immediately to the east of the marina is the Washington State ferry terminal. Ferries from here zip across the sound to Edmonds, carrying commuters to and vacationers fro. Most visitors' only view of Kingston is from the ferry holding lot. Some wander far enough to buy an ice-cream cone, but all stay within dashing distance of their cars, in case their boat approaches. In addition to the businesses clustered around the ferry landing, a small shopping area is two blocks up the highway, at the top of the hill.

A long covered pedestrian ramp at the ferry landing leads to a small waiting room whose glass walls provide an excellent overlook of Kingston, as well as a nice place to watch the docking maneuvers of incoming ferries. Between the ramp and the marina breakwater is a 350-foot-long public fishing pier, with rails drilled for holding poles and lower rail sections for junior anglers. On a clear day the entire span of Cascade summits from Mount Rainier to Mount Baker are vividly displayed.

Arness County Park (Kitsap County)

Park Area: 2 acres; 400 feet of shoreline
Facilities: Picnic tables, fireplaces, sani-can, boat launch (hand-carry)
Attractions: Boating, picnicking

Bring out the picnic lunch—here's the place to enjoy it! This little park at the head of Appletree Cove is a pleasant surprise. Small boats can be hand-launched here for paddling about the bay (when there's water in it), and the beach is nice for sunning and sand castles. Unfortunately, pollution makes swimming and shellfish gathering risky business. If lunch is all you had in mind, just soak in the salty atmosphere.

The park, operated by Kitsap County Parks Department, can be reached by turning west off Highway 104 in Kingston onto NE West Kingston Road, which curves around the cove. In ¾ mile, at a Y-intersection with NE Barber Cut-off Road, stay left on West Kingston Road (regardless of what road signs may say). At another intersection in about 350 yards, turn left on South Kingston Road NE and follow it to the park.

Eglon Beach Park (Port of Eglon)

Facilities: Picnic tables, fireplace, sani-can, changing rooms, boat launch (ramp)
Attractions: Picnicking, boating, beachcombing, wading

It's small, but it is the only public beach for quite a stretch. To find Eglon Beach Park, turn north off Highway 104 at Hansville Road NE. At an intersection in 4½ miles, turn east onto NE Eglon Road, and follow it for 2 miles as it bends through a couple right-angle turns. The park is at the intersection of NE Eglon Road and Hoffman Road NE. Aside from the single-lane concrete launch ramp and a parking lot that can accommodate a dozen or so cars, the park consists of a small grass picnic area. A pair of changing rooms was converted from old pit toilets.

Watch freighter and barge traffic in Admiralty Inlet between the park and the bluffs of Whidbey Island's Possession Point and Double Bluff and fishing boats skimming along the shoreline en route to their favorite "hot spot." The horizon is sprinkled with Cascade summits from Snoqualmie Pass to the Canadian border and capped by the glaciated cones of Glacier Peak and Mount Baker.

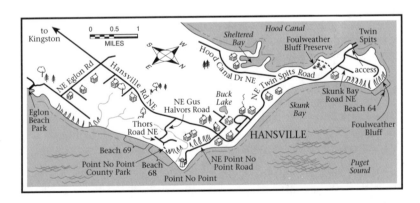

A giant glacial erratic on the beach at Point No Point County Park

Point No Point County Park (Kitsap County)

Facilities: Sani-can, hiking trails
Attractions: Hiking, beachcombing, birdwatching

A small county park a little over a mile southeast of Hansville provides a brief woodsy walk and a route to a terrific beach. To reach it, turn east from Hansville Road NE onto Northeast Gus Halvors Road, marked "Dead End." In about ½ mile, at the T-intersection with Thors Road NE, turn north, and in ¼ mile arrive at the entrance gate of Point No Point County Park. There is parking for about four cars outside the gate; the sani-can here is the park's only sanitation facility.

Beyond the gate an overgrown single-lane gravel road continues north through second-growth cedar and alder. Some clearings in the trees could accommodate a blanket-on-the-ground picnic. A pleasant ¼-mile hike through light timber leads to the top of the bluff and a one-time over-look of Puget Sound that is rapidly being overwhelmed by brush. Here a picturesque dirt and log staircase leads steeply down the bluff to the shore, arriving near a huge rock erratic that was plunked down here by a long-ago glacier.

For those wishing even more solitude for their hike, an unmarked, but obvious, footpath heads through the woods uphill and east from the main road/trail. Find the ends of this footpath about 50 feet in from the entrance gate and at a small clearing about 100 yards inland from the bluff viewpoint. The path between these two points stays about 100 yards inland from the lip of the bluff and might be a bit muddy in places, but you may see woods critters as you enjoy its solitude.

Hansville and Point No Point

Facilities: Marinas, boat launch (sling, rail, and ramp), gas, fishing tackle, bait, groceries, restaurant, cabins, boat rentals
Attractions: Fishing, boating, beach walking, historic light station

Any saltwater fisherman can tell you where Point No Point is—the area is legendary for its great salmon fishing, either by mooching from boats drifting just offshore or by casting from the beach near the point where the bottom plummets to a depth of 90 feet. Marinas at Hansville and east along Northeast Point No Point Road provide anglers with boat launches, rental boats, RV campsites, and necessary supplies. For those who would rather land their salmon at the supermarket and spend their recreation hours walking the beach, there is plenty of opportunity for beach walking, too.

Hansville is reached by turning north off Highway 104 onto Hansville Road NE; from there you can't miss it. Don't expect posh resorts—the weathered little town is for dedicated fishermen and vacationers who prefer the sting of salt air to the swank of tennis courts.

The first settlers here were Anton Husby and Hans Zachariasen. Locals insist (with a straight face) that Husby was a teetotaler, but the other man enjoyed his spirits, and when local Norwegian loggers came to town, they soon learned that "Husby von't drink with you, but Hans vill!"— and thus the town got its name.

In Hansville turn right on Northeast Point No Point Road and follow it past private homes to a resort. Parking is a problem—the resorts have space for those paying for their facilities, and the lighthouse at the end of the road has a parking lot for people visiting the light station, but people just wanting to walk the beach must fend for themselves, parking where they think they will least offend residents.

Walk down the road to the lighthouse to reach the shore. Two DNR beaches lie just around the point to the south. Beach 68 is 3,036 feet long, and Beach 69, to the south of it, is an additional 2,420 feet. The public lands on both of these beaches are below mean high water level— do not trespass on upland property. Shellfishing is not good here because of heavy wave action from the sound. Near the end of the public beach are the stairs descending from Point No Point County Park and the giant rock erratic described previously. Piles of driftwood in the soft sand provide convenient nooks for watching the scenery, reading, or snoozing.

Point No Point Lighthouse

Point No Point is well named, as it is only a minor sandy protuberance on an outward bulge on the west side of the Kitsap Peninsula; however, it serves admirably as a site for a navigational marker. The Point No Point lighthouse dates from 1880, when a lantern was first hung in the tower and a bell used as a warning signal.

The building was constructed in late 1879, and orders had been given for it to begin service on New Year's Day of 1880. Unfortunately, although the lighthouse was completed, window glass for the lantern house had not yet been delivered. Orders were to be followed, however, and the lighthouse keeper and his assistant spent a hectic month struggling to keep the kerosene lantern lit through gales of the dead of winter until the glass finally arrived and was installed.

The lighthouse is open to the public, compliments of the U.S. Coast Guard Auxiliary, between noon and 4:00 P.M. on weekends or by appointment only between noon and 4:00 P.M. on Wednesdays. The large radar tower north of the lighthouse is a component of the Vessel Tracking System that controls all the commercial marine traffic on Puget Sound and the Strait of Juan de Fuca.

Point No Point Lighthouse has been in operation since 1880.

Foulweather Bluff

Facilities: Marina, boat rental, boat launch (sling), gas, guest moorage,
  boat launch (hand-carry), cabins, groceries, tackle, bait
Attractions: Birdwatching, beachcombing

The Kitsap Peninsula ends in the dramatic headland of Foulweather
Bluff. Here waves and wind batter the shore from every direction, sculpting
the bluffs and depositing sand and silvered driftwood on the beaches.
The beach on the north, below the 200-foot-high bluff, is designated as
DNR Beach 64. A 3,364-foot strip of tideland, ending at the northeast
corner as the shore turns toward Skunk Bay, is public below the mean
high water level. The beach drops off quite steeply, with no shellfish in
evidence; its main attraction is the opportunity for a front row seat on the
ever-changing maritime scene of Admiralty Inlet.

There is no approved public access to the DNR beach other than by
boat, but people have been known to use the public access at Twin Spits
and walk around the north side of the bluff at low tide. To reach the beach
access, follow the road out of Hansville as it curves west and becomes Northeast Twin Spits Road; continue west to its end next to Twin Spits Resort.
Hand-carried boats can be put in at the road end, where there is daytime
roadside parking for a few cars. The resort has groceries, necessities for
boaters and anglers, fuel, and a sling launch.

Foulweather Bluff Preserve

Park Area: 100 acres
Facilities: Hiking trail
Attractions: Beachwalking, birdwatching

Since you are in the area, slip around to the west side of the Kitsap
Peninsula for a nice little nature walk. The Nature Conservancy has a 100-
acre preserve in marshland south of the bluff. The trailhead is on Northeast Twin Spits Road, 3 miles from Hansville. Look for a small turn-out
on the south side of the road, 800 feet east of the Skunk Bay Road NE
intersection; signs at either end of the parking area indicate no overnight
parking.

A short hike through forest leads to the rock and gravel beach. Waterfowl and shorebirds abound. Because this is a sanctuary, camping, fires,
clamming, and pets are not permitted; the park closes at dusk. Boats
launched at Twin Spits can easily be paddled the mile south to the preserve—the marsh is easily spotted from the water.

At high tide the beach is not exposed, but low water reveals a wide
rock and gravel shelf with marvelous tidepools to explore. The thick clay of
the bank north of the marsh is studded with cobbles and small boulders,

A red-winged blackbird takes flight at Foulweather Bluff Preserve.

a clear giveaway to its origin: these are deposits left behind by the continental glaciers that covered the region around 15,000 years ago. The view is south to Port Gamble, Hood Head, misty Olympic peaks, and the inviting corridor of Hood Canal—but that's another chapter.

CHAPTER FIVE

Hood Canal

In Puget Sound country, where inlets and bays and meandering channels are standard fare, this 1½-mile-wide watery finger is unique. Straight and true, it flows southward along the foot of the Olympic Mountains for over 50 miles before bending sharply to the northeast for the final 15 miles of its course.

Captain George Vancouver, who, on his voyage of discovery in May of 1792, was the first European to visit this body of water, named it Hood's Channel in his journal, but for some reason Hood's Canal was written on his charts, and "Canal" it has remained ever since. In reality it is a fjord—or as close to one as can be found here in Washington State.

The canal was carved by the advances of massive ice sheets that flowed across the area over a period of 1.5 million years. When warming weather caused the northward retreat of the glaciers about 15,000 years ago, several glacial lakes were formed, including Lake Hood. This lake drained to the east through Clifton Outlet into today's Case Inlet. As the glacial melt freed the Strait of Juan de Fuca of ice, the waters of the region dropped and rushed to this new avenue to the sea. Hood Canal took on its northerly saltwater opening of today, with its connection to Case Inlet but a memory. Most of the road cuts along the west side of U.S. 101 show thick banks of sandy sediments laced with cobbles and gravel. This glacial till is a memento left behind by the melting ice sheets.

Hood Canal boasts some of the region's most spectacular scenery year-round, as seasonal changes paint the nearby rugged peaks, glacier-carved valleys, and timbered shorelines. Nine state parks and several other public parks distributed along the length of the canal make this an ideal destination for campers or for boats ranging from kayak to cruiser. Waters of the canal yield an abundance of fish to be had for the taking, either by rod or scuba gear—but first check the Washington State Department of Fish and Wildlife brochure for gear restrictions, open seasons, and closed areas.

Opposite: *Pleasant Harbor is a secluded cruising destination.*

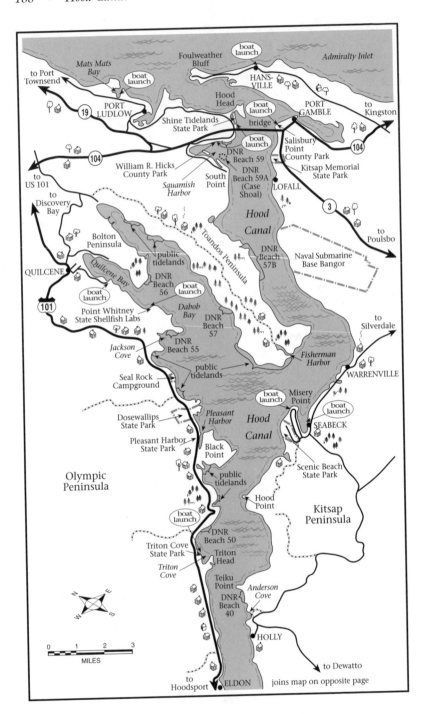

to Port
Townsend

*Mats Mats
Bay*

boat
launch

Foulweather
Bluff

boat
launch

HANS-
VILLE

Admiralty Inlet

to
Kingston

Hood
Head

PORT
LUDLOW

19

boat
launch

PORT
GAMBLE

bridge

Shine Tidelands
State Park

Salisbury
Point
County Park

104

104

to
US 101

William R. Hicks
County Park

boat
launch

DNR
Beach 59

DNR
Beach 59A
(Case Shoal)

LOFALL

Kitsap Memorial
State Park

3

to
Discovery
Bay

*Squamish
Harbor*

South
Point

*Hood
Canal*

to
Poulsbo

Bolton
Peninsula

public
tidelands

Toandos Peninsula

DNR
Beach
57B

Naval Submarine
Base Bangor

QUILCENE

Quilcene Bay

DNR
Beach
56

boat
launch

boat
launch

101

Point Whitney
State Shellfish Labs

*Dabob
Bay*

DNR
Beach
57

to
Silverdale

*Jackson
Cove*

DNR
Beach 55

public
tidelands

*Fisherman
Harbor*

WARRENVILLE

Seal Rock
Campground

Dosewallips
State Park

*Pleasant
Harbor*

*Hood
Canal*

boat
launch

Misery
Point

boat
launch

SEABECK

Pleasant Harbor
State Park

Black
Point

Scenic Beach
State Park

Olympic
Peninsula

public
tidelands

Hood
Point

Kitsap
Peninsula

boat
launch

DNR
Beach 50

Triton Cove
State Park

Triton
Head

*Triton
Cove*

Teiku
Point

*Anderson
Cove*

DNR
Beach
40

HOLLY

N

W   E

S

0   1   2   3
MILES

to
Hoodsport

ELDON

to Dewatto

joins map on opposite page

Another prime reason for visiting the canal is to invite to dinner one of the area's most important inhabitants—a succulent little gray critter that delights the palate and slides down the gullet with the greatest of ease— the Pacific oyster. Clams, crabs, and spot shrimp are other forms of canal wildlife that lure thousands of eager gourmets each year. The generally rocky beaches, however, dictate a lot of hard work for digging clams, except in the muddy alluvial fans at the mouths of rivers. The best chance for finding oysters and clams is at the public tidelands that are boat access only. Those beaches that can be reached from land are heavily harvested.

Cruise innocently into the canal on selected weekends in late May and early June, and you may think you have stumbled into a nautical convention. It is during that period that the one- or two-day-at-a-time, Hood Canal sport shrimp season opens, and residents and out-of-staters alike flock here to harvest this delicacy. Spot shrimp, which have white spots on their reddish-brown shells, are the largest species to be found in Puget Sound, reaching as much as 10 inches in size. They are caught in net traps called "pots" that are set in 200 to 300 feet of water. The best places for catching shrimp are in Dabob Bay and the south end of the canal from Hamma Hamma to Union. Special regulations apply to shrimp fishing in

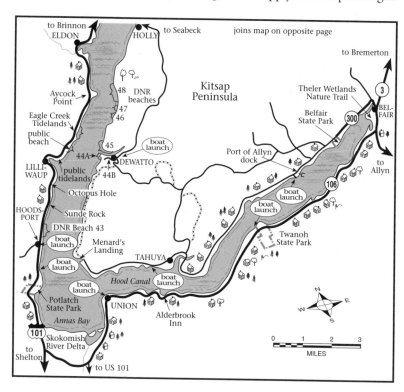

Shrimp season on Hood Canal brings hundreds of boaters to favorite spots.

Hood Canal; a stiff fine can result for those failing to comply. Before planning a shrimping expedition be sure to check the state Department of Fish and Wildlife brochure listing these regulations.

Although the nautical distance to Hood Canal from the major population centers on Puget Sound is less than the distance to the San Juan Islands, far fewer boaters cruise these waters. While most boaters enjoy the solitude, it can also cause inconveniences—there are fewer commercial facilities to serve boating needs. The small towns of Seabeck, Hoodsport, and Union each have some marine amenities, grocery stores, and restaurants; a few additional commercial marinas are at other spots along the shore.

U.S. 101 parallels the west side of the canal for almost its entire length, with plenty of places for recreational access to the shorelands. The eastern shore is wilder, and roads touch down to water in only a few spots. Once around the Great Bend, civilization sets in with a vengeance on both sides of the canal, with elbow-to-elbow homes (both vacation and year-round) and a proliferation of "private property, no trespassing" signs.

Beaches along the canal are typically narrow, dropping off quickly to a depth of 80 fathoms or more. Low, sandy points occasionally thrusting outward below the steep hillsides extend for only a couple of hundred feet. The sole exceptions are the wide alluvial fans formed at the mouths of the major rivers draining the Olympics. Here mud and sand deposited by the rivers can extend out into the canal for as much as ¼ mile at minus tides. While shores along Puget Sound are generally gray, here they are a pleasing light tan, with a high-tide band of sparkling white oyster shells.

Because of the narrowness of the underwater shelf, very few docks, either public or private, are built at the northern end of the canal, and good anchorages can be found only at a few limited bays and coves. Stops must be planned accordingly. The underwater cliffs of this rapid drop-off are a magnet for scuba divers. They may be seen at many public beaches year-round.

At the turn of the century, when settlements along the shoreline were primarily limited to logging camps, the camps relied on rafts anchored in deep water where the steamers of the Mosquito Fleet would stop to unload supplies. Barrels of crude oil for greasing the logging skids were rolled overboard and picked up by the logging boom man to be towed to shore. Horses or mules for the logging camps were pushed over the side to swim ashore.

During times of extreme tide change, the tidal current in Hood Canal can exceed 2.5 knots, causing some problems for small boats. Although usually quite benign, weather can also be a concern, for the steep hills surrounding the channel serve as a funnel for winds, and storms can be furious.

ADMIRALTY INLET

The mouth of Hood Canal opens into Puget Sound at Admiralty Inlet. Two bays along the Olympic shore, Mats Mats and Ludlow (one snug, one generous) are interesting to boaters or shore visitors.

A series of hull-claiming rocks lie just off the entrance to Mats Mats Bay and extend south for a mile to the entrance of Port Ludlow. These rocks are especially hazardous because they lie in the path of boats running between Port Townsend Canal and Hood Canal. Klas Rock, at the northern end, is covered at extreme high water. It lies ¼ mile from shore and is marked by a lighted buoy on the north side and an unlighted one on the south.

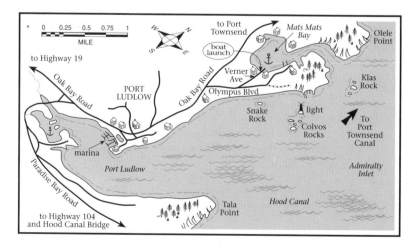

Colvos Rocks, ¾ mile farther south, are also marked by a light; a second light shows the end of a shoal running southeast from it. Snake Rock, which is unmarked, is 300 yards offshore, southwest of Colvos Rocks.

Mats Mats Bay

Access: Land, boat
Facilities: Boat launch (ramp) with float
Attractions: Boating, paddling, fishing

Whoever invented the term "gunkholing" surely had Mats Mats Bay in mind. It is the ideal little cranny for the adventuresome to explore, with a twisting, timber-shrouded channel opening up into a round little lagoon.

The entrance to the channel lies ¼ mile west of Klas Rocks on the southwest shore of Admiralty Inlet. Upon entering the narrow dredged channel, align with the range located at the west end of the first leg of the channel. The shallowest portion, 5 feet at mean low tide, extends from the dogleg where the channel turns southward to where it opens into the bay itself. Proceed cautiously, staying midchannel in this section! Once inside, good anchorages can be found in the bay in 5 to 12 feet of water.

All shoreline is private except for a small park and launch ramp operated by the Port of Port Townsend at the southern end of the bay. This ramp can be reached by land by turning east off Oak Bay Road at the Mats Mats General Store, 1¼ miles north of Port Ludlow, onto Olympus Boulevard. In ½ mile turn left onto Verner Avenue, which is signed to Boat Haven. In ¼ mile the road deadends on the shore of Mats Mats Bay.

Here there is a very nice little park boasting a single-lane concrete launch ramp with an adjoining boarding float. Although the ramp and float extend about 150 feet out into the bay, at low tide the water recedes well beyond their end, leaving a long mudflat that makes the ramp unusable.

Port Ludlow

Access: Land, boat
Facilities: Guest moorage with power and water, restrooms, showers, laundry, groceries (limited), fishing tackle, bait, marine supplies, diesel, gas, marine pumpout station, tidal grid, boat and kayak rental, bicycle rental, restaurant, resort, golf course, tennis and squash courts, swimming pool, children's play area
Attractions: Boating, paddling, fishing, bicycling

Over the course of history Port Ludlow has worn many hats. It served first as the site of a lumber mill and shipyard. After the death of the owner, the original mill ran into difficulties caused by a lengthy probate of the

The resort and marina at Port Ludlow offer fine facilities to boaters.

estate, and the shipyard was forced to relocate to Port Blakely to be near a reliable source of lumber. The Puget Mill Company (Pope and Talbot) purchased the foundering sawmill in 1878. After five years of rebuilding and improvements, it became one of the most productive in the area.

In time a dwindling lumber supply and a depressed market forced the mill to close. The small village remaining served for a while as a terminal

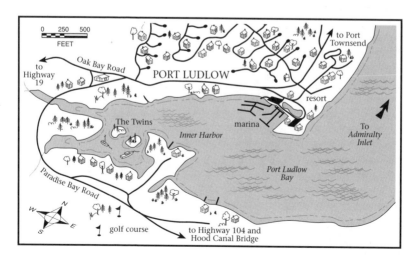

for a ferry running from Foulweather Bluff. It has now changed hats again and is a posh resort for vacationing and conferences.

For many boaters the Port Ludlow marina, with more than 100 guest slips, is not just a stopover on the way to somewhere else, but a destination in itself, with great things to do on shore for both adults and children. Visitors can maneuver paddle boats on the resort lagoon, rent bicycles to tour the quiet byroads, play a round of golf on the resort's 18-hole course (one of the best in the Northwest), or just lie in the sun and enjoy the ambiance. Shuttle service is provided to the golf and tennis courts. The swimming pool, unfortunately, is only for resort guests.

To reach the bay by land, cross the Hood Canal Bridge and turn north immediately on Paradise Bay Road, or continue west on Highway 104 and in 3½ miles turn north on Highway 19. From either road, signs will direct the way to Port Ludlow. The marina, restaurant, and resort facilities are located at the northeast corner of the inner harbor. By water, the entrance to Port Ludlow is about 24 nautical miles from Seattle's Shilshole Bay, or 12 nautical miles from Port Townsend, via the Port Townsend Canal. Colvos Rocks lie near the middle of the wide entrance, but they

A hidden cove on the Inner Harbor of Port Ludlow has delightful, secure anchorages.

are well marked and easily avoided. A shoal extending quite a distance north from Tala Point should be avoided at minus tides.

Even without the handsome resort and marina, Port Ludlow would make a dandy overnight stop, offering boaters dozens of good spots to drop a hook all along the shore. The broad outer harbor takes a 45-degree dogleg to the west and becomes the inner harbor, on which the resort marina fronts. Channel markers guide the way into the inner harbor.

The special delight of Port Ludlow, however, is the miniature bay at its extreme southwest end, tucked behind two tiny wooded islets. Enter this hidden cove through the small channel between the two islands— the eastern channel between the shore and the smaller of the islands has many snags and rocks. Be wary also of a rock lying off the south end of the smaller island.

Once inside you will find bombproof anchorages for even the worst of weather, or tranquillity for calm summer nights. Don't plan on solitude though, for the spot is well known and heavily used. The little islets, The Twins, are lovely to look at, but are used by boaters to drain their dogs, so any trip ashore might be hazardous to your Topsiders. The shoreline above the tiny cove has slowly, but inexorably, been transformed into a Port Ludlow subdivision, with homes and condos overlooking the once secluded anchorage.

HOOD CANAL BRIDGE—THE EASTERN APPROACH

Port Gamble

Access: Land, boat (bay only)
Facilities: Grocery store, historic buildings, museums
Attractions: Sightseeing, picnicking

It is certainly appropriate to begin a tour up Hood Canal with a stop at Port Gamble, a town that played a vital role in this area's early history. A. J. Pope and William Talbot (whose names still linger hereabouts), along with Cyrus Walker, founded the town in 1853. Here they built a company town and a small sawmill. The mill was enlarged and modernized several times; however, many of the homes kept closer ties to their Victorian pasts and have been historically preserved. After a long history of operation, the mill finally closed for good in 1995. Plans for the historic old company town are currently vague; however, it may include a marina and condominiums in the future.

The town's general store, which displays old-time memorabilia, has been newly remodeled. It offers picnic supplies, a deli, and gifts to visitors. The "Of Shore and Sea" museum on the second floor of the building

St. Paul's Episcopal Church, which was built in Port Gamble in 1870, is one of the town's many historic buildings.

displays a fascinating collection of over 14,000 shells and marine fossils from around the world. Picnic lunches can be enjoyed just above the beach in a grassy area that has several tables and provides a sweeping view of the bay and Hood Canal. Signs around the town give highlights of the town's history, while the historical museum, located in the basement of the general store, traces in more detail the story of the mill and the people who shaped this country. The museum is closed in the winter.

Nowhere on Port Gamble Bay is there currently a public shore access for pleasure boats. The bay, however, does offer boats heading up the canal a pleasant overnight stay, with excellent anchorages in 3 to 5 fathoms. Water immediately outside the entrance to the bay is quite shoal; boaters can locate the dredged channel entrance by heading for the outermost of two

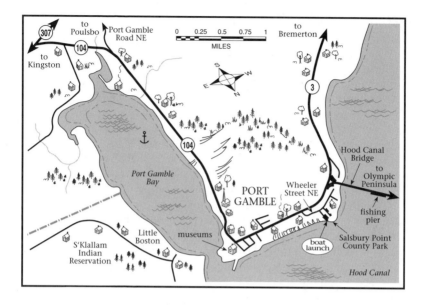

channel markers on pilings by the entrance. From there, a range located on a small point of land about a mile to the north can be used to line up on the channel. Be wary of numerous deadheads that can be found in the bay. Favored anchorages are in the small bight on the east shore at the southern end of the bay.

On the east side of the bay, the sandy spit on the S'Klallam Indian Reservation that holds a deteriorated pier was the site of Little Boston, an early Indian village. These Indians called the bay *Teekalet*—"brightness of the noonday sun." The launch ramp on the spit is reserved for tribal use.

Salsbury Point County Park (Kitsap County)

Park Area: 5.6 acres; 520 feet of shoreline
Access: Land, boat
Facilities: Boat launch (ramps) with a boarding float, picnic tables and shelter, fireplaces, children's play area, nature trail, water, restrooms
Attractions: Picnicking, swimming, hiking, boating, Cascadia Marine Trail campsite

A small park just off the northeast end of the Hood Canal Bridge provides easy access to the canal for fishing, boating, and scuba diving. Salsbury Point County Park lies ½ mile northeast of the turn-off to the bridge on Highway 104 and ¾ mile west of Port Gamble. From Highway 104 at a "County Park" sign, turn west onto Wheeler Street NE, which immediately turns south and becomes Northeast North Bridge Way. In a short distance, Whitford Road NE leads west to the boat launch ramps. A parallel road just to the south leads to the picnic grounds.

The boat launch consists of three single-lane concrete ramps and boarding floats. A voluntary contribution is asked for use of the launch. There is a large parking lot for cars and trailers above the ramps, but because of its popularity, parking often overflows along the sides of Whitford Road. A split-rail fence separates the ramps from the day-use area.

The road into the day-use picnic area has three small parking lots alongside and a path leading into the woods to picnic sites. This area was logged during the 1850s to provide lumber for the mill at Port Gamble. The path passes numerous examples of early logging techniques, such as cedar stumps with springboard notches.

The timber gives way to an open grassy area, where there are picnic tables and a picnic shelter. The sand and gravel beach slopes gently enough to allow wading or swimming during warm temperatures; a rim of driftwood marks the high tide. The picnic area is closed on Wednesdays and Thursdays and is open from noon to 8:00 P.M. other days of the week. The trees rimming the beach hold a Cascadia Marine Trail campsite—the only camping permitted here.

The park is a favorite access point for scuba divers who explore bridge abutments and cables of the Hood Canal Bridge, just ¼ mile to the southwest. The swiftly flowing current brings nourishment to extraordinary numbers of feather duster worms, plumose anemones, sponges, and other filter-feeding invertebrates. The growth of this marine life is so heavy that it must regularly be cleaned from the bridge cables, or they would break from the weight. Due to the severity of the current, only experienced divers should dive here, and only at slack tide.

Kitsap Memorial State Park

Park Area: 58 acres; 1,797 feet of shoreline
Access: Land, boat
Facilities: 43 campsites, 5 walk-in bicycle campsites, 30-person group camp, 2 mooring buoys, 2 picnic shelters, picnic tables, fireplaces, restrooms, showers, community hall, trailer dump station, baseball diamond, volleyball court, horseshoe pits, children's play equipment, hiking trail
Attractions: Camping, picnicking, boating, swimming, scuba diving, hiking, clamming, oysters

Summer afternoons find this waterfront state park jammed with local people using the numerous facilities. The park's location, close to Kitsap Peninsula towns, makes it the perfect spot to have a family outing or a scout troop camp out. For boaters, the park is a nice place to

A stairway descends to the beach at Kitsap Memorial State Park.

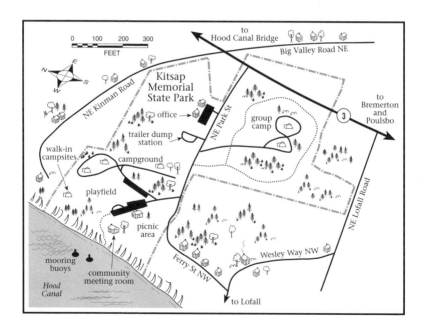

stop and enjoy an onshore barbecue after a day's recreation on Hood Canal. The two mooring buoys offshore provide a handy spot for large boats to tie up.

Kitsap Memorial State Park is located just off Highway 3, 21 miles north of Bremerton and 6 miles north of Poulsbo. By boat, it is 2¼ nautical miles southwest of the Hood Canal Bridge. Small boats can easily be carried the short distance from the parking lot down to the beach for launching.

The park's campsites are all situated in a forested area away from the water; some are tightly packed along the edge of a large playfield, but most are strung along a more spacious loop to the north. A small group camp is located in the woods in the inland portion of the park, and a trail leads from it to the other park areas above the beach.

The day-use picnic area, with tables, fireplaces, and shelters, and a large community hall sit on the embankment above the beach. A short trail, bordered by Scotch broom and madrona, drops down from the picnic area to a staircase down the bulkhead to the beach.

At high tide the water covers the sandy upper portion of the beach and reaches to the base of the log bulkhead. Low tide exposes boulders and barnacles—difficult for walking in bare feet but holding some promise of shellfish. In 1994, as a part of an experimental program, geoduck clams were planted offshore. It takes several years for them to mature to harvestable size, so in the future you may be able to gather this leviathan of shellfish!

Hood Canal Bridge and Fishing Pier

Access: Land
Facilities: Fishing pier
Attractions: Fishing

Most famous of the human-made features of the waterway is the 1¼-mile-long Hood Canal Floating Bridge, located (usually) at the northern entrance of the canal. Built over a four-year period, and finally opened in 1961, the bridge is constructed of a series of 23 floating concrete pontoons, linked together. Similar floating bridges had been built on Lake Washington in Seattle, but never before had one of such size been put on saltwater, where it would be affected by tidal changes of up to 18 vertical feet, as well as heavy currents and waves. In February of 1979, during a period of extreme tidal current, a violent gale smashed down from the north and destroyed the western half of the bridge.

The trusty state ferry, which had shuttled between Lofall and South Point prior to the building of the bridge, was pressed back into service for another four years while the bridge was reengineered and rebuilt.

Reopened in 1982, the bridge now serves as an important transportation link between Puget Sound cities and the Olympic Peninsula, as well as a handy butt for local jokes.

The bridge serves not just for transportation, however—it also functions as a dandy fishing platform. A 6-foot-wide cantilevered walkway gives access to pontoons on the east end. Parking is on the north side of the east end of the bridge, where a lot provides space for about 30 cars. The walkway follows the north side of the bridge at treetop level for a few hundred yards before descending a winding staircase to the fishing pier. Whether you are planning to fish or not, a stroll along the upper walkway provides broad views out to Admiralty Inlet and Hood Canal and knee-weakening views to the water and bridge pontoons below.

Fishing off the Hood Canal Bridge

The safety rail surrounding the pier has frequent spots for holding rods and a number of fish cleaning stations. Chunks of broken concrete have been dumped below the pier to form an artificial reef that attracts bottom dwellers such as rockfish and lingcod. The site provides a deep-water fishing opportunity without the necessity of a boat.

Hood Canal Bridge—The Western End

Shine Tidelands State Park

Park Area: 4.6 acres; 11,030 feet of shoreline
Access: Land, boat
Facilities: Boat launch (ramp, nearby), 15 campsites (primitive), pit toilets, sani-cans, no water
Attractions: Beach walking, birdwatching, fishing, clamming, crabbing

The almost-island of Hood Head, lying close to the western shore of Hood Canal, encloses a mile-long tideflat appropriately named for what it is: a bywater bay. Such bays are formed by the action of waves building a sandspit.

To reach the camping area, used predominately by self-contained RVs, turn northeast onto Paradise Bay Road at the west end of the Hood Canal Bridge, then immediately turn right on Termination Point Road, a narrow track leading downhill to a Y. The right leg of the Y ends in a boat launch ramp. The single-lane concrete ramp dropping steeply into the water is usable at all tide levels.

The left leg of the gravel road goes to a parking area and 15 primitive campsites spread along an open flat above the shore; toilets are found in the trees above the beach. The adjacent beach is sandy and gently sloping. All of the tidelands below high tide level from here north to Hood Head are state park property and are open for beach walking and clam digging.

Wolfe Property State Park

Park Area: 130 acres; 5,062 feet of shoreline
Access: Land, boat
Facilities: None
Attractions: Clamming, crabbing, oysters, beachcombing

This 130-acre parcel of lushly forested waterfront land facing Bywater Bay and Hood Canal is being held by the state for possible future development as a park. The area is open to public use but has no amenities, and usage is limited to beach areas. It adjoins the north shoreline of Shine Tidelands State Park.

The car access to the park is north of the road to the Shine Tidelands

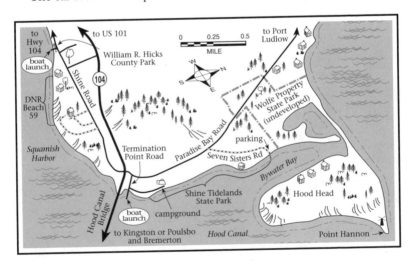

Oysters at Shine Tidelands State Park keep two oyster shuckers busy.

camping area. Continue north on Paradise Bay Road for ½ mile and turn right onto Seven Sisters Road. Follow the one-lane, unpaved road for another ½ mile to a small dirt parking area next to the bay. Property adjoining the road is private, but the road end permits public access to the beach.

Bywater Bay, which nearly dries at a minus tide, has been planted with shellfish for public harvest and provides a bounty of clams throughout the beach and a plethora of oysters near its northern end.

Explore the bay and adjacent lagoon by walking the beach. The long stretch of beach along the north shore of Hood Head and halfway down its east side is also public below mean high tide levels. Note the differences between the intertidal marine life found on the wave-washed north side and that seen in the protected bay and lagoon.

William R. Hicks County Park (Jefferson County)

Park Area: 0.7 acre; 460 feet of shoreline
Access: Land, boat
Facilities: Boat launch (ramp), picnic table, fireplace, latrine
Attractions: Clamming, crabbing, oyster picking, boating, birdwatching

Hood Canal offers very few boating detours along its narrow length; Squamish Harbor is a notable exception. The bay lies hard to the starboard immediately after passing under the Hood Canal Bridge. A lighted beacon near the northern shore marks Sisters Rocks.

A great blue heron skims over Squamish Harbor.

Navigational caution in Squamish Harbor is imperative, as lying along the southeast side is Case Shoal, a large gravel bar filling nearly half the broad bay and drying at a minus tide. The shoal is marked by a nun buoy #2 at its southern end, a marker on a piling on the north, and a small floating buoy between. Water is adequately deep along the north shore and offers some good anchoring possibilities; however, the bay is quite open and doesn't provide much shelter when strong winds kick up.

Midway along the northern shore of the bay is William R. Hicks County Park, which has a one-lane concrete launch ramp, a single picnic table, a latrine, and parking. Because the ramp runs down to a gradually sloping gravel beach, it is not usable at low tide.

To reach the park by land, turn south onto Shine Road, either just after crossing the Hood Canal Bridge or 2½ miles farther west. The park is on a spur road a little over a mile from either turn-off; however, the sign identifying the park is visible only when approaching from the west. Shine Road parallels the north side of the bay, with views out to the water through red-barked madrona and, in summer, vetch and fireweed.

The Squamish Harbor tidelands are a popular foraging area for dozens of great blue herons that nest nearby. As gracefully as dancers they wade in tidepools hunting for stranded fish.

Squamish Harbor DNR Beaches

The major attraction of Squamish Harbor is a pair of DNR beaches offering some of the best opportunities for clam, crab, and oyster harvesting on the canal. Take along a sturdy shovel and lots of determination, and try to dig for the geoducks said to be plentiful here.

Beach 59. On the north shore, DNR Beach 59 is a 2,800-foot strip beginning directly below a steep, 100-foot cliff and running westward. It can be reached by boat or by walking the beach from the county park boat launch area at low tide.

Beach 59A. The second DNR beach, 59A, includes all the tidal area of Case Shoal, which at a minus tide offers several acres of prime shellfish gathering for butter, horse, and littleneck clams.

BANGOR VICINITY

The presence of the U.S. Navy nuclear submarine base on Hood Canal at Bangor might cause some pleasure boaters to approach this section of the canal with trepidation. Boaters will encounter no problems while cruising in the vicinity of Bangor if they hold close to the western shore, staying well clear of the posted military areas lying on a 5-mile strip along the east shore. Movements of the submarines are not publicly announced, but on rare occasions one may be seen. The sight of one of these leviathans with a steel sail as tall as a four-story building cannot fail to stir awe. If a submarine is sighted, boats must keep 1,000 yards away.

A naval operations area is located in this portion of the canal from approximately Lofall to Hazel Point on the Toandos Peninsula and in Dabob Bay. Such operations are rare; however, when they are underway, flashing green lights are shown when caution is required by boaters, and flashing red lights when the area is closed to navigation. If no lights are flashing, operations are not underway. Consult navigational charts for the exact location of the operations area and the warning lights. Boaters may also receive instructions by radio. Any total closure is usually only for a few hours. Failure to observe warning lights may result in a torpedo-sized opening in one's hull.

TOANDOS PENINSULA

This 12-mile-long forested spine separates Dabob Bay from the main channel of Hood Canal. The interior of the Toandos Peninsula offers little for tourists—the main road runs the length of the ridge, and a spur traces portions of the east flank. All views are obscured by dense forest, and the few road ends touching water are all on private property. A private camping club holds a large section of waterfront and timbered uplands along the southeast end.

DNR Beaches 57B and 57

Precipitous cliffs surrounding the Toandos Peninsula rise steeply for 200 feet, and below water the seawalls drop off as sharply to depths of 25

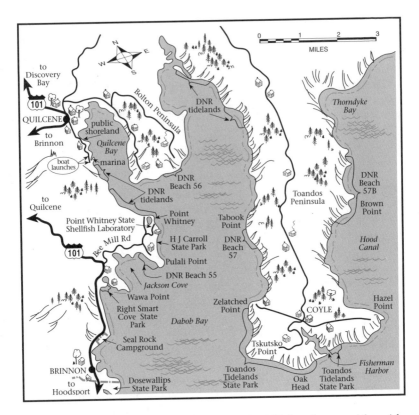

fathoms or more. Two narrow, cliff-bound DNR beaches on either side of the peninsula offer boaters several miles of shore access at low tide. DNR Beach 57B is a 12,050-foot strip on Naval Reservation property along the west shore of Hood Canal. It can be located by spotting the Brown Point light, which is approximately in the middle of the beach. Beach 57, facing on Dabob Bay, is a 3,280-foot strip of tidelands running south from Tabook Point. Both of these rocky beaches hold oysters and a variety of clams.

Fisherman Harbor

Fisherman Harbor is a narrow slot in the bluffs at the foot of the Toandos Peninsula resembling, perhaps, a fjord for elves. Merely a cozy 200 yards wide, the cleft extends for ¾ mile between rocky walls.

Venturesome boaters enter Fisherman Harbor, but only during high tide; a sandspit extending from the west shore across the entrance is nearly bare at low water. After crossing the entrance shoal, turn to the west at a right angle, keeping within 10 or 15 feet of the sandspit—the shore drops off sharply on this side. Follow the spit for almost its full length, then turn north, following the west shore into deep water. Once inside, several tight anchorages can be found in adequate depths of water.

The tidelands for 700 feet on the east side of the entrance to Fisherman Harbor, and those west from the entrance around the point to Zelatched Point, are designated as Toandos Tidelands State Park. Oysters and clams can be taken at low tide on this 10,455-foot-long stretch of sand and gravel beach.

DABOB AND QUILCENE BAYS

The forked arm of Dabob Bay, thrusting northward between steep, forested walls of the Olympics, provides a pleasant digression from Hood Canal's "main street." Here is found an even greater sense of remoteness; the intrusion of civilization is slight, and much of the shoreline remains just as natural as when it was first seen by early settlers.

Although to many people the names of Dabob Bay and adjoining Quilcene Bay are synonymous with gourmet oysters, the bays are also noted for their commercial production of oyster seed. The seed (juvenile oysters) is grown here in long net bags called cradles, which are suspended from logs floating in the water. The harvested seed is sold to oyster growers throughout the world. Quilcene Bay alone provides 75 percent of the oyster seed used by all West Coast commercial oyster growers.

Stores on Quilcene Bay have freshly shucked, commercially grown oysters for sale; or several public beaches on Dabob Bay are accessible by boat for those who thrill to stalking the wild ones.

Every year from the end of May to mid-June, Dabob Bay sees a major invasion by eager shrimp fishermen. The bottom configuration

Bald eagles perch on a snag overhanging Hood Canal.

of the bay is especially suited to the lifestyle of shrimp who spend their nights in 100 to 200 feet of water and move into deeper trenches during the day.

Because the tidal currents are weaker here than in the rest of Hood Canal, the steep, rocky underwater walls from Point Whitney to Seal Rock are prime scuba diving areas. Octopuses, lingcod, and free swimming scallops inhabit crevices in the basalt ledges.

Quilcene Bay Public Accesses

Quilcene Bay dwindles out into long, mucky tidal flat that doesn't lend itself to carefree boating. Midway into Quilcene Bay, just where the water begins to shallow, is a public tideland and a waterside park. The town of Quilcene itself is at the head of the tidal flat and has no water access. To reach the bay from Quilcene, turn off Highway 101 at signs pointing to Quilcene Boat Haven, and follow Linger Longer Road east, then south along the edge of the bay. In 1½ miles a gravel spur to the east is marked "public shellfish tidelands." At its end is a sani-can, a small parking area,

The Quilcene Bay Marina has a few guest moorages.

and access to the Quilcene Bay State Tidelands. The land was purchased a few years back from a local oyster company. The public tidelands are bounded on the north by a beached, dirt-filled barge and on the south by a saltwater lagoon. White stakes outline the limits of the public access beach.

Another ½ mile to the south is a small park and boat launch ramp. The upland park is primitive, with a sani-can, a small grass patch, a few picnic tables and fire braziers, and a single-lane concrete launch ramp. Although the gradually tapering beach dries beyond the end of the ramp at low tide, the beach below is firm cobble and gravel, permitting launch and retrieval for anyone willing to get their rear axle wet.

Quilcene Bay Marina

Access: Land, boat
Facilities: Boat launch (ramp), fuel, guest moorage (limited), marine pumpout station, restrooms, showers, picnic tables, fireplaces, swimming beach, groceries (in Quilcene)
Attractions: Picnicking, boating, swimming

The Quilcene Bay Marina, operated by the Port of Port Townsend, has a small basin with space for about 50 boats. Gas and diesel pumps are on the north shore. The marina office, restrooms, and a small picnic area are located across the road from the marina, and RV parking is permitted on the spit above the marina. The single-lane concrete launch ramp located inside the protection of the marina's rock breakwater is usable at most tide levels, but its snug proportions might give fits to less-experienced drivers.

The south side of the rock jetty spreads into a swimming area on a gently sloping gravel beach (no lifeguard). The oyster company located

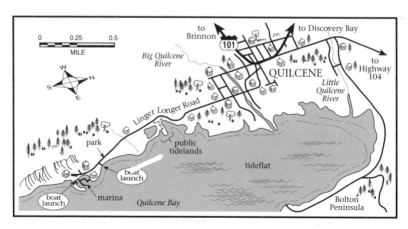

north of the marina offers fresh oysters for sale. For boaters in need of supplies, the town is a long but pleasant 1½-mile-long trudge along Linger Longer Road, with roadside blackberries in season, and some salty views across the end of the bay.

Point Whitney State Shellfish Laboratory

Area: 10 acres; 2,000 feet of shoreline
Access: Land, boat
Facilities: Boat launch (ramp), dock with float, restrooms, laboratories
Attractions: Educational displays, swimming, clams, oysters, fishing

An interesting wayside stop along the western shore of Dabob Bay puts tourists in closer touch with the shellfish they hunt in Hood Canal. The labs located here are responsible for setting the state regulations for the harvesting of shellfish. This facility also raises juvenile geoducks for enhancing the local population. The buildings, which are open during normal business hours, are not geared to visitors, but an interpretive display located outside, near the restrooms, explains the biology of intertidal life, and the reasons why regulations are imposed.

To reach the labs, turn off U.S. 101 8¼ miles south of Quilcene or 2¼ miles north of Seal Rock Campground onto Bee Mill Road, signed to Camp Parsons. Continue past the scout camp, staying on Bee Mill Road to its intersection with Point Whitney Road, then follow the latter to the labs, at 2¼ miles. A single-lane, concrete launch ramp is at the road end, with adjacent parking for several cars. Boaters who stop by can land small boats at the lab's pier, which has a short float, or beach their boats on the steeply sloping gravel shore.

A sandspit encloses a saltwater lagoon used to grow algae to feed the lab's shellfish. Although the lagoon is closed to shellfish harvest, the bay side of the spit is open to the public for shellfish gathering, beachcombing, and swimming. Because Dabob Bay is shallower than the rest of Hood Canal, the

Launching at Point Whitney

water here is generally much warmer. To the north, public lands continue to the cove south of Frenchmans Point, but on the south the open beach continues for only several hundred more feet onto the tidelands of the Navy operations area, marked by a white wooden tower on the bluff.

Dabob Bay Public Tidelands

DNR Beach 56. A 2,400-foot rocky tideland at the tip of the Bolton Peninsula is one of the best spots to find oysters, as well as clams. The beach, directly below Red Bluff, is easily located by spotting a house at the top of the bluff. The public shore is immediately east of a drainage flume coming down from that house.

Toandos Peninsula Beaches. There are three other DNR beaches on Dabob Bay. Two are on the Toandos shoreline. One extends for nearly a mile south from Camp Discovery. A second beach, more than a mile in length, runs south from a finger peninsula near the head of the bay. Both beaches, which are bare at minus tides, are accessible only by boat. The third public shoreline wraps around the head of Tarboo Bay, at the north end of Dabob Bay, and is accessible only from the water. It is best visited at high tide—at low tide it is edged by a ¼-mile-wide mudflat.

A young boater explores DNR Beach 56 on the Bolton Peninsula.

H. J. Carroll Property State Park. Less than an acre in size, this undeveloped state park is impossible to find by land but offers a short section of public beach accessible by boat. The beach is ½ mile north of Pulali Point, adjacent to Coast Guard property.

Jackson Cove. Lying midway along the western shore of Dabob Bay, the cove has a section of rocky ledge offering at low tide some promise of oysters. The public area, DNR Beach 55, is a 2,791-foot strip on the east side of the bay, lying along Pulali Point. Some clams can be found on the gravelly northern half of the beach. Boy Scout Camp Parsons is immediately adjacent to the beach, so it is heavily used by youngsters from the camp; there is no public access to the beach through the scout camp. Jackson Cove has space for several nice boat anchorages in a rocky bottom.

Right Smart Cove State Park Tidelands. This beach is located along the edge of the small cove west of Wawa Point. At one time a nearby landowner provided a pay launch ramp at the beach; however, strained relationships with various governmental agencies caused the road to the beach to be barricaded and liberally posted with "No Trespassing" signs. State Parks, in fact, has a legal easement for access to the beach, so walking to it is a legal, albeit a venturesome exercise.

Dosewallips

Seal Rock Campground

Park Area: 47 acres; 2,700 feet of shoreline
Access: Land, boat
Facilities: 42 campsites, picnic tables, fireplaces, restrooms, water, disabled-accessible interpretive trails, boat launch (hand-carry)
Attractions: Scuba diving, beachcombing, oysters, clams, walking, paddling

Near the mouth of Dabob Bay the boundaries of the Olympic National Forest dip down to touch saltwater. Here, along the shore, is Seal Rock Campground—the only Forest Service campground in the nation where oysters can be gathered.

The campground lies 10½ miles south of Quilcene on U.S. 101. The camping area is on two loops in fine, old-growth forest on a low bluff above the shore at the north end of the park. At the south end of the park a disabled-accessible interpretive trail winds uphill through the day-use picnic area, passing displays telling how the natives used the bounty of the forest and beach before the arrival of European explorers.

Stairways lead down to the beach from both ends of the day-use parking area. The upper beach ranges from cobble to boulders, all liberally

Herons cruise the tideflat at Seal Rock Campground.

covered with oyster shells. At low tide the beach tapers out gently for several hundred yards to gravel and mud.

A second marine interpretive trail follows the campground road north from the day-use area, then slips down to the bank above the beach and continues north as a disabled-accessible boardwalk. Displays along the way tell the story of the balance between the three different ecosystems found in the park, the forest, the intertidal zone, and the sea. The trail finally reaches the beach at the north end of the campground loop, where there is a short road stub that permits launching hand-carried boats.

The park has no easy access for boaters; the only option is to anchor out and land small boats on the rocky beach.

Dosewallips State Park

Park Area: 425 acres; 5,500 feet of shoreline
Access: Land, boat
Facilities: 88 standard campsites, 40 RV campsites, 2 primitive sites, 3 platform tents, 2 group camps, picnic tables, picnic shelters, fireplaces, restrooms, showers, RV pumpout station, hiking trails, wildlife viewing platform
Attractions: Beachcombing, picnicking, hiking, fishing, birdwatching, clamming, oysters, wildlife watching

The Dosewallips River, which originates in glaciers of the high Olympic peaks, meanders into Hood Canal at the mile-wide alluvial plain of Brinnon Flats. The estuary created here holds a thriving intertidal community of saltwater invertebrates, fish, and shorebirds. Search the tideflats carefully to see how many kinds of life you can find, but treat every creature with care; each is a part of the web of life. The best exploring is at low tide; wear rubber boots for wading channels and squishing through ankle-deep mud on the tideflats.

The park lies south of Brinnon on U.S. 101. The camping area is divided into two sections. The older section of the campground, containing 24 sites without hookups, is located along the Dosewallips River on the east side of the highway. The access road to these campsites runs under the bridge, and the low clearance prevents use by tall RVs. The newer campsites, many with complete hookups, are on the west side of the highway in a grassy flat broken up by planted evergreens. The picnic area is on the east side of the highway, near the salt marsh.

An upland hiking trail starts near the park office at the entrance to the campground area and wanders through a forest of Douglas-fir, hemlock, and stumps of once-majestic cedar. Native rhododendron and lush growths of ferns carpet the understory. Select from three different loop trips, ranging from 2 to 4¼ miles in length, by combining sections of trail with a

Beaches at Dosewallips State Park yield oysters and clams for the dinner table.

fire road that diagonals through the uplands. Spur trails drop from the main loops to the park's group camps. Walk quietly and perhaps spot some of the blacktail deer, elk, raccoon, beaver, or skunk known to frequent the park.

The marsh at the east side of the picnic area is heavily overgrown and laced with muddy channels, so it does not afford any easy access to the saltwater. To reach the beach, cross the river on a narrow walk- way along the east side of the bridge, and find the trailhead on the northeast side of the bridge. The trail follows the park bound- ary east, first through a thicket of brush, alder, and cedar. In little over ¼ mile a gravel path through sow thistles, Puget Sound gumweed, and beach grass leads to a viewing platform overlooking the Dose- wallips estuary. Interpretive panels around the edge of the platform tell

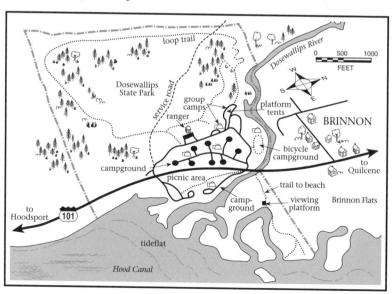

of the birds and other wildlife you may expect to see. To the east is a fenced channel. This was once a haulout spot for hordes of seals, whose feces polluted the beach and caused its closure to shellfish gathering. The fencing caused these pests to move on, and the beaches are once again safe for shellfish harvesting.

Shallow, mud-rimmed, saltwater channels give way to rock and cobble extending outward for another ¼ mile at minus tides. The vast tideflat lies waiting to be explored. Watch for great blue herons, loons, and dozens of other waterfowl frequenting the area, or join the mud-slogging crowd seeking the low tide treasures of clams and oysters. Access to the park by boat is difficult, due to the huge tideflat.

The Kitsap Peninsula Shoreline

Traveling south along Hood Canal, the eastern shore, which is the Kitsap Peninsula, becomes wilder. Land accesses are limited to a few sites, joined together by isolated roads through the densely timbered hills of the peninsula. The common starting point for land trips is Bremerton, which can be reached by ferry from Seattle or via Highway 16 from Tacoma.

Seabeck

Access: Land, boat
Facilities: Marina, boat launch (hoist), boat rentals, guest moorage, bait, fuel, groceries, restaurant, fast food, post office
Attractions: Boating, fishing, scuba diving

One of the oldest towns in the state, Seabeck was founded in 1856 when a sawmill was established at the site. The town prospered as a lumber and shipbuilding center until a fire leveled the mill in 1886. Because the nearby timber supplies were nearly exhausted, rather than rebuilding at Seabeck, the operation moved to Hadlock. The population quickly deserted the town and the mill dock was used as a landing place for a small resort, which also failed after a short period. A church conference center now occupies a good portion of the town.

Today Seabeck is a favorite spot for fishermen—the waters of the canal just west are one of the premium salmon fishing spots in the state, and prime shrimping areas are a short distance away. An artificial reef placed just northeast of the tip of Misery Point provides excellent fishing for rockfish, lingcod, and other bottomfish. Fishing from the marina dock is permitted for a fee, except during busy summer months. The smooth bottom of the bay, with its many old pilings, makes Seabeck Bay a popular scuba diving site.

The moorage at Seabeck

Seabeck Bay is the only noteworthy moorage spot south of Port Gamble along this side of the canal. The Indian name for it was *Kah-mogk*, meaning "quiet waters." The bay is well sheltered on the west by the long finger of Misery Point; however, it has little protection from strong northerlies. The marina located here solved this problem quite uniquely by chaining a mass of huge surplus iron ring-buoys together to create a floating

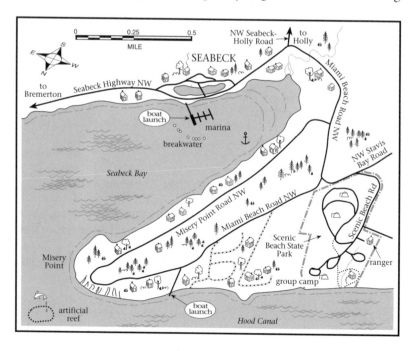

breakwater north of the marina. Several of the buoys have succumbed to the beating of waves, and some have been partially replaced by sections of old abandoned docks—not pretty, but efficient.

To reach Seabeck, take Highway 3 north from Bremerton to the Newberry Hill Road/Silverdale exit. Head west on NW Newberry Hill Road, which T's into Seabeck Highway NW in 3 miles. Follow the highway another 4½ miles to Seabeck. Total distance from Bremerton is about 13 miles. Most of the parking in Seabeck is along the road; when shrimp season or fishing derbies are on, the space can be jammed.

Misery Point Launch Ramp

Facilities: Launch ramp, vault toilets, fishing reef
Attractions: Fishing, scuba diving

An excellent public launch facility operated by the Department of Fish and Wildlife between Seabeck and Scenic Beach State Park is heavily used by shrimpers and salmon fishermen. An artificial reef, placed to attract bottomfish, lies just a stone's throw to the northeast, off the tip of Misery Point.

To reach the launch ramp, drive south from Seabeck on Seabeck Highway NW to its intersection with Miami Beach Road NW, ½ mile from Seabeck. The intersection is signed to the park and boat launch. Turn west onto Miami Beach Road NW. At a Y-intersection in ½ mile continue straight ahead, and in ¾ mile look for the spur road to the left to the single-lane concrete launch ramp. At minus tides the ramp ends above a soft sandy beach, where its use is questionable.

The area is open for use between 4:00 A.M. and 10:00 P.M. Overnight parking and camping are prohibited. A spacious parking lot has room above the ramp for 20 cars with trailers. Vault toilets are found at the entrance to the launch site. Property on either side is fenced and private.

Scenic Beach State Park

Park Area: 88 acres; 1,487 feet of shoreline
Access: Land
Facilities: 52 campsites (no hookups), group camp, picnic tables, picnic shelter, fireplaces, restrooms, community center, children's play area, log cabin, volleyball courts, horseshoe pit
Attractions: Camping, picnicking, walking, beachcombing, scuba diving, views, interpretive programs

Scenic it is, with awe-inspiring views up the imposing glacier-gouged valleys of the Dosewallips and Duckabush Rivers on the west side of the canal, and north to Dabob Bay and the steep walls of the Toandos

Peninsula. Sunsets silhouette the darkening peaks against a rosy sky, or morning mists engulf the phalanx of hills and peaks in nuances of gray.

In late May the scenic beauty is enhanced by masses of the pink blossoms of native rhododendrons. The park is said to have more rhododendrons than any other in the state; most bushes are to be found on the campground loops. Call ahead to the park ranger to find if they are at the height of their bloom, and enjoy them along the road on the drive to the park as well as in the park itself.

Campsites, located on a double loop on the southeast side of the park, are pleasantly isolated by tall western hemlock, Douglas-fir, western red cedar, and dense underbrush. The east picnic area lies above the beach in a small meadow with a scattering of tall evergreens. The trail to the beach can be found at the east side of the picnic area.

Farther west, across a marshy gully, is a large grass lawn and an orchard. Here, surrounded by carefully tended flower gardens and accompanied by a small gazebo, is the Emel House, built in 1912 and currently used as a community center. Interpretive programs are held here during summer months. Joe Emel, Sr., who owned 30 acres of what is presently park land, operated a resort and boathouse on the site, which he called Scenic Beach. The log cabin on the east side of the gully is a replica of one that was built by his son. Following Emel's death, the property was purchased for a state park.

The park's gently sloping beach is mostly gravel and cobbles below a steep, eroded bank, with access via a short trail from the picnic area. Very little beach is visible at high tide, however, as the water laps up against the bluff and bulkheads. This is a favorite area for scuba divers who swim out from shore. Hermit crabs, sea pens, sea cucumbers, and striped nudibranchs

Rhododendrons bring springtime beauty to Scenic Beach State Park.

are but a few of the animals found on the sandy bottom. Extreme low tide reveals some of these creatures to beachcombers. Do not disturb the marine life, as it is a vital part of the environment.

To reach Scenic Beach State Park, drive south from Seabeck, as previously described for the Misery Point Launch Ramp. At the intersection with Scenic Beach Road NW, bear west and follow signs to the park in another ½ mile. The park is open from April 1 to October 1. Because of its nearness to Bremerton, it is very popular with Kitsap residents.

East Shore Public Beaches

Short sections of beach along the east shore between Misery Point and the Great Bend offer some limited opportunities for harvesting shellfish. Most have no upland access (because of private land), and so can be reached only from the water.

DNR Beach 40. Existing as a beach only at low tide, DNR Beach 40 is a 2,145-foot strip of mud-to-sand, offering a chance for oysters, mussels, clams, and crabs to those who can beach a boat or anchor off and come ashore by dinghy. The beach lies between a cluster of homes north of Anderson Cove and a row of pilings extending far into the water 2,500 feet farther north.

DNR Beaches 45, 47, and 46. One long and two smaller beaches provide an opportunity to gather oysters and clams at low tide. All three beaches are cobble. Beach 48, immediately across the canal from Ayock Point, is 9,072 feet long and lies below a steep, wooded cliff about 300 feet high. Beach 47, which is 900 feet long, lies 500 feet south of Beach 48 beneath extremely steep, timbered banks. Another 600 feet farther south is Beach 46, 1,643 feet long. It lies below a recently logged area.

DNR Beaches 44A and 44B. Two short stretches of beach are located on the south side of Dewatto Bay. Both are gravel, sloping to sand and mud, where oysters, clams, and crab are found. Beach 44A, 514 feet long, surrounds a point at the southwest entrance to the bay. Beach 44B, 713 feet long, lies along the next curve of the beach, inward into the bay. The bay itself is very shallow, with most of the inner bay drying at a low tide.

Anderson Cove. As the Seabeck–Holly Road returns to the Hood Canal shoreline near Holly, a short loop to the west, Old Holly Hill Road, winds down to the north shore of Anderson Cove. Waters of the shallow little cove reflect the snow-clad peaks of the Olympics across the canal. Hand-carried boats can be launched from the beach adjacent to the road at high tide. The tidelands off the small point on the north side of the cove are public below mean high tide level.

Dewatto Bay Launch Ramp. Adjacent an abandoned cinder block building near the head of Dewatto Bay, a single-lane gravel launch ramp dips gently into the bay. At one time this was a fee ramp, but obviously it was not a money-maker. Unless the property is gated, or "No Trespassing" signs are erected, take advantage of the ramp and adjoining parking. The tidelands along the shore are public to the mean high tide level.

THE OLYMPIC SHORELINE

Pleasant Harbor

Park Area (state park): 0.8 acre; 100 feet of shoreline
Access: Land, boat
Facilities (at the state park): Dock, picnic table, vault toilet; **(at the marina)** guest moorage with water and power, groceries, restaurant, gift shop, restrooms, showers, fuel, swimming pool, hot tub, laundry, fishing supplies, picnic pavilion
Attractions: Boating, fishing

In summer evenings when nighthawks sweep across the bay, capturing insects in their open beaks, and the last rays of light glimmer across the darkening water, "pleasant" barely begins to describe this harbor—"superb" may be more apt. A bit more than ½ mile long and 300 yards across, this snug little evergreen-rimmed cove is one of the few well-protected niches on Hood Canal. Located on the west side of the canal just across from Seabeck, the harbor is hidden behind Black Point and is reached through a narrow channel lying on the north side of the point.

Pleasant Harbor shelters a short dock that is billed as a "state park" and a sizable commercial marina/resort complex. The second dock just inside the harbor entrance is the principal facility of Pleasant Harbor State Park. The float has room for about six boats but has no power or water. The only other amenities of the park are a picnic table and a few garbage

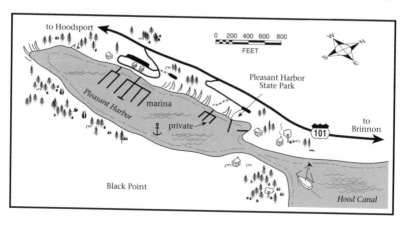

Pleasant Harbor State Park has moorages on a float.

cans located at the head of the dock and a vault toilet at the small parking area above. Private land bounds both edges of the property, leaving about 100 feet of beachfront for the park. Just beyond the state park float is a private marina, whose floats are plainly posted.

The commercial marina at the west end of the harbor more than compensates for the Spartan nature of the state park. Six long sets of floats are capable of accommodating more than 150 boats, and although more than half are filled with permanent residents, ample guest moorage is usually available. Onshore facilities provide most of the necessary amenities. If the marina is full, or if boaters do not want to take advantage of its facilities, the harbor has generous space to anchor in about 5 fathoms of water.

To reach Pleasant Harbor by land, follow U.S. 101 along the west side of Hood Canal to 1½ miles south of Brinnon. A paved road, signed to the marina, drops downhill to a road looping around the grocery store, with parking at the top side of the loop.

The unmarked road to the state park leaves the highway at a deserted grocery store slightly less than ¼ mile north of the marina. Kayaks or inflatable boats could be carried down to the float and put in for exploration of the bay and shore of Hood Canal.

Triton Cove State Park

Facilities: Launch ramp, fishing pier, picnic tables, sani-cans
Attractions: Boating, fishing, picnicking

This former trailer park north of Hoodsport was acquired by the State Parks and Recreation Commission in 1990 and was totally rebuilt. The original dock and float were replaced with a fishing pier, the launch ramp was relocated, and the launch ramp approach was modified to make it less steep and easier to use. It is a fine launching facility; however, the only shoreside amenities are picnic tables, sani-cans, and a large parking lot for cars and boat trailers.

The park lies adjacent to U.S. 101, 10½ miles south of Dosewallips State Park, just north of the Mason County/Jefferson County line. The entrance can be missed, because there are no advance warning signs along the highway.

West Shore Public Beaches

The glaciers that gouged out Hood Canal carved deeply into bedrock along its west shore, and the rocky ledges now lying underwater paralleling the shoreline are a scuba diving mecca, home to a kaleidoscope of marine animals that love niches and crannies. Divers should be aware that although the tidal current may be weak near the surface, it can be much stronger at greater depths, as it flows through the subterranean canyons.

Property owners along this portion of the canal zealously guard their tidelands and the tasty critters they harbor, and visitors will do well to heed posted property. Fortunately, a number of brief sections of beach lying just below U.S. 101 are open to the public for gathering shellfish.

Duckabush River to McDaniel Cove. Most of the alluvial fan of the Duckabush River is a DNR beach, but it holds little appeal, because it becomes a mucky mudflat at low tide.

About 1½ miles southwest of the Duckabush River bridge, as U.S. 101 swings close to the shoreline, is a 4,000-foot-long public beach that extends to the southwest to the end of McDaniel Cove. The beach is very

Harbor seals are often seen in Hood Canal.

narrow and drops away steeply, except in the cove itself. Uplands above most of the beach are private, so it is best approached by boat.

DNR Beach 50. Located 2 miles southwest of the outflow of the Duckabush River, and ½ mile southwest of McDaniel Cove, DNR Beach 50 is 2,610 feet long. The north half of the beach is almost nonexistent, as rock slabs taper steeply into the water. The south half of the beach is on the alluvial fan of Fulton Creek; the sand here harbors oysters, clams, geoducks, and crabs for the harvest at low tide. Although the beach lies just below the highway, the bank is so steep the upland approach is hazardous; it is best reached by boat.

Eagle Creek Recreational Tidelands. Directly across the road from a tavern on the south side of Eagle Creek, 2¾ miles north of Lilliwaup, are extensive tidelands that dry out about 2,000 yards at a minus tide. The rocky beach is an excellent harvesting spot for oysters. There is parking for about 15 cars on a wide paved road shoulder south of the Eagle Creek bridge. When the tide is out and oysters are prime, numerous cars are usually parked here. The beach north of the creek is private.

Lilliwaup State Park Tidelands. As U.S. 101 continues north from Lilliwaup, the highway bends west around Lilliwaup Bay. North of the bay, ½ mile from the town, the road curves northeast again, and a 4,122-foot rocky stretch of public beach lies below the bluffs. Although the beach and adjoining bluffs are owned by the State Parks and Recreation Commission, the area is not developed. Parking is at an unmarked gravel pullout above the bluff. A crude access trail has been worn into the bluff on the south end of the parking area. Very steep underwater rock walls below the beach are favorite sites for scuba diving.

Octopus Hole. This offshore rock ledge is a popular scuba diving spot. The rock ledge, in about 30 feet of water, is riddled with cracks and holes providing homes for wolf eels and octopuses. The area can be visited by divers of any skill level; tidal currents are minimal. However, it is closed to the harvest of marine life. The site is 3¼ miles north of Hoodsport and 1¼ miles south of Lilliwaup. Uplands are posted as "No Trespassing," but the site can be approached by boat from the water.

Sunde Rock. An offshore rock 1½ miles south of Lilliwaup is of interest primarily to scuba divers. The top of the rock is exposed at all times, but it is the myriad ledges lying below the water, with their wealth of fish, numerous kinds of crabs, and colorful starfish, anemone, and nudibranchs that attract divers. A turn-out on U.S. 101 just north of Virginia Avenue on the north end of Holiday Beach has parking for several cars. A short trail to the beach leads past an interpretive sign describing the subtidal ecosystems; respect private property flanking the path.

THE GREAT BEND

Hoodsport

Access: Land, boat
Facilities: Guest moorage, marine supplies and repairs, boat launch (sling), groceries, ice, restaurants, fuel, scuba air fills, shopping, motels
Attractions: Fishing, shrimping, scuba diving, salmon hatchery

Hoodsport is the only town of any size on U.S. 101 between Shelton and Quilcene. It marks the beginning of the Great Bend of the canal as it heads westward, and also the beginning of greater population.

The community of around 600 residents is oriented to tourists, with numerous gift shops, restaurants, and motels catering to visitors touring the Olympic Peninsula. In late May, during shrimp season, the town is crammed with sport shrimpers when up to 20,000 of them descend on Hood Canal to set pots in offshore waters for the big shellfish.

The Port of Hoodsport dock provides guest moorage for pleasure boaters who want access to shoreside facilities. Caution: The innermost section of the three-fingered float almost rests on the mud at a minus tide. Immediately south of the Port facility is a marina with a sling launch, floats, repair facilities, and marine supplies.

A salmon hatchery operated by the Washington Department of Fish and Wildlife, located immediately north of Finch Creek in Hoodsport, is open for public viewing. Outdoor rearing tanks can be visited at any time; the hatchery office is open from 8:00 A.M. to 4:30 P.M., weekdays. The 600-foot-long gravel beach in front of the hatchery is public and may be accessed from the north side of the hatchery. Saltwater fishing

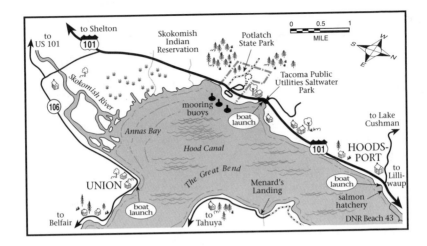

is restricted in a radius of 100 feet from the confluence of Finch Creek.

DNR Beach 43, lying immediately adjacent to the highway ¼ mile north of the center of Hoodsport, just north of the town limits, is accessible from both land and water. The cobblestone beach is 2,951 feet long; adjacent beaches are private. At low tide you may find oysters, clams, mussels, and crab, although the area is heavily used because of its closeness to the town. The beach also provides a scuba diving access. Parking space along the highway at this point is very limited.

Tacoma Public Utilities Saltwater Park (Cushman Park)

Park Area: 4.7 acres; 1,000 feet of shoreline
Access: Land, boat
Facilities: Picnic tables, fireplaces, restrooms, boat launch (ramp)
Attractions: Picnicking, fishing, boating, swimming, scuba diving

Tacoma City Light, which operates the large hydroelectric plant 2½ miles south of Hoodsport, provides this day-use picnic area and launch ramp immediately across Highway 101 from their facility. A large parking lot, ample for 75 to 80 cars and trailers, is adjacent to the highway. On the bank above the beach is a wide grass strip with fruit trees, evergreens, and about 50 picnic tables. Generator flywheels and other castoffs from the hydro plant are mounted at several places in the park as decoration and for kids to scramble on.

The long cobblestone beach is open for wading or swimming. A two-lane concrete launch ramp drops steeply from the southeast corner of the parking lot down to the water.

Potlatch State Park

Park Area: 57 acres; 9,570 feet of shoreline
Access: Land, boat
Facilities: 17 standard campsites, 18 RV campsites, 2 primitive campsites, picnic tables, fireplaces, restrooms, showers, trailer dump station, swimming beach, bathhouse, picnic shelter, group day-use area, 5 mooring buoys
Attractions: Camping, picnicking, swimming, clamming, boating, scuba diving, hiking

Potlatch State Park, a small facility along Highway 101, 3 miles south of Hoodsport, occupies the site of a former private resort. The park's campground lies on the west side of U.S. 101, and the picnic area and beach on the east. A single campground loop has 35 sites (18 with hook-ups) and two primitive walk-in spots. The wooded campground isn't particularly spacious, so privacy between campsites is limited.

A short trail leaves the back of the campground, joins a service road,

Good anchorages can be found off Potlatch State Park.

A flotilla of pigeon guillemots on Hood Canal

and then loops back to its beginning. The woodlands attract a variety of creatures such as squirrels, skunks, rabbits, and deer.

The picnic area is a large, open, grass field overlooking the beach. The beach below tapers gently into Annas Bay and varies from rock to gravel and mud. Offshore are five mooring buoys for visitors arriving by water. Although clamming is a favorite sport here, the beach is heavily dug, and a sturdy shovel is necessary to find the few remaining shellfish down through the rocks and cobbles. Better to save the energy and leave them to repopulate. Seals are frequently seen cavorting in Annas Bay, and waterfowl frequent the salt marshes.

The Skokomish (meaning "River People") originally inhabited the river delta and adjoining valleys at the southern end of Hood Canal. The Point No Point Treaty of 1855 set aside a portion of their land as a reservation, which they were to share with the Toandos and Chimakum tribes. Although the broad flat north of the Skokomish River delta was a traditional gathering site, it was not included as part of the reservation.

It was here that the Skokomish held their "potlatches"—ceremonies popular among Northwest Native Americans in which the host chief proved his status and wealth by giving away or destroying vast amounts of his possessions. These elaborate ceremonies often required years of preparation, with dances and songs to be rehearsed, speeches to be composed, and offerings of furs, blankets, food, oil, ornaments, and slaves to be amassed.

Union

Access: Land, boat
Facilities: Marina, guest moorage, groceries, ice, boat launch (ramp), fuel, restaurant, bait
Attractions: Boating, fishing

The small community of Union lies on a point of land east of the delta of the Skokomish River, where Hood Canal makes its hook to the northeast.

The town consists mostly of a few businesses catering to recreational boat traffic on the canal and tourists on the highway.

The marina at Union and adjoining businesses provide full facilities for visitors. Immediately west of the marina is the Mason County public launch area, a two-lane concrete ramp. Adjacent parking is limited.

Union is 5 miles east of Highway 101 on State Highway 106 or 24 miles southwest of Bremerton on that same highway.

THE SOUTH SHORE

Once past the Great Bend, the nature of the Hood Canal shoreline changes drastically, becoming wall-to-wall cabins, beach houses, and year-round homes, and the water becomes busier with small pleasure craft and water skiers. Pollution in the ever-more-shallow water, along with the population density, make for slimmer pickings of shellfish at the few available public accesses. In short, here civilization has virtually conquered the natural state of the waterway.

The shoreline on either side of the canal in this reach is most often approached by land from Bremerton. Follow State Highway 304 west out of Bremerton to where it joins State Highway 3 as it skirts the north shore of Sinclair Inlet. Continue southwest on Highway 3 for another 10 miles to reach Belfair, a small community at the far east point of Hood Canal. Here at a Y in the highway, Highway 300 heads down the north side of the canal and in ½ mile, at a second Y, Highway 106 heads down the south side.

If approaching from either the north or south via U.S. 101, turn onto Highway 106, 2 miles south of Potlatch State Park, or reach it via the Purdy Cutoff Road which leaves U.S. 101 another 2½ miles farther south.

Alderbrook Inn

Access: Land, boat, floatplane
Facilities: Resort, conference center, restaurant, swimming pool, hot tub sauna, shops, golf course, guest moorage (power, water), showers, marine pumpout station, paddle boat and sailboat rentals, bicycle rentals, tennis, volleyball, and badminton courts, horseshoes, children's play area, jogging course
Attractions: Swimming (saltwater and pool), golfing, boating, hiking, scuba diving

Whether touring Hood Canal by boat or car, visitors cannot miss the striking facilities of Alderbrook Inn, located on the south side of the canal 13 miles southwest of Belfair on Highway 106. By boat, the dock at the inn lies on the south side of the canal, 2 miles east of Union.

An historic waterwheel can be seen along the road near Alderbrook Inn.

Alderbrook Inn, one of the finest resorts in western Washington, has complete resort and conference facilities, and a justifiably renowned dining room. Reservations are recommended for stays at the rooms or cottages of the resort. Guest boat moorage is available on 1,200 feet of floating dock (for a fee). A small additional charge is made for use of the indoor swimming pool. The resort has neither groceries nor marine supplies; the closest spot for these is Union.

Near Alderbrook Inn, just south of the Union Post Office, is an ancient waterwheel, one of the first hydroelectric plants on Hood Canal, built by Edwin J. Darby in 1923. Situated just off the east side of the road on private property, the historic wheel with its decrepit wooden flume still functions despite the ravages of age. Walk from the resort, or park at the post office and walk along the road (being careful of traffic) to view it.

Twanoh State Park

Park Area: 182 acres; 3,167 feet of shoreline
Access: Land, boat
Facilities: 38 standard campsites, 9 RV campsites, group camp, restrooms, showers, picnic tables, fireplaces, kitchen shelters, dock, 7 mooring buoys, boat launch (ramp), marine pumpout station, swimming beach, wading pool, bathhouses, tennis court, horseshoe pits, hiking trails, concession stand
Attractions: Boating, fishing, swimming, hiking, camping, picnicking, scuba diving

Flanked by miles of beachfront homes and near the population centers of Bremerton, Port Orchard, and Shelton, Twanoh State Park has many of the features of a well-developed city park, yet it manages to blend in the camping and hiking found in more remote state parks. The park is

7½ miles southwest of Belfair on Highway 106. The highway splits the park into two sections: on the south the camping and hiking area, and on the north the picnic grounds and beach.

Campsites along the single loop road are fairly open, separated by second-growth cedar with sparse underbrush. Only nine of the campsites have hookups. At the south end of the campground loop are eight walk-in campsites. A primitive group camp is located at the trail intersection atop the ridge. The park is open to camping from April 1 to September 30.

An interesting feature of the park is numerous large cedar stumps with springboard notches, remnants of the 1890s when the area was first logged. Many of the park buildings—built with large stones and heavy timbers—were constructed in 1936 to 1937 by the Depression-era Civilian Conservation Corps.

Although Twanoh is best known for its beach, most of the park consists of densely wooded hillsides above the small stream flowing through the park. A 2-mile-long hiking trail swings through this area, with a shorter 1¼-mile loop option. Both ends of the loop start at the parking lot west of the campground.

The west leg of the trail is a fire road climbing steeply through moss-covered cedar to top a 350-foot-high ridge. Here is the option of the short or long loop, with the short trail dropping steeply downhill in a series of switchbacks through fir and hemlock forest to the east side of

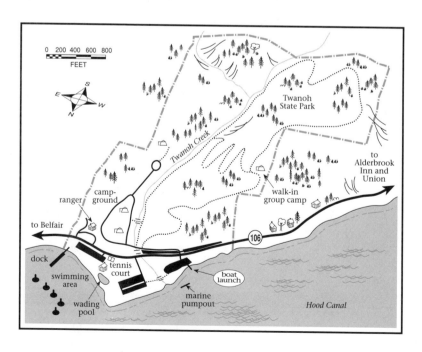

Picnic tables lie in the shade of ancient firs at Twanoh State Park.

the loop just above the creek bed. Continue on the longer loop to break out onto an open hilltop covered with huckleberry bushes. From here the trail drops gradually downhill to the south park boundary, then switchbacks down to the bank above the creek. As the trail follows the creek downhill, the moist forest sprouts devil's club, ferns, and moss. The shorter loop trail joins in at an open grassy spot, and the converged trails continue along the creek back to the parking lot.

The park's day-use area, on a small point protruding into the canal, is open 6:30 A.M. to dusk, year-round, although most of the facilities (such as restrooms) are available only in the summer. A small creek divides the area in two; each section has a parking lot and picnic facilities. The two-lane concrete boat launch ramp is at the west section of the park. The eastern section has a roped-off swimming beach (unguarded); a shallow wading pool for toddlers has been scooped out of the gravel beach near the swimming area.

At the southeast corner of the park, a 40-foot-long float extends off the end of a dock. The float is quite close to shore; approach cautiously at low tide. Seven mooring buoys are spaced offshore for visiting boaters.

Theler Wetlands Nature Trail

Access: Land

Facilities: Tourist information office, 2 miles of trails, interpretive signs, vault toilets, picnicking, children's play area, disabled-accessible

Three different kinds of wetlands are on display at Theler Wetlands: a saltwater wetland, a freshwater wetland, and a freshwater swamp. As the sign at the trailhead will tell you, wetlands are the most productive ecosystem in the world, without which life on this planet would not be the same. The trail offers visitors an opportunity to experience first hand the subtle differences of three different wetland environments. Interpretive signs along the paths provide more details about the plants and animals that inhabit the areas, and their critical link in the ecological web that eventually affects the health and well-being of humans.

The saltwater marsh lies on the tideflat at the end of Hood Canal, which is exposed twice daily by low tides. The freshwater marsh is manmade; it was initially created behind

A tiny barn swallow rests on a railing at Theler Wetlands Nature Trail.

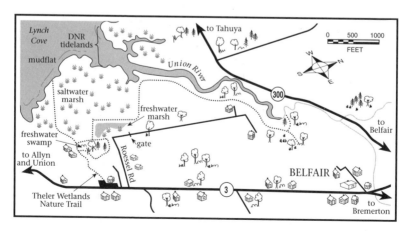

Boardwalks cross marshy spots at Theler Wetlands Nature Trail.

dikes as a place in which to compete hunting dogs. The dikes were also used to reclaim farmland, which is now being managed to protect and enhance the wetlands of the estuary. The freshwater alder/cedar swamp is a forested version of a wetland, where the forest growth cycle of these two species of trees is seen.

The longest section of trail is about 3 miles, round trip. The way is nearly flat, either on a gravel path atop old dikes or on boardwalks over marshy areas. All paths are disabled-accessible. A quick circuit of all of the trails takes about 1½ hours, but more time should be spent to listen to the marsh sounds, and watch for marshland birds and waterfowl such as red-tailed hawks, red-winged blackbirds, Virginia rails, barn swallows, mergansers, and many more. With luck you may also spot river otter, raccoon, muskrat, or beaver.

To reach the trailhead, take Highway 3 about 1 mile south from the center of Belfair to the Mary E. Theler Community Center at 22871 East Highway 3. The trail leaves from the center's parking lot.

THE NORTH SHORE

Belfair State Park

Park Area: 62.5 acres; 3,720 feet of shoreline
Access: Land, boat (shallow draft)
Facilities: 134 standard campsites, 47 RV campsites, 3 hiker/biker sites, disabled-accessible restrooms, showers, picnic tables, fireplaces, swimming beach (unguarded), bathhouse, trailer dump, horseshoe pits, children's play area
Attractions: Picnicking, camping, beachcombing, swimming, scuba diving, crabbing, fishing

The farthest reach of Hood Canal dwindles down to a shallow tideflat that bares at the hint of a minus tide. Belfair State Park, the largest park on the canal, is located at this end, 3 miles west of the town of Belfair, on State Highway 300. The park provides an interesting combination of freshwater and saltwater shoreline, as two good-sized streams, Big and Little Mission Creeks, flow through it to reach the canal.

Because of the shallowness of the water, only small boats can approach the park, and even those with care, lest they become mired. The advantage of the tideflat, however, is that water flowing over it warms more quickly than that in deeper portions of the canal, making it ideal for summertime wading and swimming. A saltwater lagoon formed in a diked-off area at

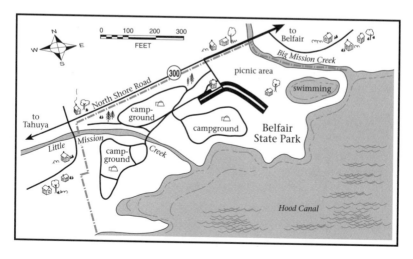

Belfair State Park has terrific places for kids to splash.

the mouth of Big Mission Creek provides an even warmer and more protected bathing spot.

Camping is in two distinct areas. The loops of the older section of the park are in old-growth Douglas-fir and rhododendrons; however, these sites have no RV hookups. Many of the campsites in the newer section of the park have hookups, although they are more in the open. Camping is permitted year-round, although the park hours vary by season. Picnic sites are on the east side of the park, scattered along a grass strip between the parking lot and Big Mission Creek.

A rock bulkhead defines the park shoreline. The beach below is gravel baring to sand and mud at low tide. Seagulls, ducks, and geese populate the shore, while woodpeckers and a variety of other birds inhabit the wooded upland areas.

The tiny peninsula that juts out from the shoreline on the west edge of the park, according to Indian legend, carried supernatural powers that caused people loitering there to become possessed. Its Indian name meant "Snail Woman," an evil person who carried a large basket on her back and who stole children and ate them (no child psychologists back in those days!). She was transformed into the tiny snails with shells on their backs that can be found there today.

Port of Allyn Dock and Launch Ramp

Area: 30 feet of shoreline
Access: Land, boat
Facilities: Dock with float, launch ramp with boarding float, sani-can
Attractions: Boating

West on State Highway 300, 1½ miles from Belfair State Park, a small bulge of land provides a site for a dock and launch ramp operated by the Port of Allyn. The ownership seems a bit incongruous, because the town of Allyn lies 8 miles away on Case Inlet, at the end of Puget Sound, but one cannot complain of the existence of this fine, well-maintained facility.

The launch ramp and dock are separated by a two-block-long section of private beach homes. The ramp has a large parking area, a boarding float, and a smaller supplemental parking area across the road to the north.

The dock extends out to a U-shaped float that has room for about 15 boats. Although the area is intended primarily for day use, overnight moorage is permitted after registering at the fee box at the head of the dock. All adjacent beach is private. From land, the dock may be identified by a sign, "Caution, Pedestrian Crossing–Boat Ramp Ahead." Parking and a sani-can are at a pull-off across the road from the head of the dock.

Tahuya

Facilities: (Nearby) bait, fuel, guest moorage, boat launch (ramp), boat rentals, RV camping

The community of Tahuya surrounds a pretty little bay at the mouth of the Tahuya River. Half a mile west of the residential area is a commercial resort with RV camping, cottages, boating facilities and supplies, a launch ramp, and a dock with floats. It can be reached by land by driving 12½ miles southwest of Belfair on North Shore Road, the county road extension of State Highway 300.

The melodious name *Tahuya* is an Indian word meaning "that done." It refers to some memorable (but since-forgotten) event that took place here long ago.

Menard's Landing (Port of Tahuya)

Park Area: 8 acres; 1,405 feet of shoreline
Access: Land, boat (shallow draft)
Facilities: Pavilion, picnic tables, sani-can, boat launch (hand-carry)
Attractions: Picnicking, beachcombing

A small section of land owned by the Department of Natural Resources is located at the far southwest point of the Kitsap Peninsula, just across Hood Canal from Hoodsport. The area consists mainly of a tiny peninsula covered with stumps and driftwood at the mouth of Rendsland Creek. Recently, funds from the agency's Aquatic Lands Enhancement Account were used by the Port of Tahuya to develop a delightful little park, Menard's Landing, at the site. Driftwood and native plantings surround a small graveled flat with picnic tables, rustic

Menard's Landing is a delightful little park near Tahuya.

log benches, and a small pavilion. A narrow gravel ramp leads down to a saltwater finger from Hood Canal where hand-carried boats may be launched.

The park is 18½ miles southwest of Belfair on North Shore Road, the county road continuing on from Highway 300. There is parking space next to the road for a few cars.

Appendices

A. Emergency Phone Numbers and List of Contacts

All western Washington cities and counties use 911 as an emergency number. The following phone numbers are listed as additional contacts for *nonemergency* situations.

Sheriffs

Jefferson County (Port Townsend): (360) 385-3831
King County (Seattle): (206) 296-3311
Kitsap County (Port Orchard): (360) 876-7101
Mason County (Shelton): (360) 427-9761
Snohomish County (Everett): (425) 388-3393

U.S. Coast Guard

Seattle

Emergencies: (206) 217-6000
Search and Rescue Coordination Center: (206) 220-7001
Other: (206) 220-7000

Everett

USCGC Point Duran: (425) 252-5281
Cellular telephone quick-dial for the Coast Guard: *CG

Radio Contacts

Marine VHF

Coast Guard distress or hailing—Channel 16
Coast Guard liaison—Channel 22
Coast Guard Vessel Tracking Center—Channel 14 (1 watt only)
Hiram Chittenden Locks—Channel 13 (1 watt only)

Marine Operator
> Everett—Channel 24
> Tacoma—Channel 28
> Seattle—Channels 25 and 26

NOAA Weather Service—Channel WX1

Seattle Ship Canal Bridges—Channel 13 (1 watt only)

U.S. Customs

Everett: (425) 259-0246; after-hour arrivals and weekends: 1-800-562-5943

Seattle (private yacht arrivals): (206) 553-4678 (weekdays and Saturday, 8:00 A.M. to 5:00 P.M.) or 1-800-562-5943 (evenings, Sundays, and holidays)

Other Contacts

Red Tide Hotline: 1-800-562-5632

Whale Hotline (to report sightings or strandings): 1-800-562-8832

Ferries

Horluck Foot Ferry (Bremerton, Port Orchard, and Annapolis): P.O. Box 87, Port Orchard, WA 98366. Phone: (360) 876-2300.

Kitsap Fast Ferry: Kitsap Harbor Tours, 290 Washington Beach Avenue #7, Bremerton, WA 98337. Phone: (360) 377-8924.

Washington State Ferries Information: 801 Alaskan Way, Pier 52, Seattle, WA 98104. Phone: (206) 464-6400 (Seattle) or 1-800-843-3779 (toll free).

Persons with hearing or vision impairments may call one of the following numbers: 1-800-833-6388 (TTY relay service), 1-800-833-6385 (Tele-Braille), or 1-800-833-6384 (Voice).

The web site is located at http://www.wsdot.wa.gov.

Washington State Parks

General information regarding the state parks is available from Washington State Parks and Recreation Commission, 7150 Cleanwater Lane, Olympia, WA 98504. Phone: (360) 902-8500.

Campsite reservations can be made for selected parks via a two-state reservation system operated for Washington and Oregon state parks. The reservation center operates from 8:00 A.M. to 5:00 P.M., weekdays. Telephone 1-800-452-5687, or use Telecommunications Device for the Deaf at 1-800-735-2900 (TTY/Voice).

Belfair: NE 410 Beck Road, Belfair, WA 98528. Phone: (360) 275-0668.

Dosewallips: P.O. Box K, Brinnon, WA 98230. Phone: (360) 796-4415.

Fay–Bainbridge: 15446 Sunrise Drive NE, Bainbridge Island, WA 98110. Phone: (360) 842-3931. *

Fort Ward (satellite to Fay–Bainbridge): 15446 Sunrise Drive NE, Bainbridge Island, WA 98110. Phone: (360) 842-3931 or (360) 842-4041 (seasonal).

Illahee: 3540 Bahia Vista, Bremerton, WA 98310. Phone: (360) 478-6460.

Kitsap Memorial: 202 NE Park Street, Poulsbo, WA 98370. Phone: (360) 779-3205.

Manchester: P.O. Box 36, Manchester, WA 98353. Phone: (360) 871-4065.

Potlatch: Route 4, Box 519, Shelton, WA 98584. Phone: (360) 877-5361.

Scenic Beach: P.O. Box 7, Seabeck, WA 98380. Phone: (360) 830-5079.

Twanoh: East 12190 Highway 206, Union, WA 98592. Phone: (360) 275-2222.

Other Parks

Bainbridge Island Park District: P.O. Box 10089, Strawberry Hill Park, Bainbridge Island, WA 98110. Phone: (360) 842-2306.

Bremerton Department of Parks and Recreation: Sheridan Park Recreation Center, 680 Lebo Boulevard, Bremerton, WA 98310. Phone: (360) 478-5305.

Discovery Park: 3801 W Government Way, Seattle, WA 98199. Phone: (206) 386-4236.

Edmonds Parks and Recreation: 700 Main Street, Edmonds, WA 98020. Phone: (425) 775-2525.

Everett Parks and Recreation Department: 802 Mukilteo Boulevard, Everett, WA 98203. Phone: (425) 259-0300.

Jefferson County Parks and Recreation: Lawrence and Taylor, Port Townsend, WA 98369. Phone: (360) 385-2221.

King County Parks and Recreation Division: 2040 84th SE, Mercer Island, WA 98040. Phone: (206) 296-4232 (general information) or (206) 296-2956 (scheduling use of park facilities).

Kitsap County Parks Department: 1200 NW Fairgrounds Road, Bremerton, WA 98310. Phone: (360) 692-3655.

Seal Rock Campground: Quilcene Ranger Station, Quilcene, WA 98376. Phone: (360) 765-3368.

Seattle Parks and Recreation Department: 600 4th Avenue, Seattle, WA 98104. Phone: (206) 684-4075 (general information) or (206) 684-4081 (picnic site reservations).

Snohomish County Parks and Recreation Division: P.O. Box 310, Monroe, WA 98272. Phone: (425) 339-1208.

Museums

Bremerton Naval Museum: 130 Washington Avenue, Bremerton, WA 98337. Phone: (360) 479-7447.

Edmonds Museum: 118 5th Avenue N, P.O. Box 52, Edmonds, WA 98020. Phone: (425) 774-0900.

Firefighters Museum: 13th Street Dock, Everett Marina, Everett, WA 98201. Phone: (425) 259-8709.

Kitsap County Historical Museum: 280 4th Street, Bremerton, WA 98337. Phone: (360) 692-1949.

Log Cabin Museum: 416 Sidney Avenue, Port Orchard, WA 98366. Phone: (360) 876-3693.

Naval Undersea Museum: Garnett Way, Keyport, WA 98345-7610. Phone: (360) 396-4148.

Of Sea and Shore Museum: Port Gamble, WA 98364. Phone: (360) 297-2426.

Port Gamble Historic Museum: Port Gamble, WA 98364. Phone: (360) 697-6626.

Suquamish Museum: P.O. Box 498, 15383 Sandy Hook Road, Suquamish, WA 98392. Phone: (360) 598-3311.

Other

The Marine Science Center of the Pacific Northwest: 18743 Front Street, Poulsbo, WA 98370. Phone (360) 799-5549.

Point Whitney State Shellfish Laboratory: 1000 Point Whitney Road, Brinnon, WA 98320. Phone: (360) 796-4601.

Seattle Aquarium: Pier 59, Seattle, WA 98101. Phone: (206) 625-4358.

Seattle Mounted Police Stables: Discovery Park. Phone: (206) 386-4238.

USS *Turner Joy*: Bremerton Historic Ships Association, 300 Washington Beach Avenue, Bremerton, WA 98337. Phone (360) 792-2457.

Washington Water Trails Association: 4649 Sunnyside Avenue N, Suite 345, Seattle, WA 98103-6900. Phone: (206) 545-1961.

Hiram M. Chittenden Locks web site: www.nps.usace.army.mil/opdiv/lwsc/ lakewsc.htm

B. Nautical Charts, Maps, and Tide Tables

Charts

Sketch maps in this book are intended for orientation only. When traveling by boat in waters covered by this book, it is imperative that the appropriate nautical charts be used. The following list of charts covers the area included in this book. They may be purchased at map stores or many marine centers.

NOAA Chart 18445 SC, Puget Sound—Possession Sound to Olympia, including the Hood Canal. (Scale 1:80,000—folio of charts including some detailed insets)

NOAA Chart 18441, Puget Sound—Northern part. (Scale 1:80,000)

NOAA Chart 18448, Puget Sound—Southern part. (Scale 1:80,000)

NOAA Chart 18443, Approaches to Everett. (Scale 1:40,000)

NOAA Chart 18473, Puget Sound—Oak Bay to Shilshole Bay. (Scale 1:40,000)

NOAA Chart 18476, Puget Sound—Hood Canal and Dabob Bay. (Scale 1:40,000)

NOAA Chart 18449, Puget Sound—Seattle to Bremerton. (Scale 1:25,000)

NOAA Chart 18458, Hood Canal—South Point to Quatsop Point including Dabob Bay. (Scale 1:25,000)

NOAA Chart 18477, Puget Sound—Entrance to Hood Canal. (Scale 1:25,000)

NOAA Chart 18444, Everett Harbor. (Scale 1:10,000)

NOAA Chart 18446, Puget Sound—Apple Cove Pt. to Keyport Agate Passage. (Scale 1:10,000)

NOAA Chart 18450, Seattle Harbor, Elliott Bay, and Duwamish Waterway. (Scale 1:10,000)

NOAA Chart 18452, Sinclair Inlet. (Scale 1:10,000)

Maps

USGS topographic maps are not required for any hiking described in this book, but the 7½' series maps are both useful and interesting. Those covering areas in this book are Belfair, Bremerton East, Bremerton West, Brinnon, Duwamish Head, Edmonds East, Edmonds West, Eldon, Everett, Hansville, Holly, Hoodsport, Lake Wooten, Lilliwaup, Lofall, Marysville, Mukilteo, Port Gamble, Port Ludlow, Poulsbo, Quilcene, Seabeck, Seattle North, Seattle South, Shilshole Bay, Skokomish Valley, Suquamish, Tulalip, and Union.

For detailed street maps the following are useful:

King, Snohomish counties—Thomas Brothers Maps.

Bremerton, Port Orchard, Silverdale, Poulsbo, Winslow, Kitsap County— King of the Road Map Services.

Tide Tables

Tide Tables—19__, West Coast of North America and South America. NOAA (published annually)

Tidal Current Tables—19__, Pacific Coast of North America and Asia. NOAA (published annually)

19__ Current and Tide Tables for Puget Sound, Deception Pass, the San Juans, Gulf Islands, and the Strait of Juan de Fuca. Island Canoe, Inc., Bainbridge Island. (Extract from the above NOAA tables for local areas.)

C. Quick Reference to Facilities and Recreation

Some types of marine recreation, such as boating, shore fishing, and beach-combing, are found throughout Middle Puget Sound and Hood Canal. Others, however, are more specific to a particular area. The following table provides a quick reference to the facilities and activities in the major areas covered by this book.

- Marine Services includes fuel and marine supplies and repair; in some places they may be of a very limited nature.
- Food/Shopping generally includes groceries, cafes or restaurants, and a varying range of other types of stores. These too may be of a limited nature.
- Floats/Buoys refers to marinas that have guest moorage as well as to public facilities at marine parks.
- Launch Facilities may be only a shore access for hand-carried boats. Hoists and slings are always located at commercial marinas. Ramps may be at either commercial or public facilities.
- Point of Interest includes historical or educational displays, museums, and self-guided nature trails.

Some facilities listed may be entirely at commercial marinas; some may close off-season. For detailed information read the description of a specific area in the text.

( ) = Nearby
Fuel: D = On Dock; S = Service Station
Launch Facilities: H = Hoist; R = Ramp; C = Hand-carry
Fishing: P = Pier; A = Artificial Reef

	Fuel	Marine Services	Charters/Rentals	Food/Shopping	Restaurants	Floats/Buoys	Launch Facilities	Fishing Pier/Reef	Shellfish	Paddling	Scuba Diving	Swimming	Camping	Marine Trail Site	Picnicking	Walking/Hiking	Beachcombing	Point of Interest
1. POSSESSION SOUND AND EDMONDS																		
Tulalip Bay Marina	D			•	•	•	R			•					•	•		•
Ebey Slough Launch Ramp							R											
Langus Riverfront Park and Trail							R	P	•					•	•			
Spencer Island										•						•		
Lowell Riverside Trail							R								•	•		
Port of Everett Marina	D/S	•	•	•	•	•	H			•								•
North and South View Parks																•		•
Marine Park						•	R	P		•					•			
Everett Jetty Park						•				•					•			•
Howarth City Park										•					•	•	•	
Mukilteo	S	•	•	•	•			P		•					•			•
Mukilteo State Park				(•)	(•)	•	R			•	•	•						(•)
Picnic Point County Park										•	•				•	•	•	
Meadowdale Beach Co. Park									•					•	•	•		
Port of Edmonds Marina	D/S	•	•	•	•	•	H								•			
Edmonds Underwater Park											•							
Edmonds Public Fishing Pier				(•)	•			P/A							•			
Marina Beach							C			•	•				•	•	•	
2. THE SEATTLE AREA																		
Richmond Beach Park										•	•	•			•	•	•	
Boeing Creek Fishing Reef								A										
Carkeek Park															•	•	•	
Golden Gardens										•	•	•			•		•	
Eddie Vine Boat Launch					•		R	P										
Shilshole Bay Marina	D	•		•	•	•	H	P										
Hiram M. Chittenden Locks				(•)											•			•

	Fuel	Marine Services	Charters/Rentals	Food/Shopping	Restaurants	Floats/Buoys	Launch Facilities	Fishing Pier/Reef	Shellfish	Paddling	Scuba Diving	Swimming	Camping	Marine Trail Site	Picnicking	Walking/Hiking	Beachcombing	Point of Interest
Ship Canal Fish Ladder																		•
Commodore Park							C	•		•					•			
Discovery Park															•	•	•	•
Smith Cove Park															•			
Elliott Bay Marina	D	•	•	•	•	•												
Elliott Bay Park					•			P/A							•	•		•
Myrtle Edwards Park															•	•		•
Seattle Waterfront			•	•	•	•		P		•					•	•		•
Pier 30															•			•
Terminal 23 Fishing Pier								P										•
East and West Waterways							C			•								
Harbor Island Marina	D			•	(•)	•												
Diagonal Avenue S Access							C			•					•	•		•
S River Street Boat Launch							R											
Terminal 107 Public Access										•					•	•		•
Terminal 105 Public Access							C			•					•			
Southwest Harbor Project															•	•		•
Seacrest Park	•		•	•	•	•		P			•				•	•		
Don Armeni Park							R			•					•	•		
Duwamish Head										•						•	•	
Alki Beach Park												•			•	•	•	•
Alki Point Lighthouse																		•

3. BAINBRIDGE ISLAND

	Fuel	Marine Services	Charters/Rentals	Food/Shopping	Restaurants	Floats/Buoys	Launch Facilities	Fishing Pier/Reef	Shellfish	Paddling	Scuba Diving	Swimming	Camping	Marine Trail Site	Picnicking	Walking/Hiking	Beachcombing	Point of Interest
Eagle Harbor and Winslow	S			•	•	•	R			•					•	•	•	•
Eagle Harbor Marinas		•		•	•	•												•
Eagle Harbor Waterfront Park							R			•					•	•		•
Blakely Harbor										•	(•)							•
Fort Ward State Park						•	R	A		•	•				•	•	•	•

	Fuel	Marine Services	Charters/Rentals	Food/Shopping	Restaurants	Floats/Buoys	Launch Facilities	Fishing Pier/Reef	Shellfish	Paddling	Scuba Diving	Swimming	Camping	Marine Trail Site	Picnicking	Walking/Hiking	Beachcombing	Point of Interest
Point White Fishing Pier							C	P										
Reitan Road Access											•						•	
W Port Madison Nature Preserve														•	•	•		
Inner Port Madison																		
Fay–Bainbridge State Park						•	R		•	•	•	•	•	•	•	•	•	•
4. EAST KITSAP PENINSULA																		
Manchester	(S)			(•)	(•)	•	R								•			
Manchester State Park							C			•	•		•	•	•	•	•	•
Waterman								P							•			
Annapolis Recreation Area							R											
Port Orchard	D	•		•	•	•	R								•			•
Port Orchard Marina	D			(•)	(•)										•			
Port Orchard Boat Launch					(•)		R								•			
Port of Bremerton Marina				(•)	(•)	•												
Bremerton Boardwalk															•	•		•
USS *Turner Joy*																		•
Puget Sound Naval Museum																		•
Kitsap Co. Historical Museum																		•
Bachmann Park							C			•					•		•	
Evergreen Park							R	•							•			
Lebo Street Recreation Area					•		R	P				•			•	•		
S.P. "Pat" Carey Viewpoint							C								•			
Shell Bank																	•	•
Naval Ammo Depot Marine Park														•	•	•		
Chico Launch Ramp							R											
Silverdale Waterfront Park				(•)		•	R	P		•		•			•			
Smith Children's Park										•				•	•	•		•

	Fuel	Marine Services	Charters/Rentals	Food/Shopping	Restaurants	Floats/Buoys	Launch Facilities	Fishing Pier/Reef	Shellfish	Paddling	Scuba Diving	Swimming	Camping	Marine Trail Site	Picnicking	Walking/Hiking	Beachcombing	Point of Interest
Tracyton Launch Ramp							R											
Illahee State Park						•	R	P		•	•			•	•	•	•	•
Illahee	(S)			(•)		•		P/A			•							
Brownsville Marina	D	•	•	•	•	•	R								•			
Naval Undersea Museum																		•
Port of Keyport Marina	(S)			(•)		•	R											
Poulsbo Marina	D			(•)	(•)	•	R				•				•			
Legion and Liberty Bay Parks															•	•	•	
Suquamish Museum																•		•
Old Man House State Park							C				•	•			•		•	•
Suquamish				•	•		R	P										•
Miller Bay	S	•				•	R											
Indianola						•		P										
Kingston	D	•		•	•	•	H	P		•					•			
Arness County Park							C			•					•		•	
Eglon Beach Park							R								•			
Point No Point County Park																•	•	
Hansville and Point No Point	S		•	•	•		•	•								•	•	•
Foulweather Bluff	S		•	•			C/H											
Foulweather Bluff Preserve																•	•	

5. HOOD CANAL

	Fuel	Marine Services	Charters/Rentals	Food/Shopping	Restaurants	Floats/Buoys	Launch Facilities	Fishing Pier/Reef	Shellfish	Paddling	Scuba Diving	Swimming	Camping	Marine Trail Site	Picnicking	Walking/Hiking	Beachcombing	Point of Interest
Mats Mats Bay							R	•		•					•			
Port Ludlow	D		•	•	•	•				•		•			•			
Port Gamble				•	•										•			•
Salsbury Point County Park							R					•		•	•	•		
Kitsap Memorial State Park						•			•		•	•	•		•	•		
Hood Canal Fishing Pier								P/A										
Shine Tidelands State Park							(R)		•	•				•		•		
Wolfe Property State Park									•							•		•

	Fuel	Marine Services	Charters/Rentals	Food/Shopping	Restaurants	Floats/Buoys	Launch Facilities	Fishing Pier/Reef	Shellfish	Paddling	Scuba Diving	Swimming	Camping	Marine Trail Site	Picnicking	Walking/Hiking	Beachcombing	Point of Interest
William R. Hicks Park							R		•						•			
Squamish Harbor DNR Beaches								•										
DNR Beaches 57B and 57									•									
Fisherman Harbor									•	•								
Dabob and Quilcene Bays	S			(•)	(•)	•	R	•	•	•	•	•			•			
Quilcene Bay Marina	S					•	R					•			•			
Point Whitney Shellfish Lab						•	R		•								•	•
Dabob Bay Public Tidelands									•									
Seal Rock Campground							C		•	•	•		•		•	•	•	•
Dosewallips State Park									•				•		•	•	•	
Seabeck	D		•	•	•	•	H	P			•							
Misery Point Launch Ramp							R	A			•							
Scenic Beach State Park											•		•		•	•	•	•
East Shore Public Beaches							R		•									
Pleasant Harbor	D			•	•	•			•						•			
Triton Cove State Park							R	P							•			
West Shore Public Beaches									•		•							
Hoodsport				•	•	•	H	•	•		•							•
Cushman Park							R	•			•	•			•			
Potlatch State Park						•			•	•	•	•	•		•	•		
Union	D	•		•	•	•	R	•										
Alderbrook Inn			•	•	•	•				•	•	•				•		•
Twanoh State Park						•	R			•	•	•	•		•	•		
Theler Wetlands Nature Trail																•		•
Belfair State Park				(•)				•			•	•	•		•		•	
Port of Allyn Dock						•	R											
Tahuya	S		•	•		•	R						•					
Menard's Landing							C			•						•	•	•

INDEX

ABOUT THE AUTHORS

MARGE AND TED MUELLER are outdoor enthusiasts and environmentalists who have explored Washington State's waterways, mountains, forests, and deserts for nearly 40 years. Ted has taught classes on cruising the Northwest waters, and Marge and Ted have instructed mountain climbing. They are members of The Mountaineers, the Nature Conservancy, The Sierra Club, and the Washington Water Trails Association.